A SPORTING VISION

The Paul Mellon Collection of British Sporting Art from the Virginia Museum of Fine Arts

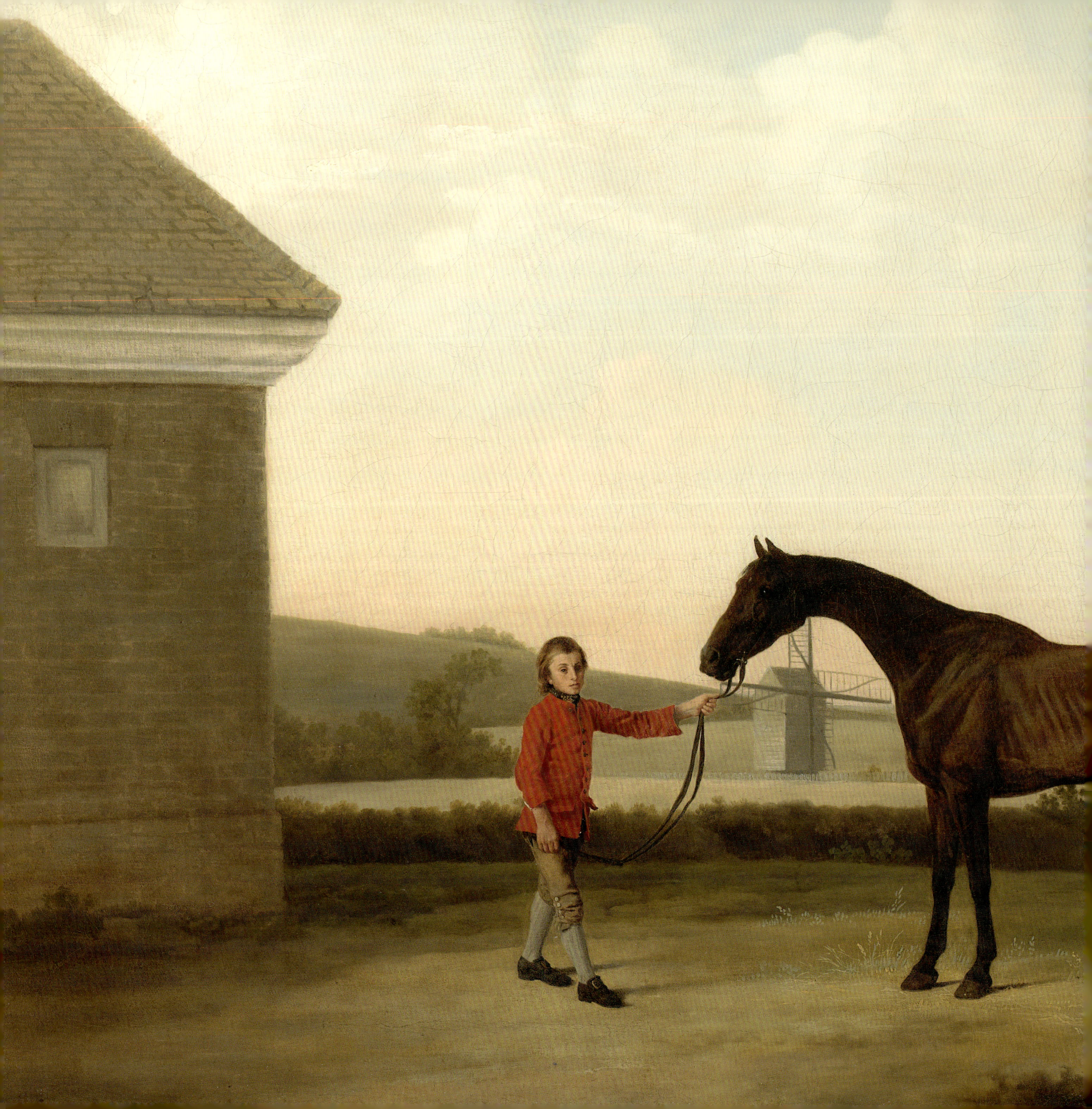

A SPORTING VISION

The Paul Mellon Collection of British Sporting Art from the Virginia Museum of Fine Arts

Dr. Colleen Yarger
Curatorial Research Specialist for the Mellon Collection, VMFA

Exhibition curated by Dr. Mitchell Merling
Paul Mellon Curator and Head of the Department of European Art, VMFA

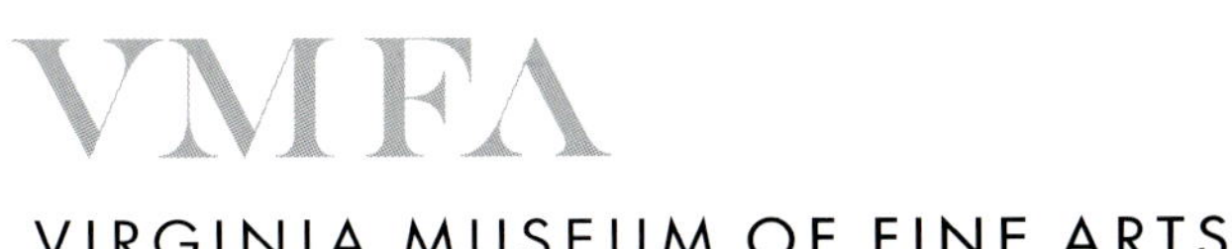

VIRGINIA MUSEUM OF FINE ARTS

This catalogue accompanies the exhibition *A Sporting Vision: The Paul Mellon Collection of British Sporting Art from the Virginia Museum of Fine Arts.*

Catalogue by Dr. Colleen Yarger

Exhibition curated by Dr. Mitchell Merling, Paul Mellon Curator and Head of the Department of European Art, VMFA

Venues

NATIONAL SPORTING LIBRARY & MUSEUM
April 13–July 22, 2018

MUSÉE DE LA CHASSE ET DE LA NATURE, PARIS*
September 3–December 2, 2018

THE FRIST CENTER FOR THE VISUAL ARTS
January 26–May 5, 2019

THE FRICK ART & HISTORICAL CENTER
June 15–September 8, 2019

**selections only*

ISBN 978-1-934351-12-3

Produced by the Department of Publications
Virginia Museum of Fine Arts
200 N. Boulevard
Richmond, Virginia 23220-4007
www.VMFA.museum

Rosalie West, Editor in Chief and Project Editor
Sarah Lavicka, Chief Graphic Designer
Lauren Kitts, Designer
Travis Fullerton, Katherine Wetzel, and David Stover, Photographers

Composed and typeset in Adobe InDesign with Garamond Premier Pro
Printed on GardaMatt paper by Conti Tipocolor, Italy

Front cover: *The Final Lengths of the Race for the Doncaster Gold Cup* (detail), 1826, John Frederick Herring, Sr., cat. no. 32; **Back cover:** *Linin' 'em Up, Newmarket* (detail), ca. 1940–53, Sir Alfred J. Munnings, P. R. A., cat. no. 38; **Frontispiece:** *Hyena (or Hyaena) at Newmarket with One of Jennison Shafto's Stable Lads* (detail), ca. 1765–67, George Stubbs, cat. no. 1; **p. ix:** *Hunting Scenes: A Hunting Morn* (detail), ca. 1840, John Frederick Herring, Sr., cat. no. 20a; **p. x:** *Paul Mellon,* 1983, Yousuf Karsh (Canadian, 1908–2002), gelatin silver print. VMFA, Paul Mellon Collection, 87.414; **p. 3:** *Tiger (or Tigress)* (detail), ca. 1769–71, George Stubbs, cat. no. 2; **p. 11:** *Colonel Henry Campbell Shooting on a Moor* (detail), ca. 1806, Benjamin Marshall, cat. no. 13; **p. 37:** *Doncaster Races, 1830: Passing the Judges' Stand* (detail), 1831, James Pollard, cat. no. 34b; **p. 59:** *Two Durham Oxen* (detail), 1827, Thomas Weaver, cat. no. 49; **p. 79:** *Count Sandor's Hunting Exploits in Leicestershire, A Set of Ten Sketches, No. 4: The Count in a Brook up to His Waist in Water and Mud* (detail), 1829, John E. Ferneley, Sr., cat. no. 58d

Contents

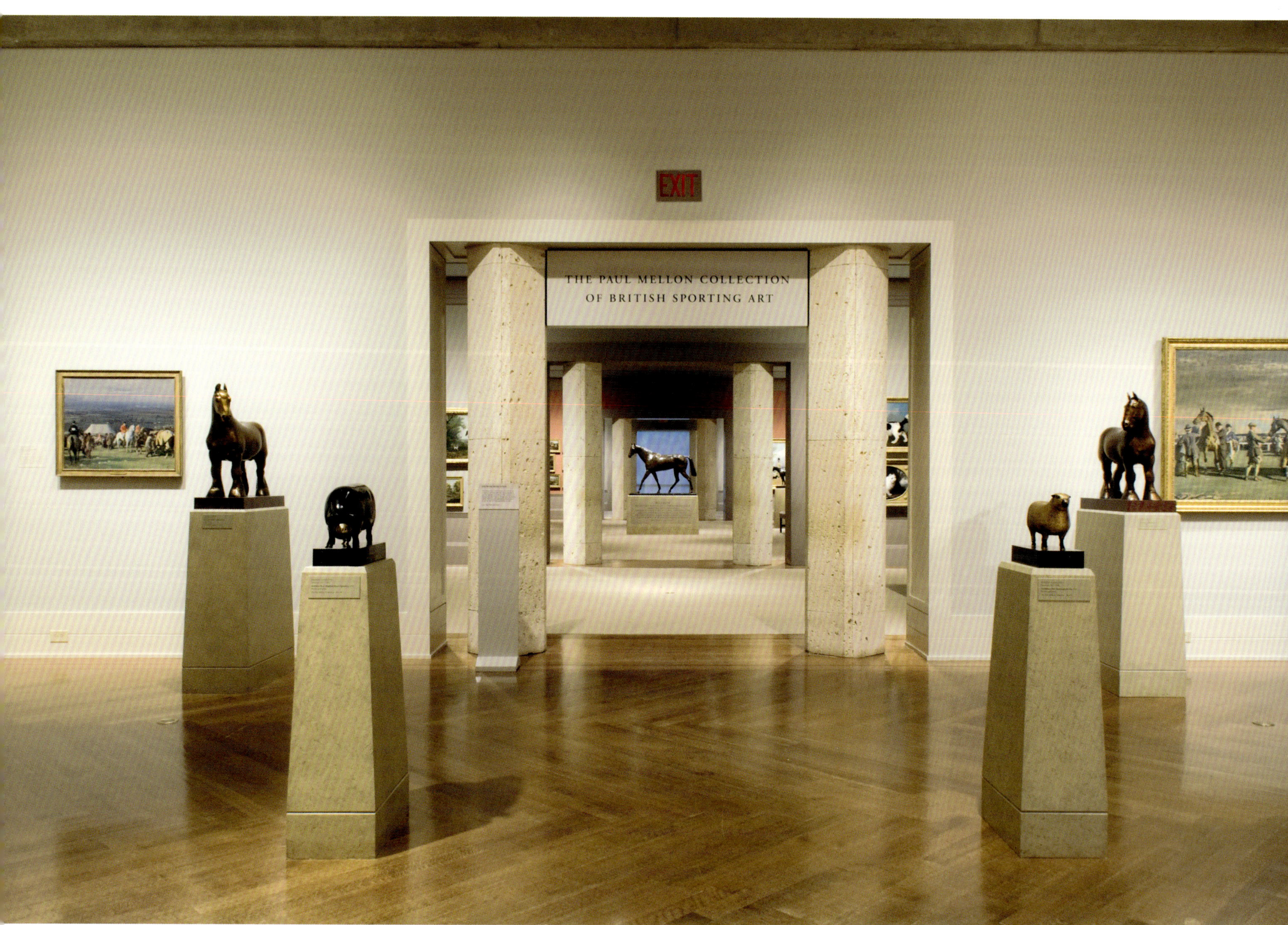

Mellon Sporting Art Galleries, VMFA

Director's Foreword

Paul Mellon became a trustee of the Virginia Museum of Fine Arts in 1938, a tenure that would last more than forty years and allow him to become one of the most influential benefactors in the museum's history. His decades on the Board were highlighted by two exhibitions of Sporting art, *Sport and Horse* (1960) and *Painting in England, 1700–1850* (1963), to which Mellon lent several major works from his collection—exhibitions that inspired both his efforts to collect British Sporting art with fervor, and his vision for its legacy at VMFA.

By the time Mellon retired from VMFA's Board of Trustees in 1979, he and his wife, Rachel Lambert Mellon, had lent more than one hundred works to the museum. As their plans for a major donation of French and British Art developed, Richmond collectors Sydney and Frances Lewis were also planning their own significant gifts to VMFA. With an outpouring of public and private support, the museum constructed its West Wing, which was dedicated in 1985 and houses the Mellon collections of French, British, and American art, and the Lewis Collections. *A Sporting Vision* contains thirty of the works that were given for the 1985 opening; works selected to ensure a comprehensive range of sporting subjects and artists, including the celebrated George Stubbs, James Seymour, and Henry Thomas Alken, alongside the lesser known Pieter Angellis, William Williams, and Robert Wilkinson Padley.

Yet the Mellons' legacy is not limited to their passion for European works. In 1952, Paul Mellon funded the construction of the five-hundred-seat Leslie Cheek Theater, the first performing arts venue inside an art museum in the United States, and in 1968 he anonymously funded the purchase of 150 Indian and Himalayan objects that would become the foundation for VMFA's world-renowned collection of South Asian art. Paul Mellon also established important endowments that have funded curatorial positions in Ancient art and European art at VMFA, and since 2000, Mellon's multimillion-dollar bequest has made possible numerous exhibitions, publications, and programs.

In total, Mr. and Mrs. Mellon donated almost 1,800 works to the Virginia Museum of Fine Arts, and we celebrate their generosity with this once-in-a-lifetime traveling exhibition that honors their legacy.

I would like to thank Dr. Mitchell Merling, Paul Mellon Curator and Head of the Department of European Art, for his careful selection of more than eighty remarkable works to share with new audiences. Dr. Colleen Yarger, Curatorial Research Specialist for the Mellon Collection, has written this excellent volume, which captures the depth and importance of the collection while also conveying Paul Mellon's passion for British Sporting art. Dr. Michael R. Taylor, Chief Curator and Deputy Director for Art and Education, has expertly guided the project, along with Courtney Freeman, Director of Exhibition Planning, and Courtney Burkhardt, Manager of Exhibitions, with tremendous support from our Design, Photography, Publications, and Registration departments. Finally, I would like to thank my colleagues at each of our venues—Claude d'Anthenaise, Director, Musée de la Chasse et de la Nature; Susan Edwards, Executive Director and CEO, Frist Center for the Visual Arts; Melanie Mathewes, Executive Director, National Sporting Library & Museum; and Robin Nicholson, Executive Director, The Frick Art & Historical Center—and their institutions for their enthusiasm in presenting *A Sporting Vision* to audiences outside of Richmond.

A Sporting Vision is exactly that—a vision of extraordinary focus and breadth from a single collector, come to life in this remarkable exhibition from the Virginia Museum of Fine Arts. We are honored to present these works in esteemed venues around the world, and invite you to join us in Richmond as we reopen our permanent galleries for the Mellon collections in 2020.

Alex Nyerges
Director

Preface and Acknowledgments

My first interaction with the Mellon British Sporting Art collection at the Virginia Museum of Fine Arts (VMFA) came in 2009 during a graduate seminar on the British sporting print at Virginia Commonwealth University. Led by Dr. Mitchell Merling, this seminar explored topics and ideas that became the basis for the 2013 VMFA exhibition *Catching Sight: The World of the British Sporting Print*. Since then, I have been privileged to be involved with the Mellon collections in VMFA positions ranging from intern to adjunct faculty and, currently, Curatorial Research Specialist for the Mellon Collection.

The entries in this catalogue provide brief introductions to stellar examples of British sporting paintings. Some include biographical anecdotes to help answer the often-asked question, "What was it about his particular work of art that made Mr. Mellon collect it?" Without a doubt, this collection was amassed with great enthusiasm and a deep love for the subjects. A complete section has been dedicated to the works by Mr. Mellon's favorite sporting artist, George Stubbs. The country pastimes of foxhunting, shooting, and fishing can be found together in "In Pursuit," and horse racing and coaching are grouped within the section "In Motion." The section "Animal, Man, Country" contains additional images illustrating these themes, and the catalogue concludes on a note of levity with humorous images in "The World Upside Down."

It would not be possible to share this familiar and fabulous collection without the fantastic efforts of Mitchell Merling, who conceived the exhibition's concept; the tremendous leadership of Dr. Michael R. Taylor, Courtney Burkhardt, and Courtney Freeman; the editing expertise of Rosalie West; the beautiful catalogue design by Sarah Lavicka; the wonderful photography skills of Travis Fullerton; and the photo management of Howell Perkins. A very special thanks belongs to Moriah L. Webster, who took time out of her busy graduate school schedule to re-open a paper topic she authored in college on John Collet's *Rising Woman and Falling Man* to complete the corresponding entry in this text. Ever willing to listen to ideas, Kristie Couser, Ashley Holdsworth, and Shannon Petska deserve my gratitude. Lastly, but no less importantly, I would like to thank my family: my husband, Chris; my parents, Ruth and Steve Truax; and my children, Robin and Basil, who have lived through countless drafts and revisions right along with me.

Colleen Yarger
Curatorial Research Specialist for the Mellon Collection

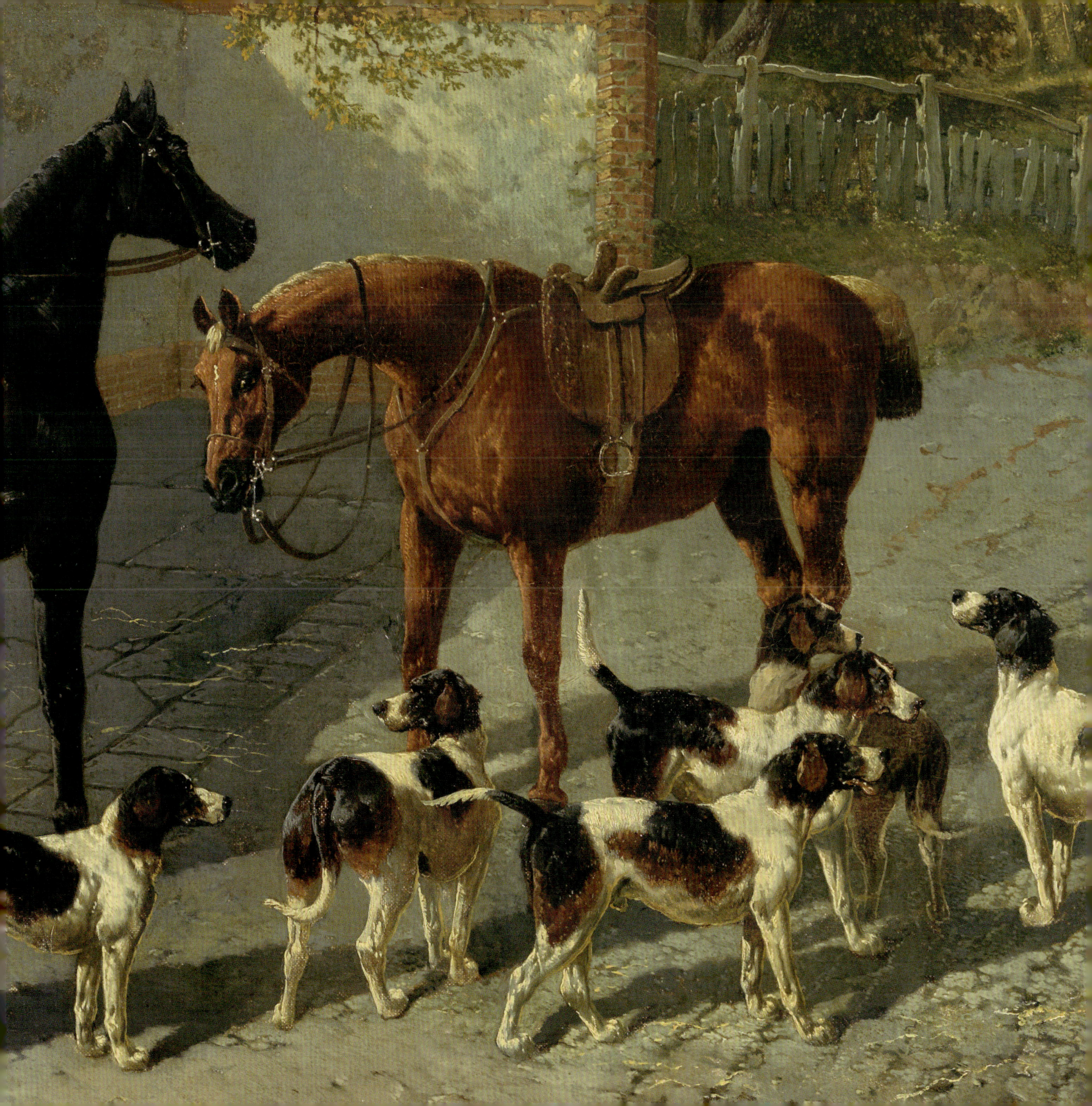

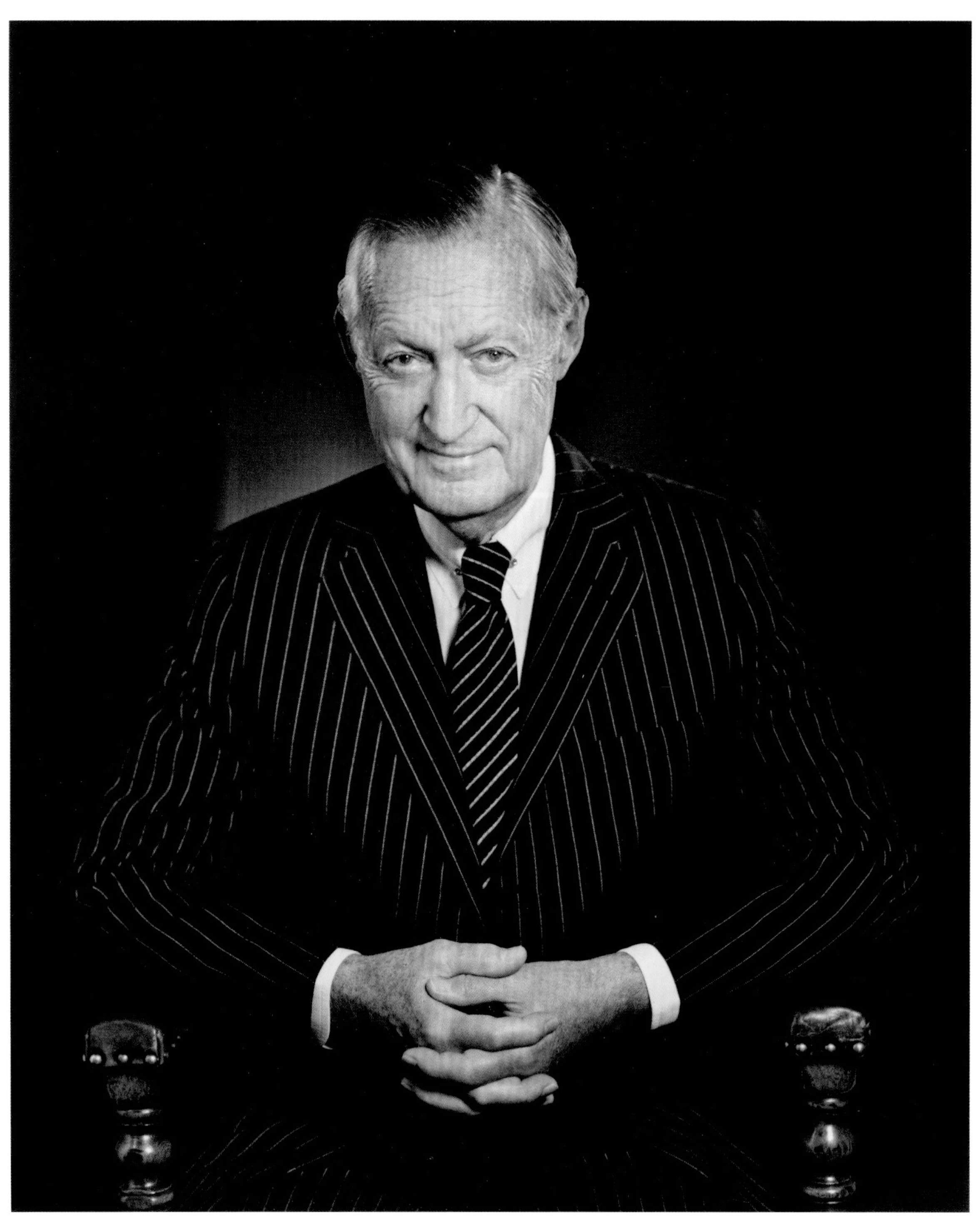

Paul Mellon (1907–1999)

Curator's Statement:
THE IDEA OF SPORTING ART

> I don't believe many motives in life are clearcut or self-evident. Collecting especially is such a matter of time and chance—intellectual bent, individual temperament, personal taste, available resources, changing fashion—and the psychologists tell us, even very early child-training—and my own motives as a collector seem to myself extremely mixed. Although temperamental trends or subjective impulses were perhaps uppermost, I won't say it was done entirely without thought, without reason, without plan. English Art, as well as being personally desirable, seemed to me long neglected or even abandoned, not only in this country but also in its homeland.
>
> So that expanding the Collection, increasing its breadth and depth, and filling in important historical or chronological gaps as well as adding artists and schools in which we were weak, or which we lacked entirely—all seemed part of the logical, deliberate attempt to say to ourselves and to the public—this is English Art, not just the Duchess of Devonshire or the Age of Innocence; let's take it seriously, let's reevaluate it, let's look at it, let's enjoy it.
>
> — Paul Mellon, "A Collector Recollects," 1963

The title of this catalogue and the exhibition it accompanies, *A Sporting Vision,* is meant to affectionately evoke something of Paul Mellon's self-deprecating and wry humor, evident throughout his spellbinding autobiography, *Reflections in a Silver Spoon.* There, he describes his own "sporting vision" as the basic impetus for his happenstance but radical purchase of a plainspoken painting of a stable lad offering some oats to a horse (George Stubbs's *Pumpkin with a Stable-lad,* now at the Yale Center for British Art), which led eventually to his rejection of the entire existing canon of British art (essentially the collecting taste of his father, perceived by Mellon as imposed on him by a dealer, Lord Duveen, which formed the basis of the collections of the National Gallery of Art in Washington). Mellon thereafter collected sporting art as avidly as he pursued sport itself, and he encouraged others to study and appreciate it for its straightforward aesthetic approach, its sense of community, and its essential humanity.

Although Paul Mellon was to divide his sporting art collection more or less equally between the Virginia Museum of Fine Arts (VMFA), the Yale Center for British Art, and Tate Britain, it is only at VMFA that his gifts can be appreciated as an integral collection—and the most important dedicated display of this material anywhere in the world.

VMFA's British sporting art galleries are located in the museum's West Wing, added in 1985 to house the collections of Mr. Mellon and his wife, Rachel Lambert Mellon, as well as those of Sydney and Frances Lewis. The Mellon collections include not only British but also European and American art, representing artists from Vincent van Gogh, Claude Monet, and Edgar Degas to George Catlin and Winslow Homer. Although the British sporting galleries have recently been updated, they still preserve the flavor of the installation created with input from Mr. Mellon himself and reflect his aesthetic ideals as well as his historic purpose to emphasize the continuity of past and present. They will continue to shine as a vision of perfection, sporting or not, and as a valid and considered idea of what a museum ought to be, which we might yet well take into account.

Mitchell Merling
Paul Mellon Curator and Head of the
Department of European Art

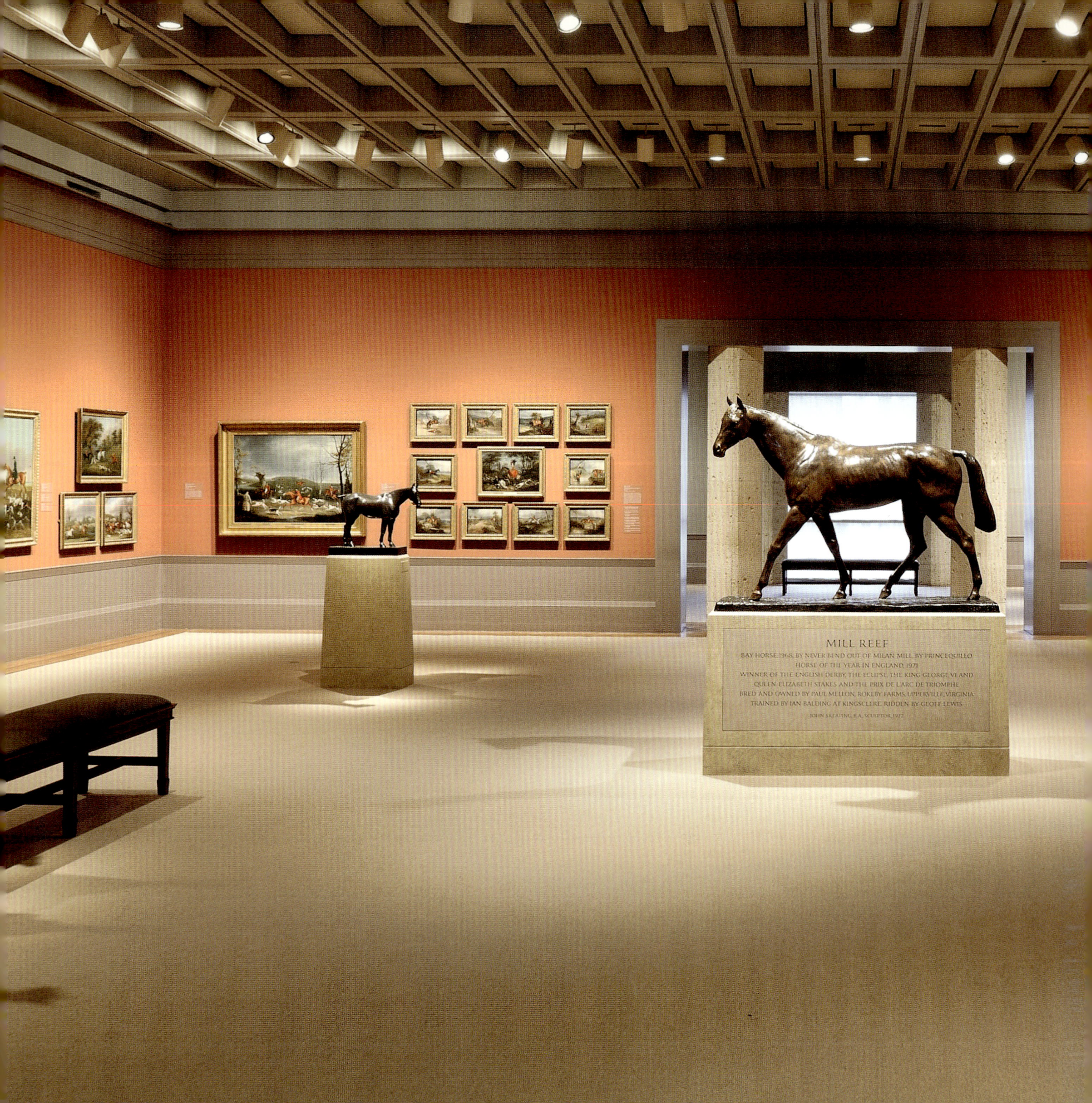
MILL REEF
BAY HORSE 1968, BY NEVER BEND OUT OF MILAN MILL, BY PRINCEQUILLO
HORSE OF THE YEAR IN ENGLAND 1971
WINNER OF THE ENGLISH DERBY, THE ECLIPSE, THE KING GEORGE VI AND
QUEEN ELIZABETH STAKES AND THE PRIX DE L'ARC DE TRIOMPHE
BRED AND OWNED BY PAUL MELLON, ROKEBY FARMS, UPPERVILLE, VIRGINIA
TRAINED BY IAN BALDING AT KINGSCLERE, RIDDEN BY GEOFF LEWIS
JOHN SKEAPING, R.A., SCULPTOR, 1972

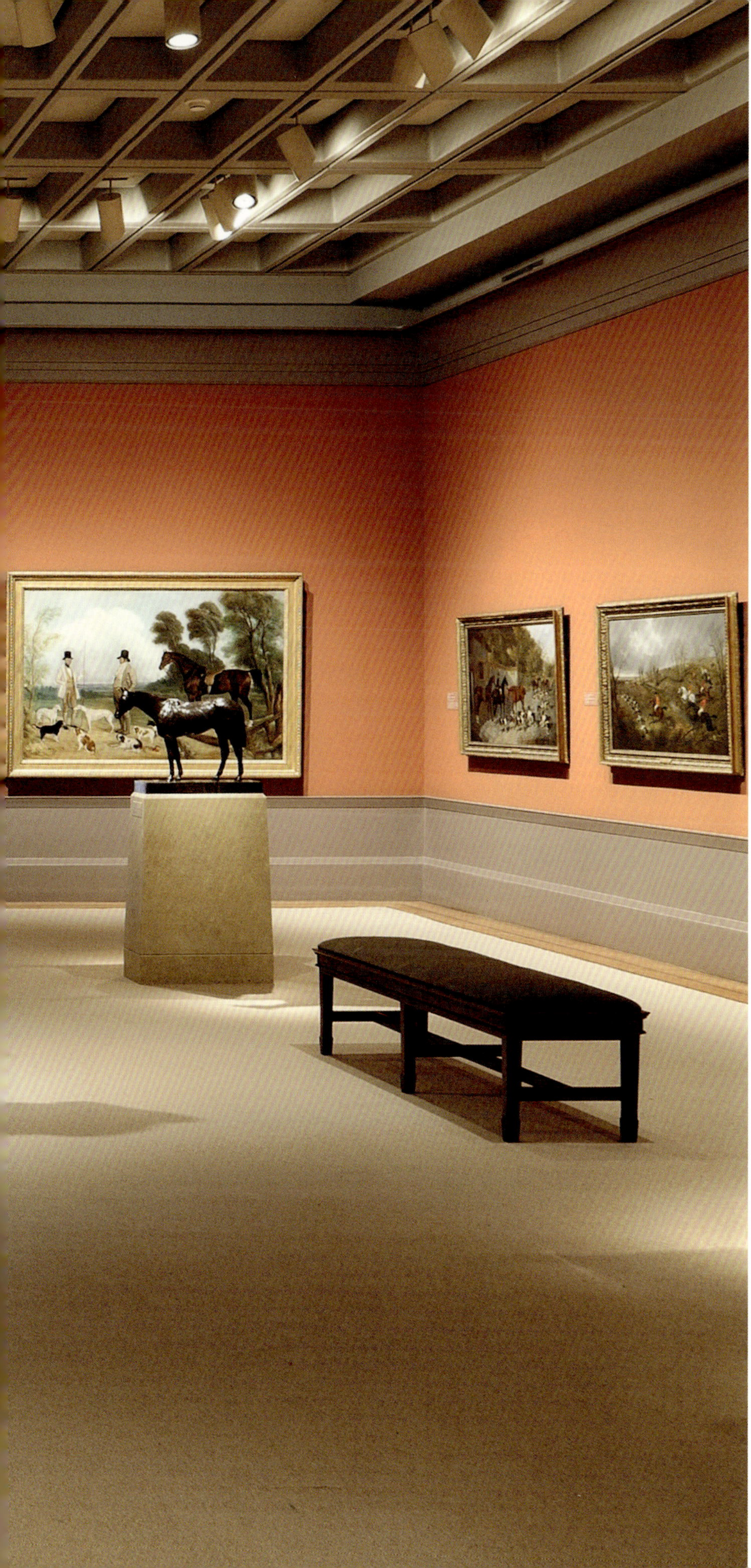

Hunting is another example of the reaction which has set up inside me against business, the city, modern industrial drabness, the suppression of the natural emotions and feelings. . . . It involves the use of the horse, that instinctive animal, and man's mastery of the horse.

—PAUL MELLON, 1936

Mellon Sporting Art Galleries, VMFA

GEORGE STUBBS

GEORGE STUBBS was one of the greatest practitioners of British sporting art. An accomplished painter and engraver whose intensive studies of anatomy included the dissection of horses, he achieved an unparalleled realism that appealed to patrons inspired, as he was, by the Enlightenment's emphasis on scientific inquiry.

In 1936 Paul Mellon bought his first painting, Stubbs's masterpiece *Pumpkin with a Stable-lad* (Yale Center for British Art). In his memoirs, Mr. Mellon reminisced about this first purchase:

> It was during our hunting tour in the Cotswolds back in 1936 that I met Angus Menzies, one of the partners of Knoedler's in London. He told me that the gallery had a beautiful Stubbs, and Mary and I agreed to go see it. We both were bowled over by the charming horse, the young boy in a cherry-colored jacket, and the beautiful landscape background. The price was five thousand dollars, and I bought it immediately. It was my very first purchase of a painting and could be said to be the impetus toward my later, some might say gluttonous, forays into the sporting art field.[1]

In the decades that followed, Stubbs remained a personal favorite of Mr. Mellon, who collected many more of his paintings. Mr. Mellon's interest did much to resuscitate Stubbs's image in the twentieth century. The six examples contained in this section span almost forty years of Stubbs's career. They highlight his ability to portray horses suited to different kinds of work, as well as the range of animals he represented naturalistically.

---

1. Paul Mellon, *Reflections in a Silver Spoon: A Memoir, with John Baskett* (New York: Morrow, 1992), 280–81.

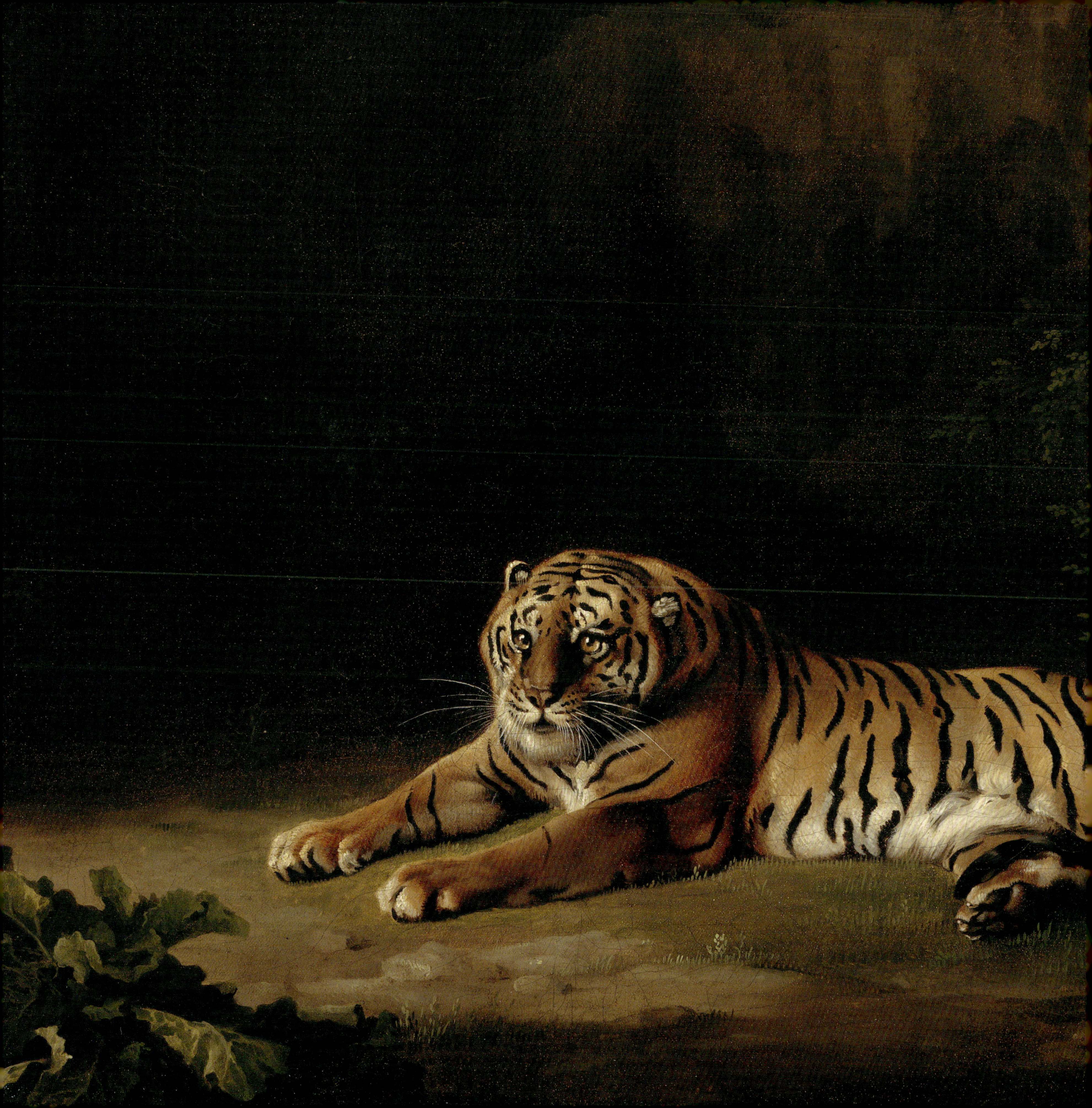

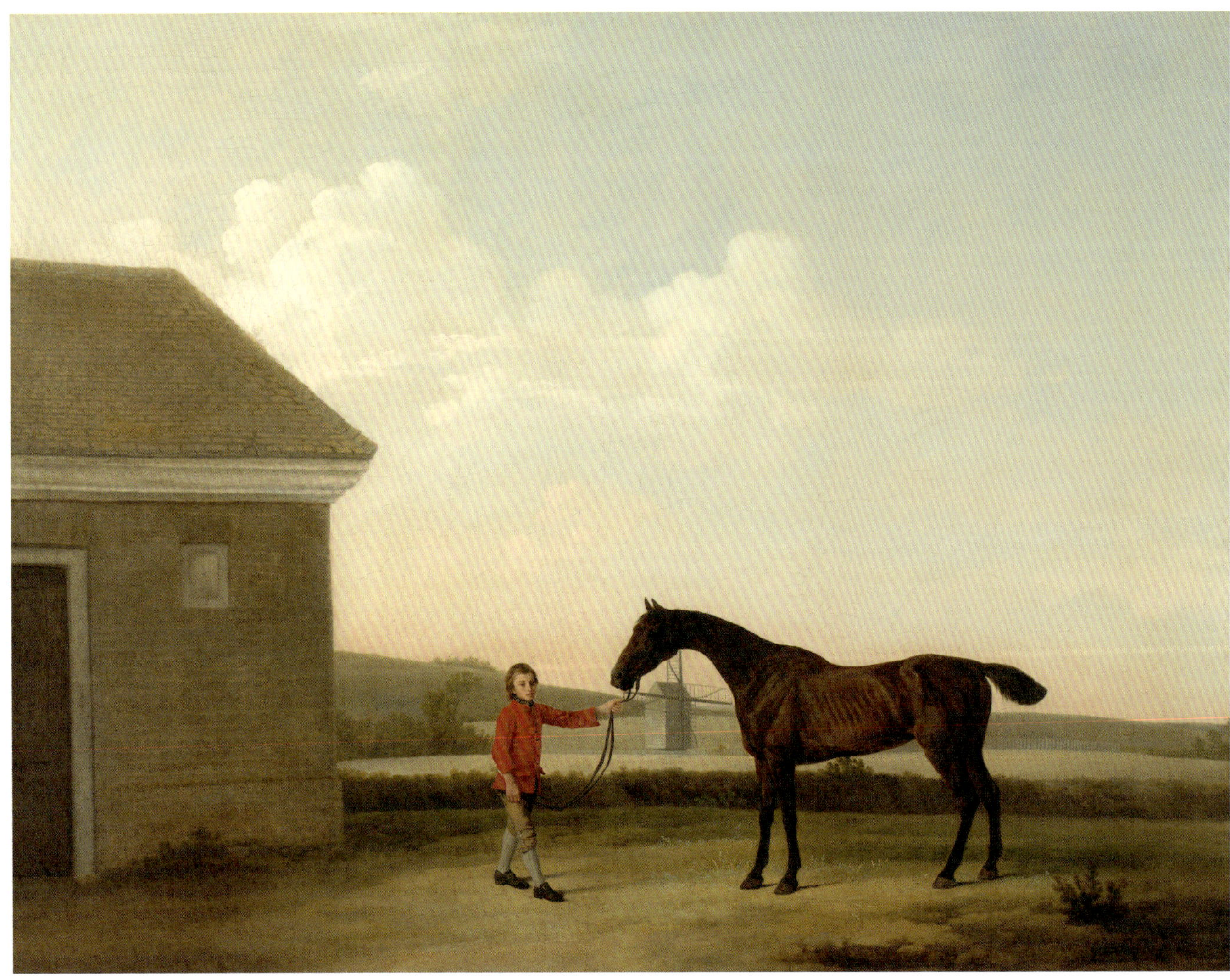

1 George Stubbs (English, 1724–1806)

Hyena (or Hyaena) at Newmarket with One of Jennison Shafto's Stable Lads, ca. 1765–67

Oil on canvas, 40 1/8 x 50 1/8 in., Paul Mellon Collection, 99.93

From 1756 to 1758 Stubbs's interests in horses, realism, and science converged as he dissected horses and made detailed drawings from three different perspectives (front, back, and side). It took almost ten years for Stubbs to turn these drawings into engravings and publish them as *The Anatomy of the Horse* (1766). This text was unrivaled in its exactitude and soon earned the artist renown, especially among sports enthusiasts.

This painting of Hyena—a successful racehorse and a famous dam of English and American winners—was produced around the same time that *The Anatomy of the Horse* was published. The painting is thus not only a portrait of an excellent racehorse but also an advertisement for Stubbs's superior knowledge of equine anatomy. At this time no one but Stubbs would have been better able to translate Hyena's physique, accentuated in the raking light, onto canvas. Her leanness was likely a result of running her long distances wearing layers of blankets to induce weight loss through sweating.

Though Hyena has been rendered with meticulous detail, it would be wrong to ignore the rest of the composition. Not wanting to be pigeonholed as a horse portraitist, Stubbs took pains to show Hyena's gentle relationship with the stable lad, who seems to be outgrowing his clothes. The landscape includes a cropped rubbing-down house at left, a windmill fitted under Hyena's neck, and an empty but voluminous sky. Perhaps Stubbs included these details to reinforce his commitment to a new kind of realism.

2 George Stubbs (English, 1724–1806)

Tiger (or Tigress), ca. 1769–71

Oil on canvas, 24 $\frac{3}{16}$ x 28 $\frac{11}{16}$ in., Paul Mellon Collection, 99.95

With his unsurpassed knowledge of anatomy, George Stubbs became the foremost Enlightenment painter not only of horses but of other animals as well. This tiger was likely kept in the menagerie of one of his English patrons.

In eighteenth-century texts, tigers were generally portrayed as

> the most rapacious and destructive of all carnivorous animals. Fierce without provocation, and cruel without necessity, its thirst for blood is insatiable: Though glutted with slaughter, it continues its carnage, nor ever gives up so long as a single object remains in its sight: Flocks and herds fall indiscriminate victims to its fury: It fears neither the fight nor the opposition of man, whom it frequently makes its prey; and it is even said to prefer human flesh to that of any other animal.[1]

Tigers were usually portrayed as fierce, but here Stubbs deviates from expectation by presenting this one in an equally natural state of repose.

1. T. Bewick, *A General History of Quadrupeds,* 3rd ed. (Newcastle upon Tyne: Hodgson, Beilby & Bewick, 1792), 186.

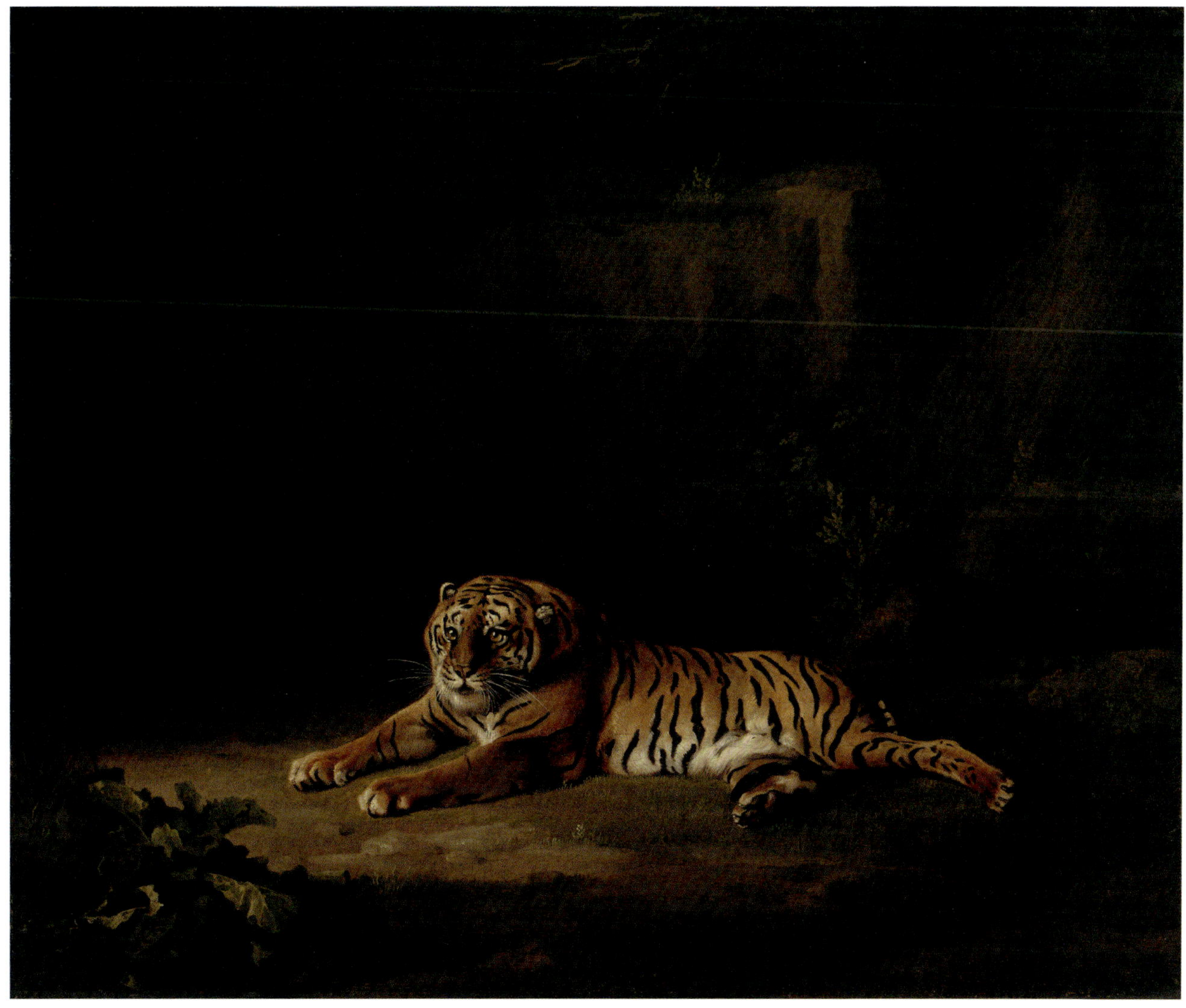

3 George Stubbs (English, 1724–1806)
A Dapple Grey Hunter with Two Foxhounds beside a Lake, ca. 1759–60

Oil on canvas, 12 x 12 in., Paul Mellon Collection, 99.91

This painting may have been a sketch for Stubbs's major commission, *The Third Duke of Richmond with the Charlton Hunt* (1759–60). Though the poses in the two paintings align, the attribution of the smaller one—an unusual size for Stubbs—has been questioned.

Would Mr. Mellon have been bothered if the painting turned out not to be by Stubbs? The answer is probably not. In his memoirs, Mr. Mellon explained that he and his wife never "felt a driving urge to own any picture just because it is important and certainly not because we considered it a good investment. We both like to wander down the byways of art, too, looking for something that catches our eye or for minor works that nonetheless recall happy memories or otherwise appeal to our hearts."[1]

Mr. Mellon is known to have turned down works by Stubbs—his favorite sporting artist—if they did not appeal to him, and his gifts to museums were accompanied by the "hope that the latest and best scholarship should prevail, let the chips fall where they may"—a sporting vision of art history indeed![2]

1. Mellon, 273.

2. Mellon, 281–82; 295.

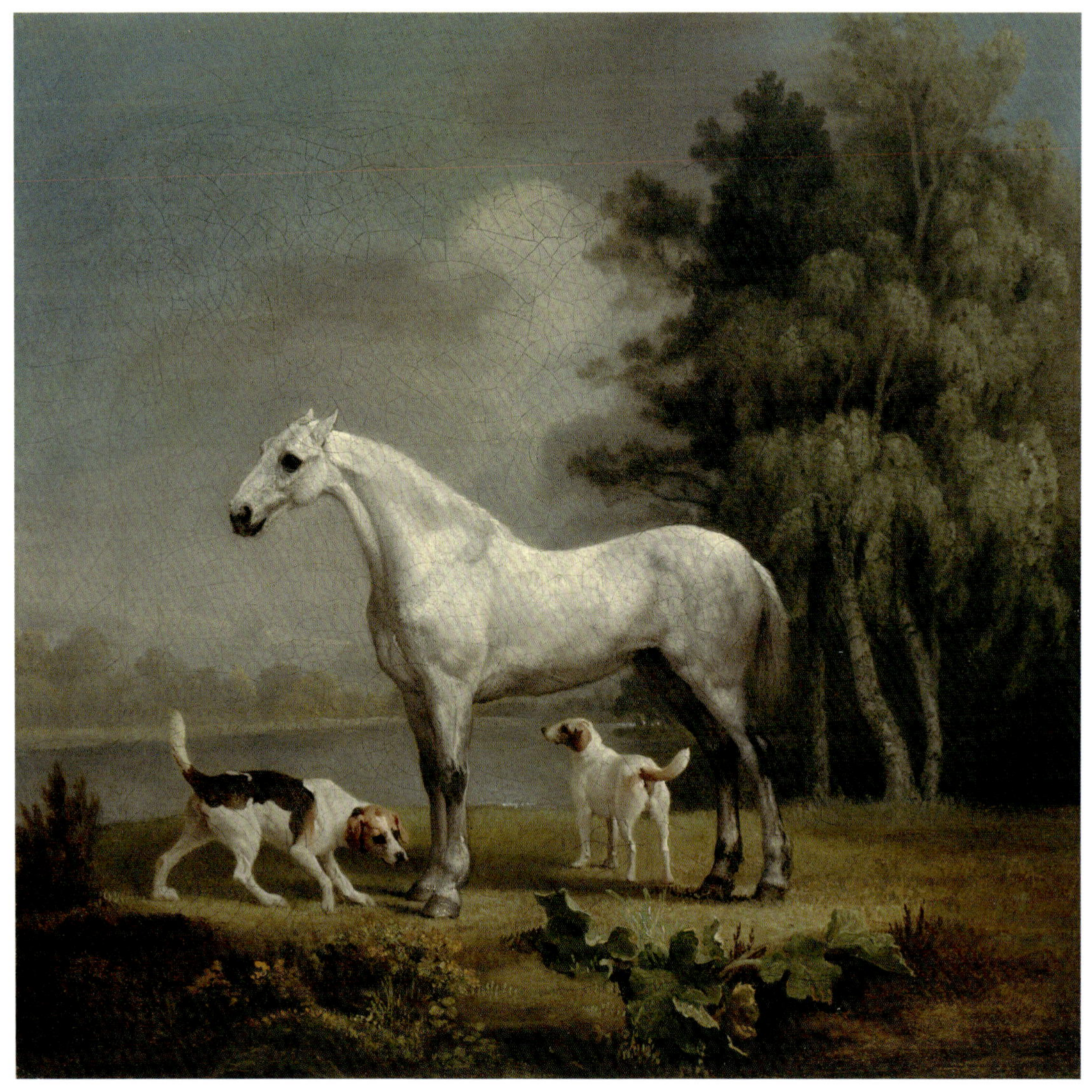

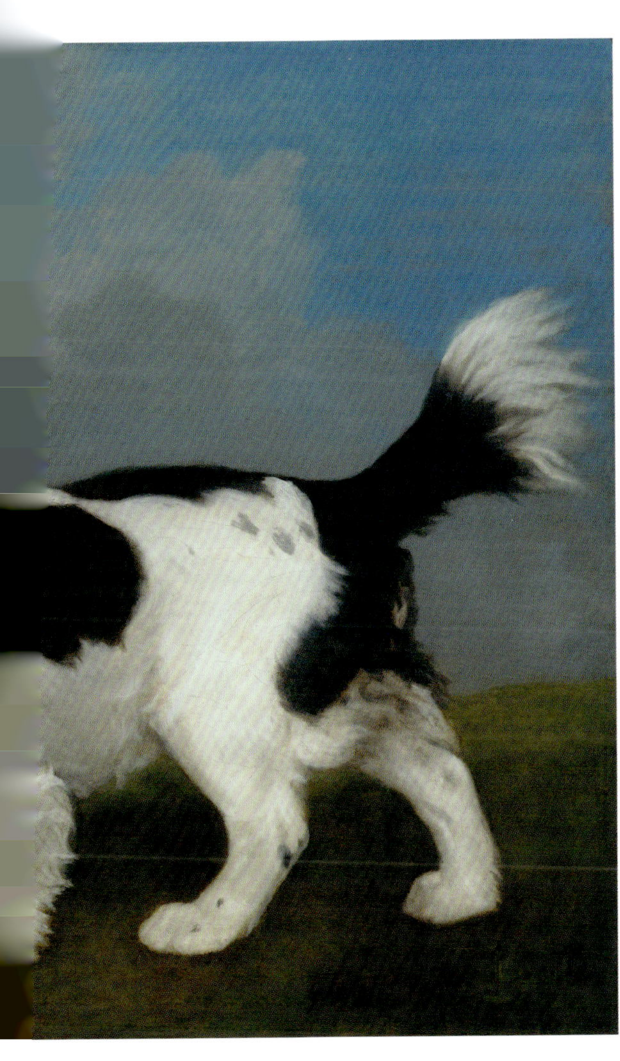

spaniel. Unfortunately, the name of this dog—or even that of its owner—has not come down through history with absolute certainty. The first documented owner of the painting was Thomas Villiers, the 2nd Earl of Clarendon, who purchased it shortly after Stubbs's studio dispersal sale on May 26, 1807.

Mr. Mellon purchased this painting in 1964, and it became the first work by Stubbs he gave to the Virginia Museum of Fine Arts.

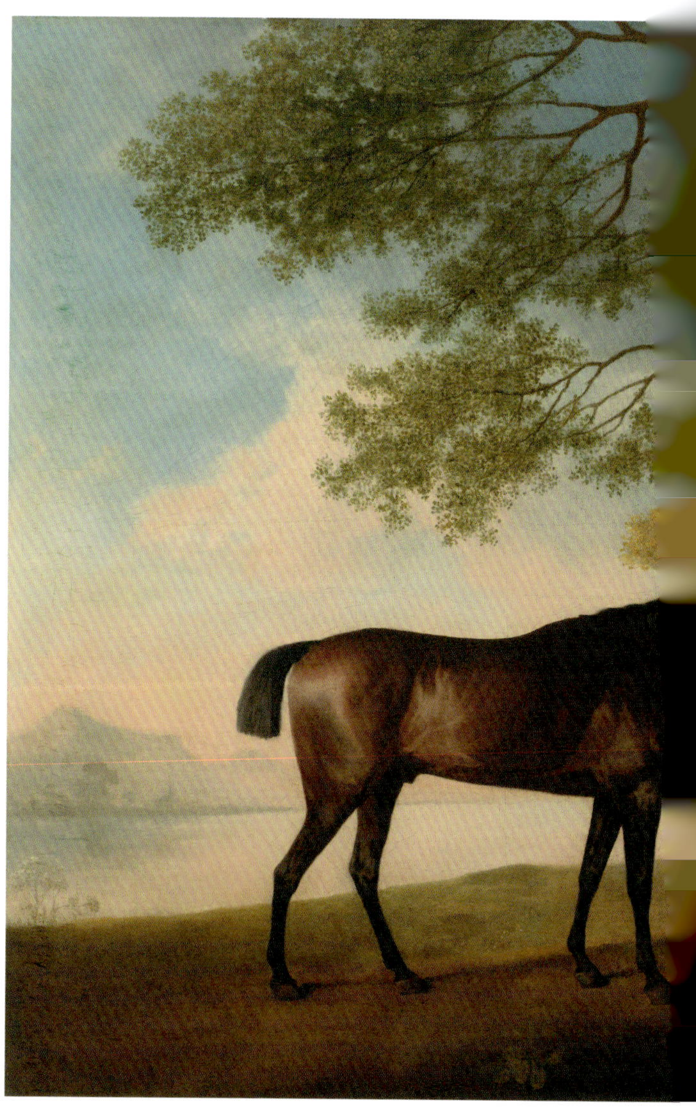

5 George Stubbs (English, 1724–1806)

Shark (or Sharke) with His Trainer Price, ca. 1790s

Oil on canvas, 40 ⅛ x 50 ⅛ in., Paul Mellon Collection, 99.94

Shark was a brown colt descended from the Darley Arabian, one of the three most important Middle Eastern sires of English thoroughbred racing stock, and Flying Childers (cat. no. 28). Foaled in 1771, Shark had a successful career racing exclusively at Newmarket racecourse between 1774 and 1779, where he amassed more winnings than any horse before him.[1]

After retirement, Shark's early career at stud was deemed disappointing. In 1786 he was eventually sold and exported to America, where he would go on to prove a successful sire in Virginia. A writer in the *American Turf Register* of 1830

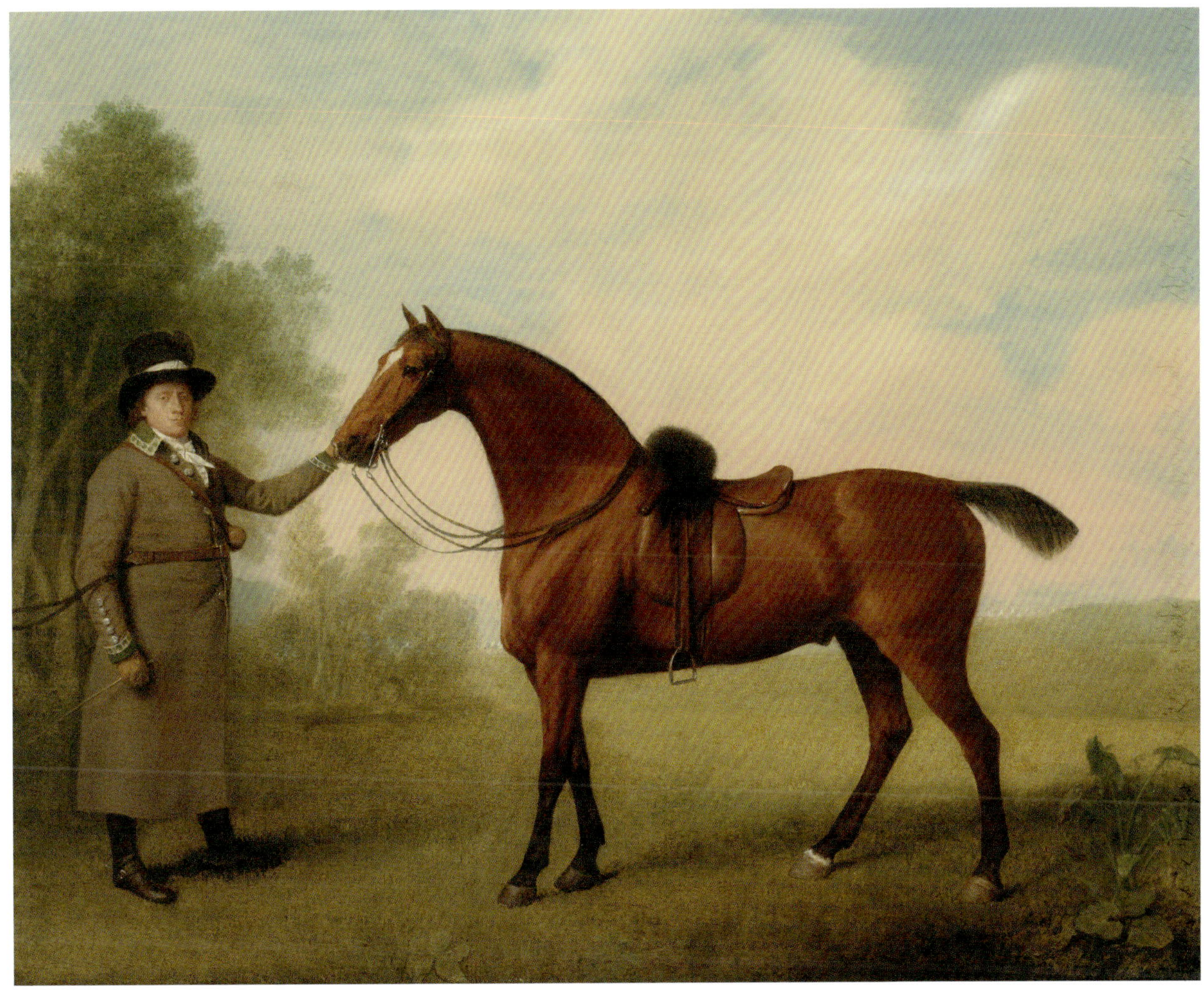

6 George Stubbs (English, 1724–1806)

Charger with a Groom, 1798

Oil on canvas, 25 x 29 ¾ in., Paul Mellon Collection, 99.92

Stubbs's subjects may seem to be simple, but they often prove to be highly sophisticated in both the choice and presentation of details. This charger, or military horse, is harnessed with tack borrowed from several sources. The fur-covered holster rests on a lightweight saddle similar to those used in hunting and at the racetrack. The double bridle comes from dressage training but appeared in battle because it provided superior communication between horse and rider. The charger is held by a well-dressed groom wearing a black cockaded hat and a long brown coat with green collar and cuffs. He seems to be holding the reins of another horse that is beyond the limits of this canvas.[1] The owner of this proudly displayed charger remains unknown because the livery of the groom has not yet been identified. Perhaps this charger belongs to a hussar, a member of the light cavalry encamped with his regiment in one of the white tents just visible in the distance.

1. Cormack, 197.

IN PURSUIT

IN PURSUIT assembles paintings by leading sporting artists to depict the three major types of country pastimes: hunting, shooting, and fishing. Foxhunting receives special focus, as it was one of Mr. Mellon's favorite endeavours—he hunted for more than fifty years on both sides of the Atlantic. In his memoirs he wrote about his attraction to this sport: "Hunting is another example of the reaction which has set up inside me against business, the city, modern industrial drabness, the suppression of the natural emotions and feelings. . . . It involves the use of the horse, that instinctive animal, and man's mastery of the horse."[1]

The grouping of works dedicated to foxhunting is noteworthy for its breadth. These paintings illustrate the evolution of the hunt and its social impact over almost two hundred years, from the 1730s to the 1920s. Starting in the eighteenth century, as a series of laws called the Enclosure Acts gradually transformed open heaths and forests to a regular field system and available prey changed from deer to foxes, attention turned to the opening up of country sports beyond the aristocracy to the upper middle class.

Shooting and fishing paintings round out this section. These images can be enjoyed for their own sake but also understood in specific contexts such as the advancement of gun making or the enactment of the Game Acts. Beginning in 1671 and revised many times thereafter, this legislation limited the shooting of particular birds and hares to the elite. By the time shooting laws were relaxed in 1831, allowing the middle class to participate, there were few unenclosed shooting grounds left.

Fishing, perhaps the greatest test of sporting skill, was also limited to those who could obtain permits from landowners possessing particularly well-stocked streams. The two fishing images in this section present game and coarse fishing, the names of which suggest their status.

In depicting sport and those who participated in it—from king to earth stopper—the paintings in this section add greatly to our knowledge of Britain and its rapidly changing landscape during the Enlightenment and Industrial Revolution.

1. Mellon, 152.

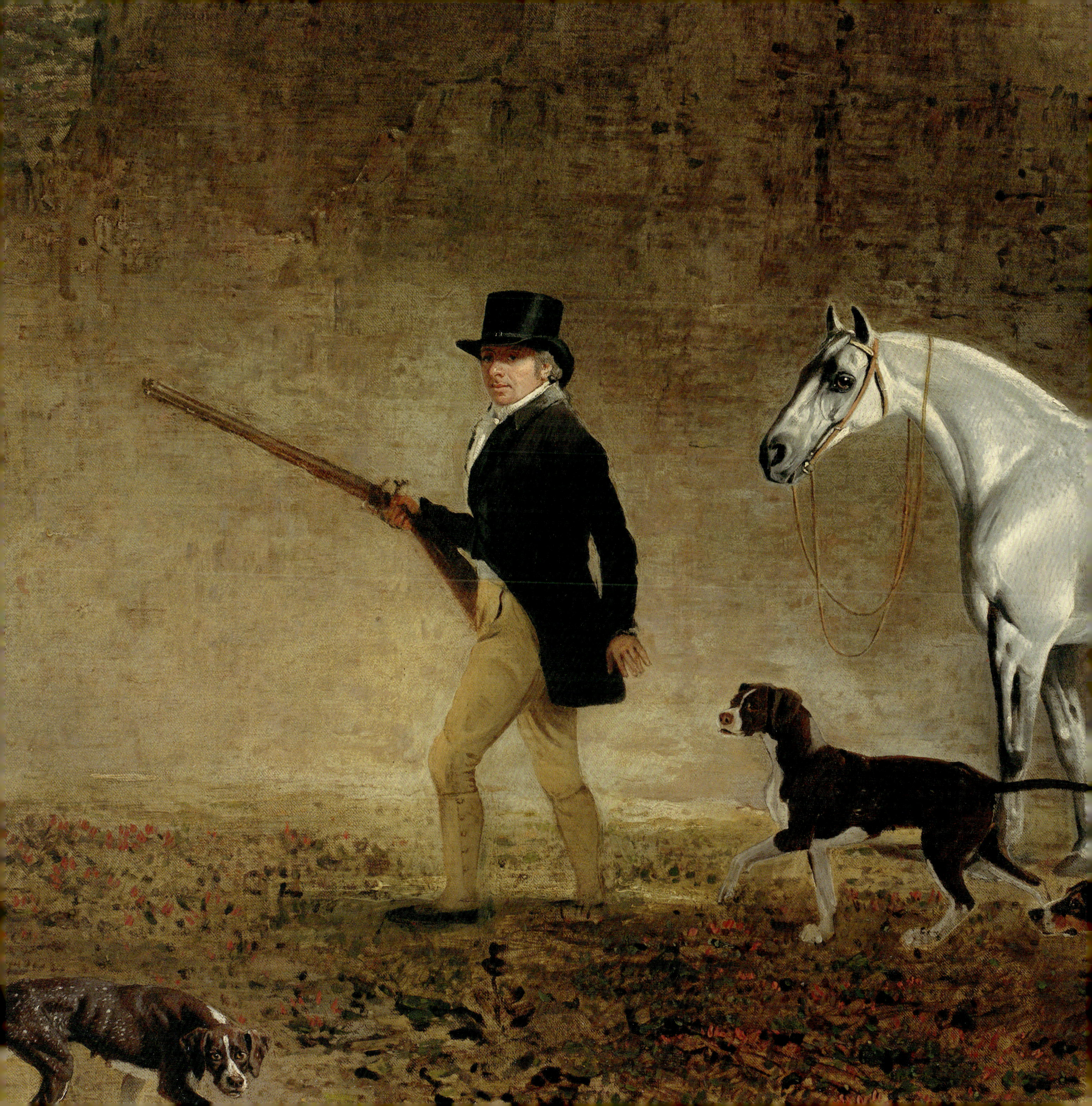

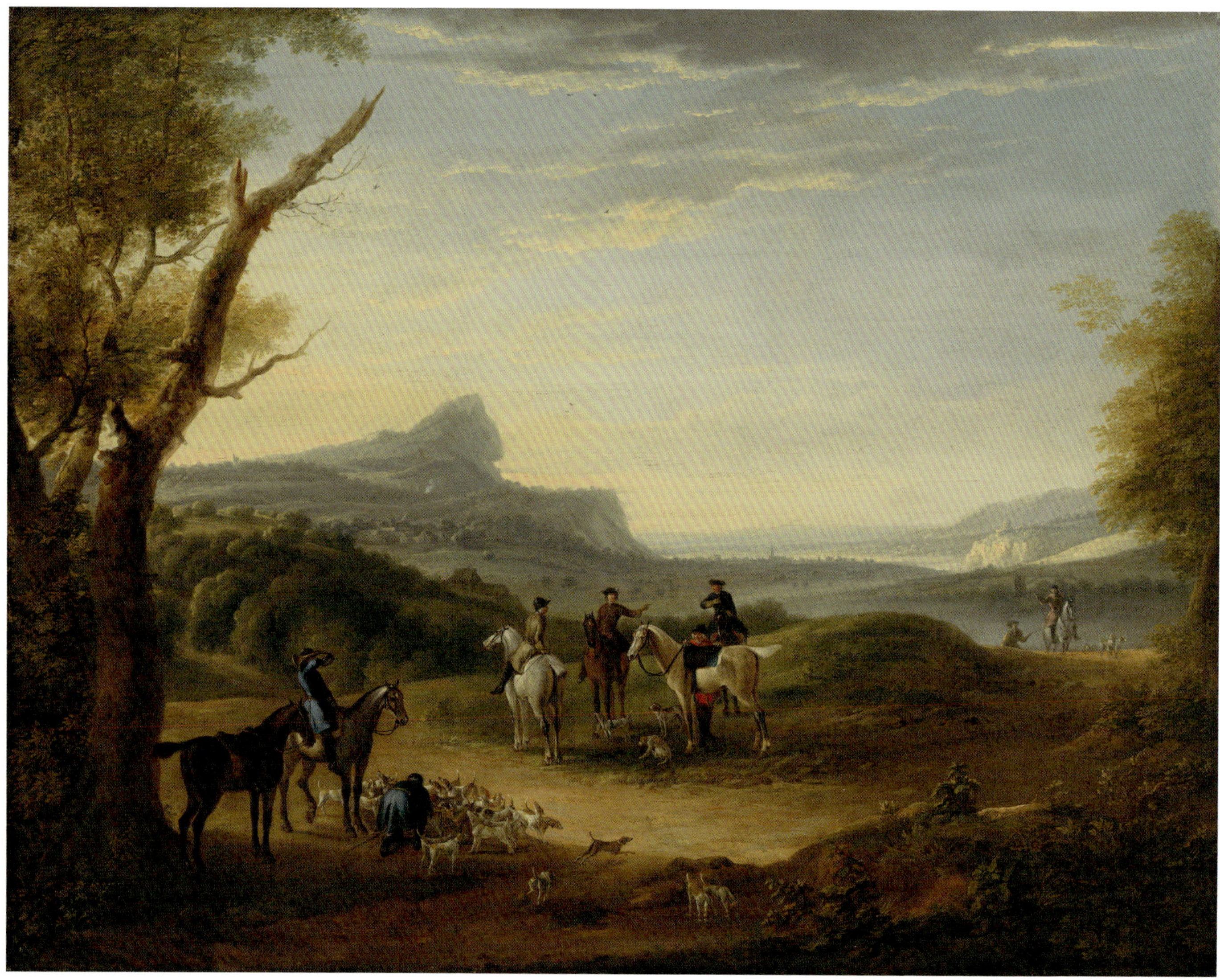

7 James Ross (English, active 1729–1733)

A Meet of Foxhounds, 1732

Oil on canvas, 40 ¼ x 49 ⅞ in., Paul Mellon Collection, 85.461

One of the earliest works in the catalogue, this hunting scene provides a point of reference for the development of the genre. Ross's composition is indebted to the continental landscape tradition, especially to seventeenth-century French and Flemish artists who popularized tree-framed foregrounds, detailed middle grounds, and atmospheric backgrounds. Ross has enhanced this open landscape by adding castellated ruins, cottages, and churches in the middle ground with rolling hills, a body of water, and a view of the Prating Rock looming in the distance. Lack of fences indicates that the gentlemen will be hunting in unenclosed land.

This work accurately conveys the social aspect of early eighteenth-century hunts. That there are so few hunters suggests that this is an exclusive affair. Indeed, the gentlemen depicted seem to be familiar with each other—those in the center are chatting, oblivious to their surroundings, the foxhounds (never referred to as dogs by huntsmen), and even the blare of the hunting horn.

Other details place the scene during the early development of hunting. The curved French horn would, in time, be replaced by the short straight English horn. The huntsman leaning down to couple, or uncouple, two foxhounds demonstrates one of the training techniques that were becoming popular: a coupling collar linked together an experienced hound with an inexperienced one in order to teach the latter how to hunt. This practice would lead to such phrases as "seven and a half couple of hounds," which meant a total of fifteen.

8 James Seymour (English, 1702–1752)

Mr. Peter Delmé's Hounds on the Hampshire Downs, 1738

Oil on canvas, 40 x 50 in., Paul Mellon Collection, 85.508

Born and trained in London, James Seymour was one of the first artists to make a living from sporting art. Though he was not a great technician and never mastered equine anatomy, he was able to produce works with enough naturalism to attract commissions.

This work's patron, Peter Delmé (1710–1770), is probably the young man in green livery leaning forward to talk to the rider turned away from the viewer; he lived the life of a country gentleman thanks to the wealth amassed by his father, Sir Peter Delmé, who served as a governor of the Bank of England and Lord Mayor of London.

Compared to the compact, focused narrative that Seymour uses for *Three Riders Following Hounds towards a Five-Barred Gate* (cat. no. 9), here he has taken great care to accurately represent the open landscape and atmosphere of Hampshire Downs on a wintry morning. The lack of larger vegetation has led some to compare the landscape to a desert, an allusion furthered by the horse at bottom right in the grounded-gallop pose who displays the distinctive dished face and high tail carriage of its Middle Eastern ancestors.[1]

1. Donna Landry, *Noble Brutes: How Eastern Horses Transformed English Culture* (Baltimore: Johns Hopkins University Press, 2008), 60–61.

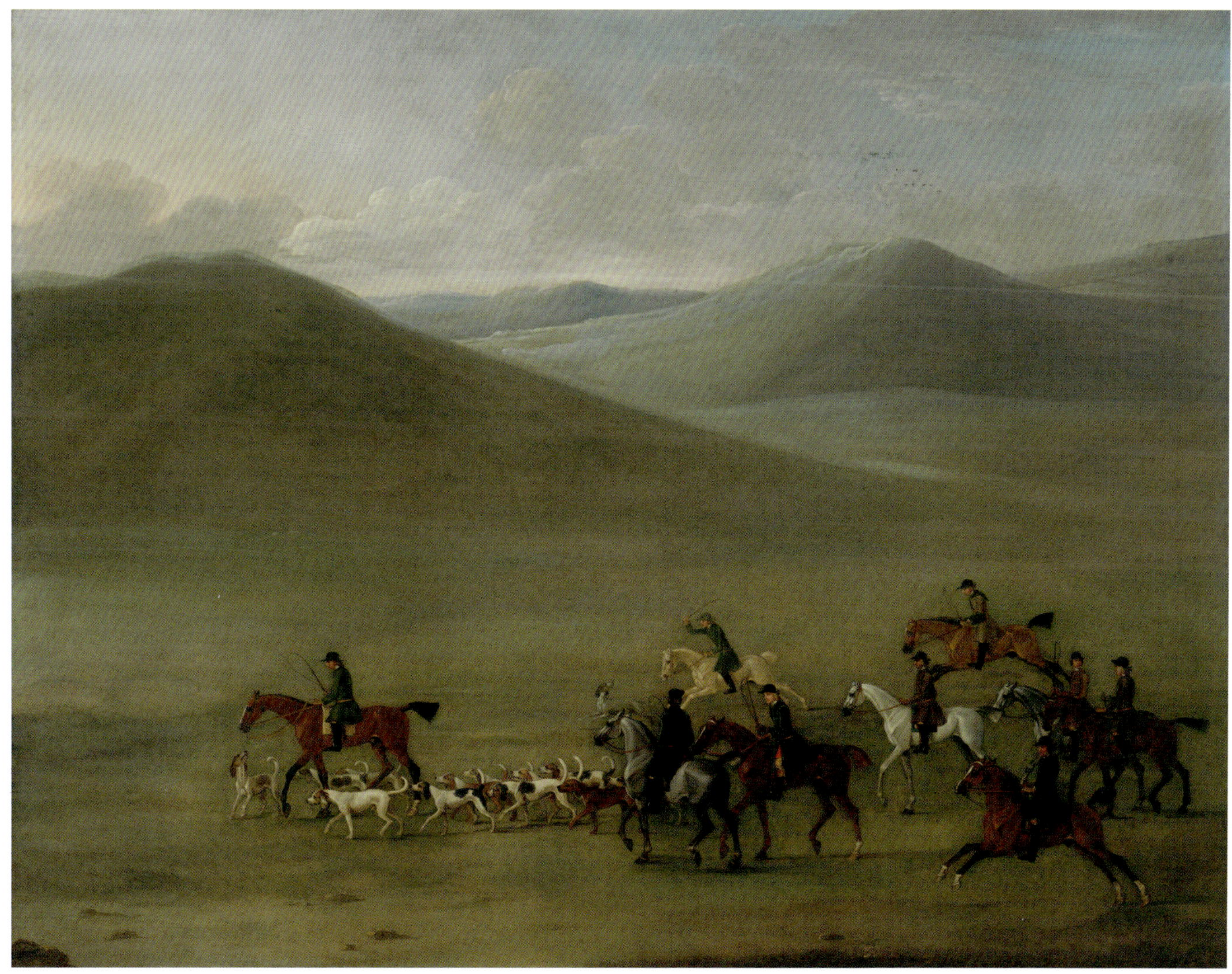

9 James Seymour (English, 1702–1752)

Three Riders Following Hounds towards a Five-Barred Gate, 1735–40

Oil on canvas, 28 x 90 ½ in., Paul Mellon Collection, 99.88

Seymour has solved the challenge of the long narrow canvas (perhaps designed to fit over a door) in a brilliant manner. A bullfinch, or high hedge, along the back and a five-bar gate at right set the scene within an area that has been reclaimed by enclosure. Strung out across this rectangle are three riders following three hounds in pursuit of unknown quarry. Seymour added a further level of visual balance to the composition by making the color schemes of the horses' and hounds' coats mimic each other.

In the fifty years leading up to the production of this image, horses of Middle Eastern descent were being imported to England.[1] Their progeny, crossbred with British horses to produce a version of modern thoroughbreds noteworthy for their speed, size, and endurance, were used for racing and hunting. To indicate

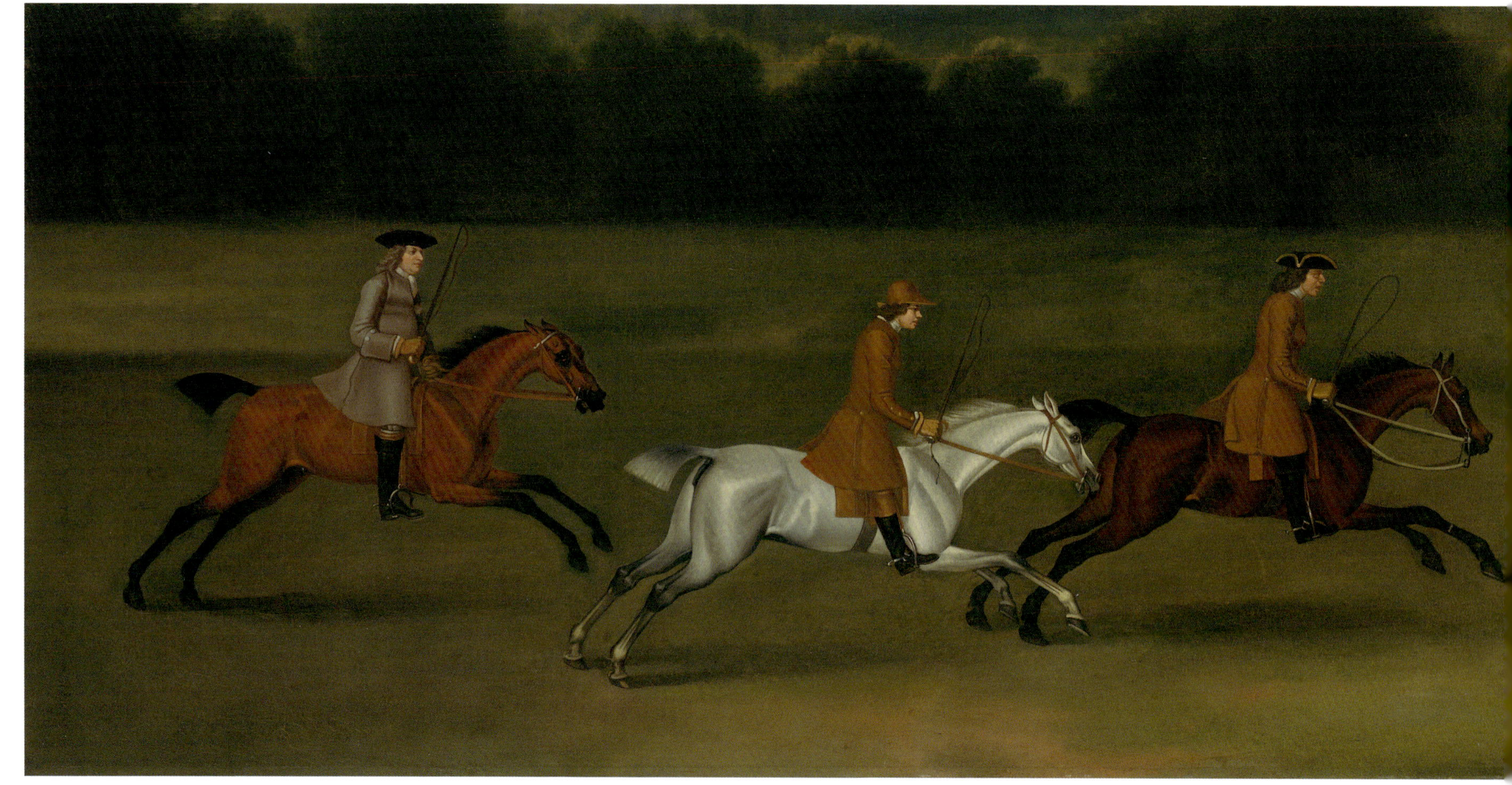

these horses' speed, Seymour has used the established European convention of the grounded gallop, with forelegs bent up and hind legs straight on the ground.[2]

As horses became faster, new tack was needed. Our three riders are all equipped with newer, smaller saddles (borrowed from jockeys) instead of large dressage saddles. Two of them have also given up another dressage element, the double bridle, and are using a single snaffle bridle instead. (Note that the rider out in front has left one of his reins a bit loose.) Additionally, stirrups were shortened—another jockey practice—to allow riders to lean forward as the pace of their mounts quickened in preparation for jumping, which the three horses in this painting are about to do.[3]

Shorter stirrups, in turn, led to a change in hunting fashion. Tall boots that came above the knee were now rolled down below the knee—as the middle rider has done—to make it possible to sit comfortably in the saddle.

1. In period equine manuscripts these horses are usually referred to as Arabians, Turks (from Central Asia), and Barbs (from the Barbary Coast).

2. Irma B. Jaffe and Gernando Colombardo, "The Flying Gallop: East and West," *The Art Bulletin* 65, no. 2 (June 1983), 183.

3. Landry, 57-61.

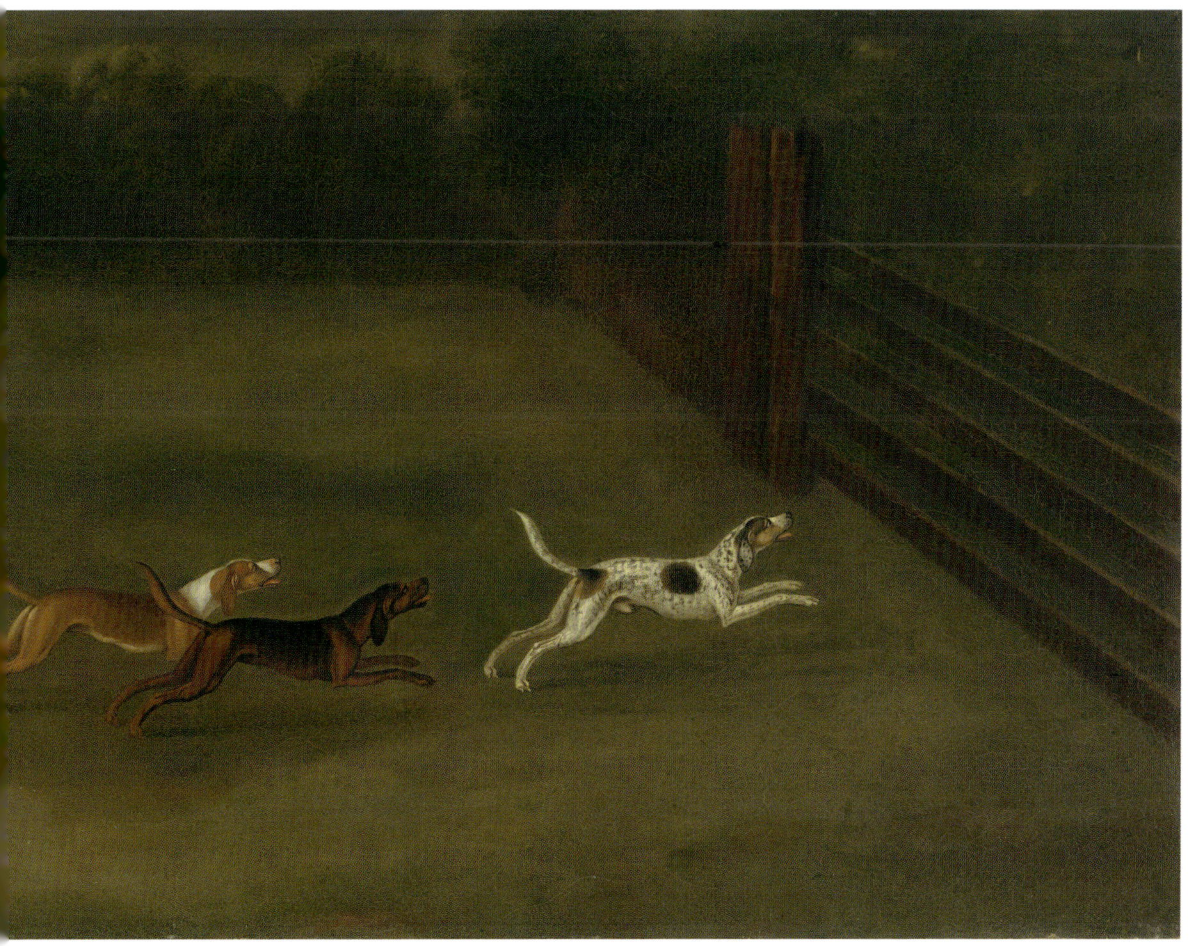

10 John Nost Sartorius (English, 1759–1828)

a. *Fox Hunting: Setting Out,* 1787

Oil on canvas, 14 1/8 x 19 1/8 in., Paul Mellon Collection, 85.468.1

b. *Fox Hunting: Full Cry,* 1787

Oil on canvas, 13 13/16 x 19 1/16 in., Paul Mellon Collection, 85.468.2

c. *Fox Hunting: Gone Away,* 1787

Oil on canvas, 13 7/8 x 19 1/4 in., Paul Mellon Collection, 85.468.3

d. *Fox Hunting: The Kill,* 1787

Oil on canvas, 14 1/8 x 19 1/16 in., Paul Mellon Collection, 85.468.4

John Nost Sartorius belonged to the third of four generations of sporting artists in his family.[1] His subjects included racing, coaching, and animals, but he is best remembered for his images of fox hunting. His popularity was due in part to the many prints made after his paintings.

This set of paintings was completed when Hugo Meynell was Master of the Quorn Hunt (1753–1800). During those years, Meynell bred his hounds to have a uniform look, greater speed, and better endurance. With these last two characteristics, he thus transformed the hunt from a slow slog to a fast and exciting event. For Meynell, there was no greater pleasure in hunting than watching his hounds do what he had bred them to do. Unfortunately, this was not the case for some of the sportsmen who rode with him.

Between 1750 and 1800, hunting became increasingly associated with wealthy landowners, or their sons, whose money allowed them unlimited access to food, drink, pleasure, and sport. To accommodate this lifestyle, Meynell moved the starting time of meets from early morning to mid-morning.[2] On the field, a definite uptick in reckless behavior occurred. Around 1780, thrusting, or riding too close to the hounds or hunting staff and jumping every obstacle in sight, became popularized by the foxhunter Childe Kinlet.[3] Indeed, sportsmen would throw caution to the winds to be first at the kill (perhaps seen in the last canvas).

Huntsman and writer Peter Beckford attempted to undo this cliché about sportsmen. In his text, *Thoughts on Hunting* (1779), Beckford emphasized the rules that one had to follow in order to participate and downplayed both the recklessness of sportsmen and their enjoyment in the brutality of the kill.[4]

These sportsmen commissioned artists like Sartorius to document their long, satisfying chases. In order to convey the multiple stages that took place during the hunt, it became common practice to use numerous canvases—generally three or four.[5] For this series, Sartorius narrows down the entire chase to four scenes: *Setting Out, Full Cry, Gone Away,* and *The Kill.*

1. Cormack, 454.
2. Martin Wallen, *Fox* (London: Reaktion, 2006), 102.
3. Wallen, 101.
4. Wallen, 102–3.
5. Wallen, 109.

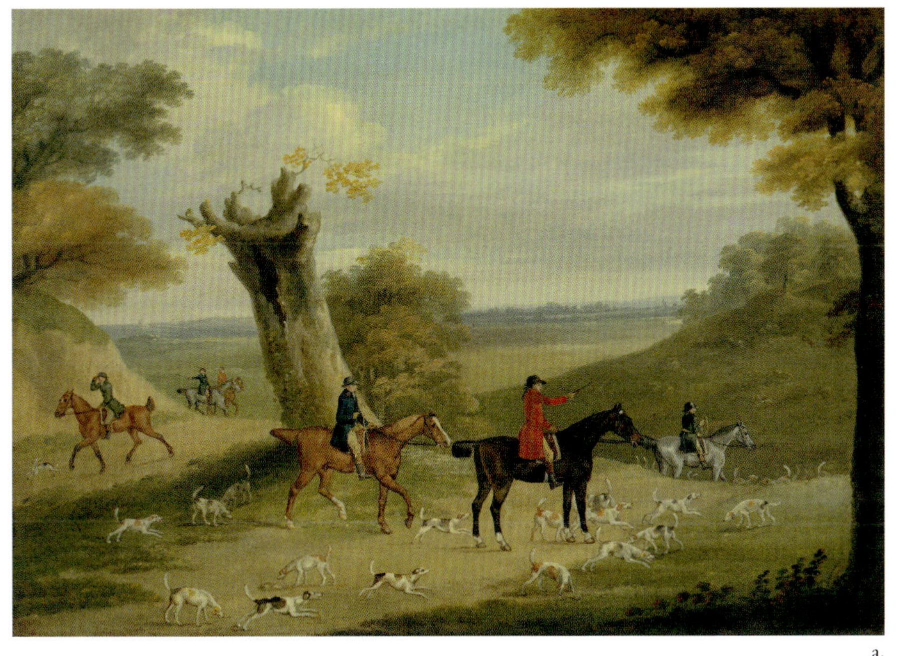

a.

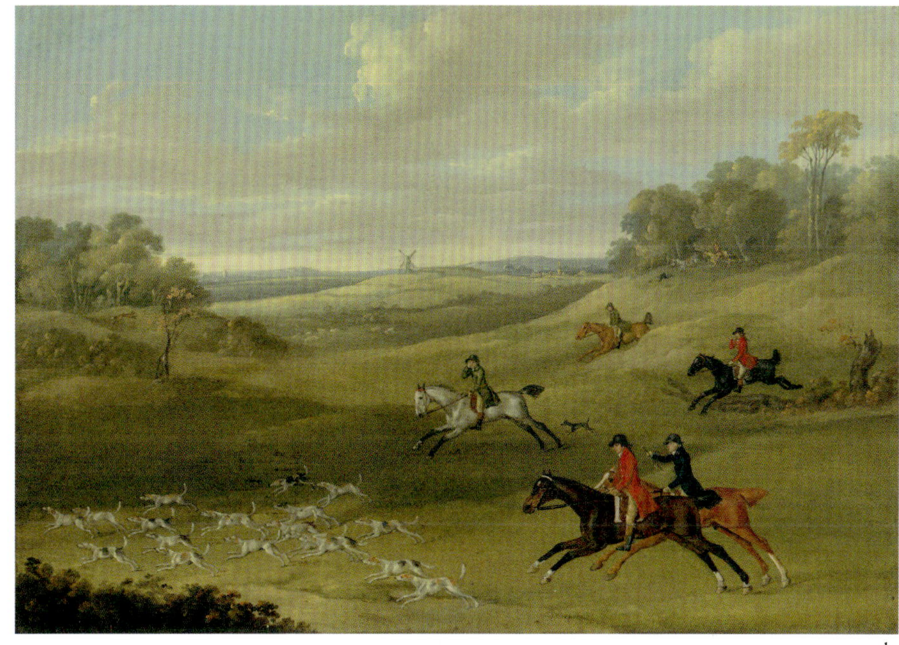

b.

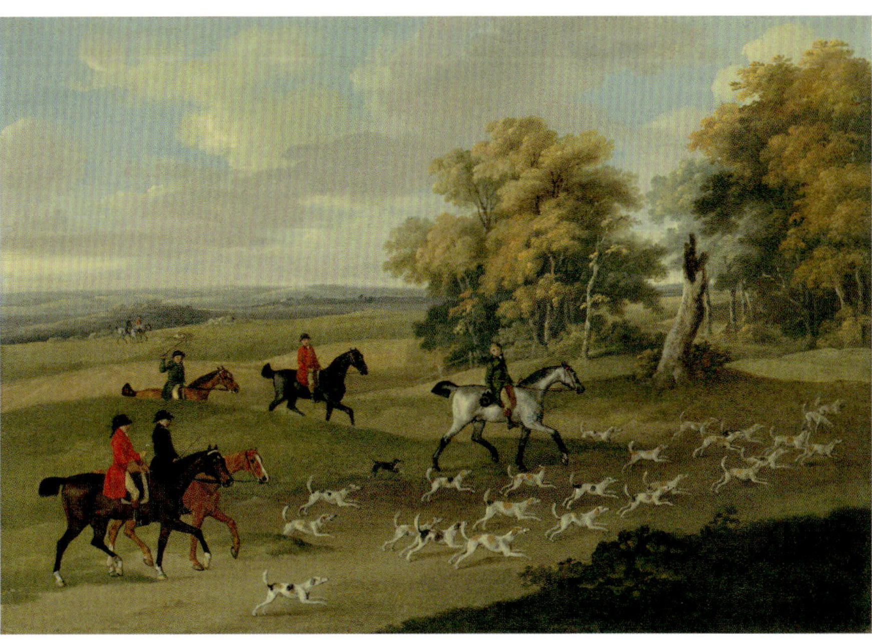

c.

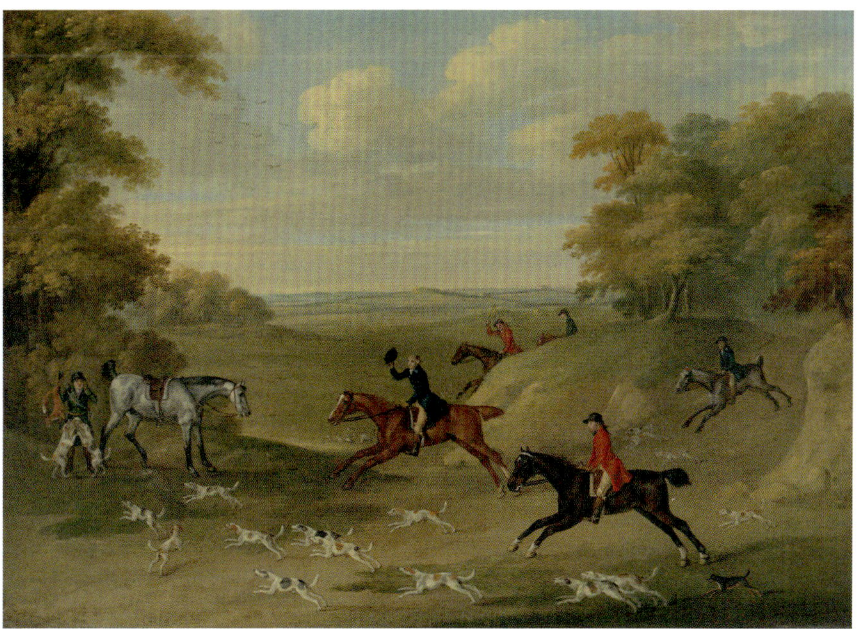

d.

11 John Nost Sartorius (English, 1759–1828)

Fox-Hunting: The Kill, ca. 1800

Oil on canvas, 38 x 48 in., Paul Mellon Collection, 85.469

In this foxhunting scene Sartorius downplays the sport's perceived recklessness and brutality, creating a piece of propaganda for the continuation of foxhunting.

Sartorius has devoted this large canvas to just one stage of a hunt, the kill. As in the last panel of his series of four (cat. no. 10d), the huntsman has dismounted and holds the fox aloft, out of reach of the hounds, while two members of the hunt in their pinks (as the scarlet hunting coats are called) approach at a slow, decidedly non-reckless speed. The rider on the brown horse turns to his companion while gesturing toward the fox—and maybe also to the woman in the cottage opening her window to see what's going on.

By placing the kill in front of a cottage, Sartorius is perhaps underscoring the beneficial nature of a sport that keeps the country safe for farmers' and villagers' animals by freeing it of vermin.[1]

1. Wallen, 108–9.

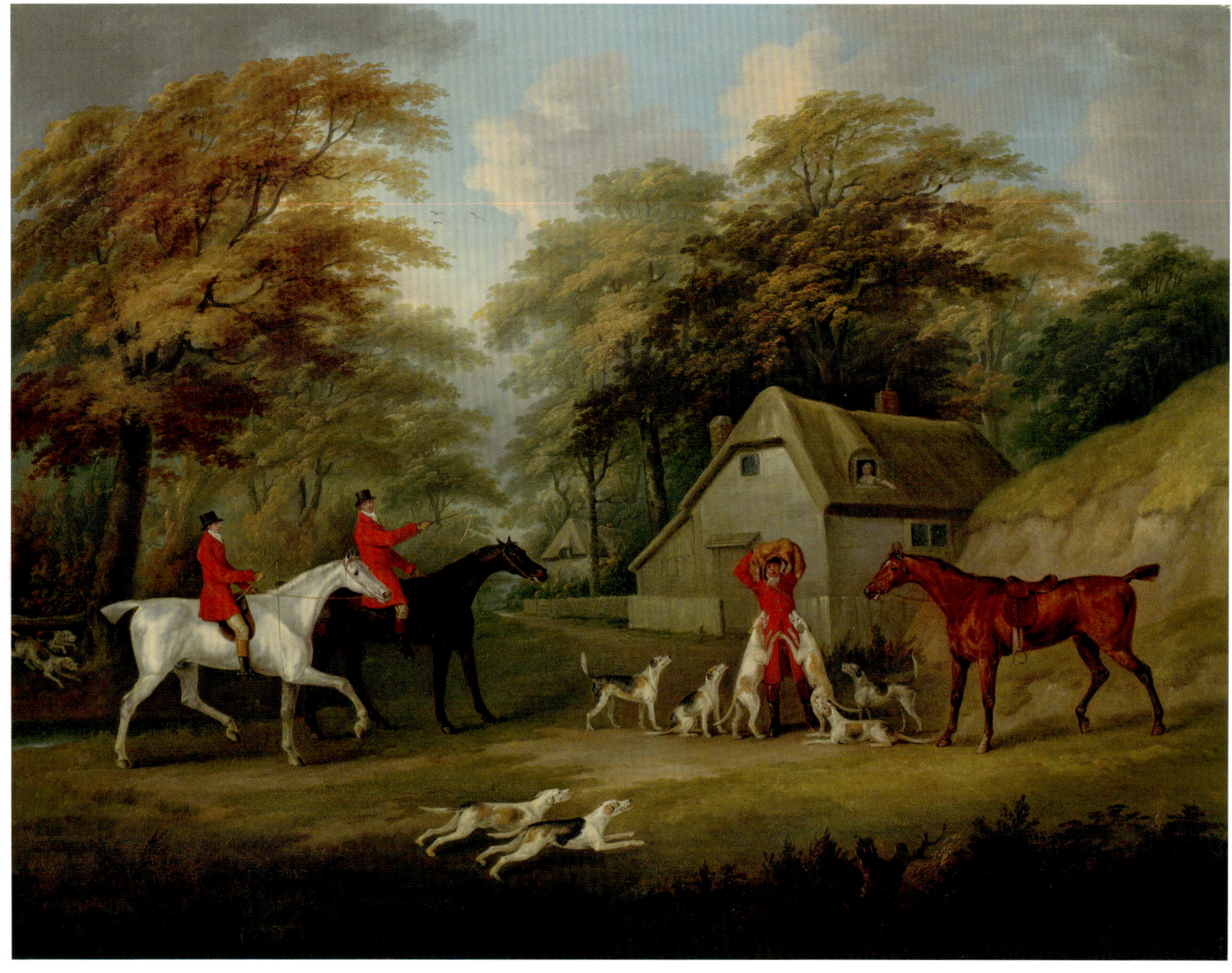

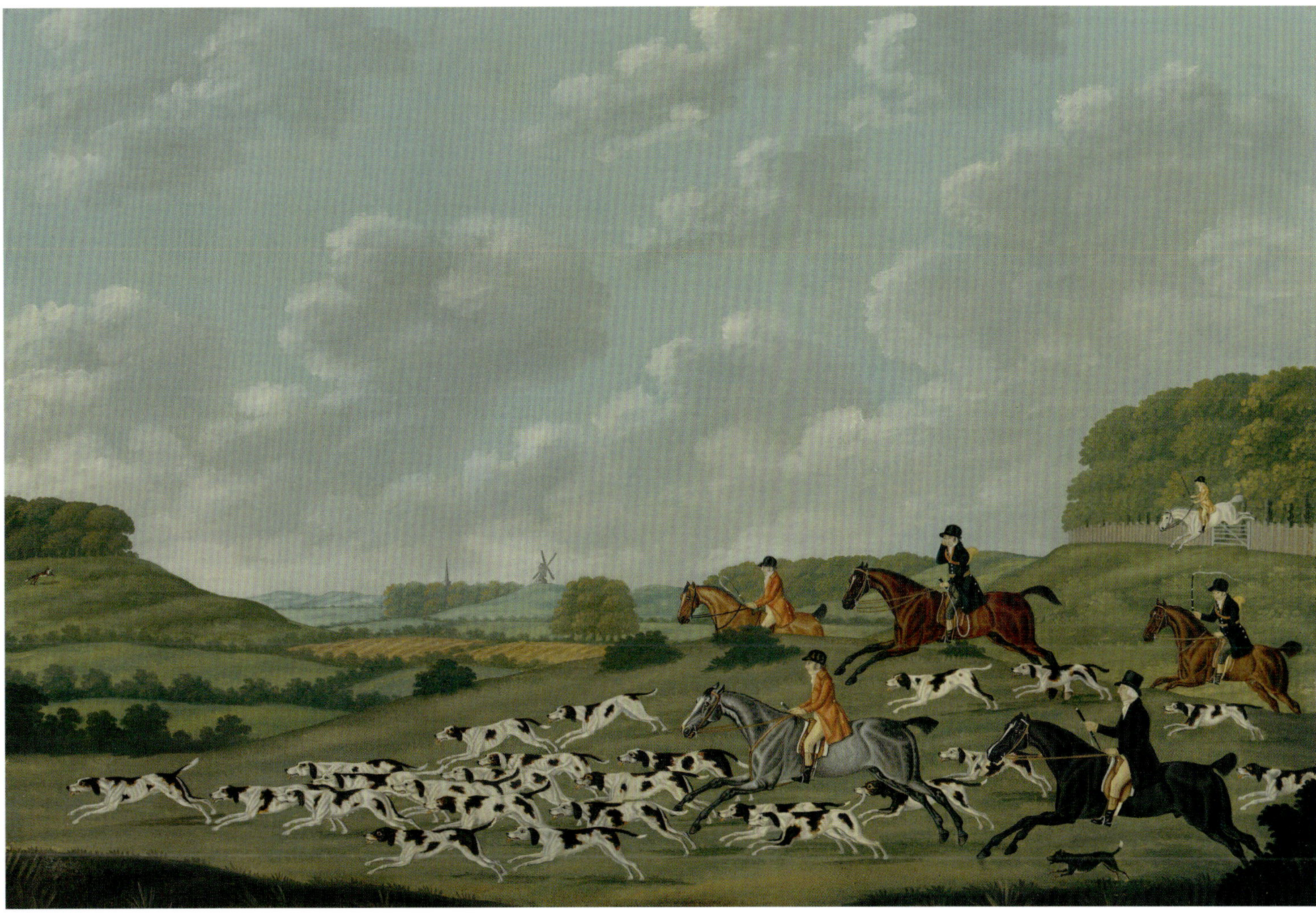

12 John Cordrey (English, active 1765–1825)

Fox-Hunting: Full Cry, 1819

Oil on canvas, 21 x 30 1/8 in., Paul Mellon Collection, 85.475

Almost nothing is known about John Cordrey. His naïve style was perhaps the result of having gotten his start painting coaches and then teaching himself how to paint pictures—mostly coaching and hunting scenes. This scene depicts the stage of the chase known as the "Full Cry," which occurs after the scent of the fox has been found and the entire pack of hounds are running hard and giving tongue (barking) while in pursuit.

Indeed, the twelve couple (or twenty-four) hounds are all depicted in the same type of grounded gallop pose that is used to show great speed in horses. Following in their wake are the members of the hunt staff. The two wearing blue coats are carrying large curved French horns. The gentleman on the black horse in the lower right corner is perhaps the patron of this work, as in actuality it would be of questionable form to follow so close to the hounds and the hunt staff. The fox, in the distance at left, seems to be heading for covert (pronounced "cover"). Beneath the black horse, a terrier keeps up with the chase; it will be sent in after the fox if the fox goes to earth (enters its den).

There are many incongruences in this particular work. French horns were popular a century earlier, as seen in James Ross's *A Meet of Foxhounds* (cat. no. 7). Produced at a time when scarlet—or pink—coats were becoming ever more common, the lack of uniformity among the members of the hunt may be another indicator that Cordrey was attempting to evoke nostalgia for earlier times.[1] The setting is another faux pas: hunting happens in the late autumn and winter—after the harvest—whereas in this countryside the trees are green.

1. Roger Longrigg, *The History of Foxhunting* (New York: Potter, 1975), 117.

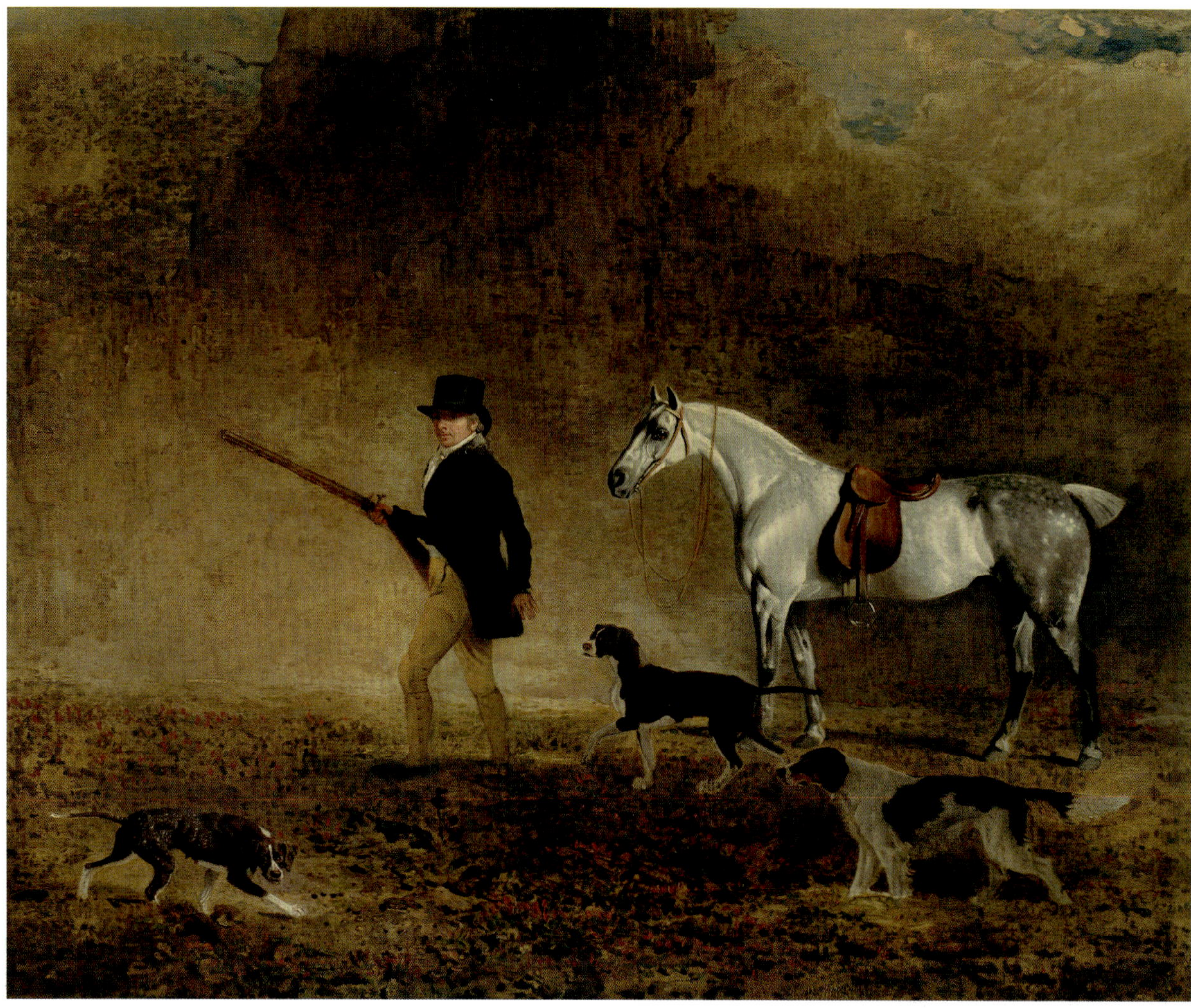

13 Benjamin Marshall (English, 1768–1835)

Colonel Henry Campbell Shooting on a Moor, **ca. 1806**

Oil on canvas, 33 7/8 x 40 1/8 in., Paul Mellon Collection, 99.81

The Game Act passed by the English Parliament in 1671, and its twenty-four subsequent revisions over the next two hundred years, restricted game hunting to only the wealthiest landowners. Such limitations were justified as a way to avoid insurrection by keeping weapons out of the hands of the lower classes, but they also ensured a plentiful supply of game. Landowners employed game-keepers to watch over their land and impose stiff punishments for poaching.[1]

Marshall depicts landowner Colonel Henry Campbell with his double-barrel rifle on a northern moor. The Campbell family was known for their well-trained "Kingston" breed of pointers, as evidenced by the dog in the left foreground that is correctly "backing off" the quarry so as not to get too far ahead of the rest of the party. This painting was engraved by J. Romney and appeared in *The Sporting Magazine* of May 1833. The engraving accompanied the article "Grouse Shooting in the North," which describes the pedigree of Colonel Campbell's pointer (or setter): "The Setter that is backing so patiently is descended from the breed long in the possession of Capt. William Churchill of the Guards, the friend . . . of His late Royal Highness the Prince of Wales, who invariably declared that of all four-footed animals he ever knew, these were nearest to perfection."

The breeding in the colonel's dogs is echoed in the conformation of his hunter (as a horse to be ridden by someone hunting is called), which appears to be a descendant of the Middle Eastern and African horses that had been imported to England in the seventeenth and eighteenth centuries.

1. Corey Piper, "The Social World of the British Sporting Print," *Catching Sight: The World of the British Sporting Print* (Richmond, Virginia: Virginia Museum of Fine Arts, 2013), 41–54.

14 Benjamin Marshall (English, 1768–1835)

Noble, a Hunter Well Known in Kent, ca. 1805–10

Oil on canvas, 40 1/8 x 50 in., Paul Mellon Collection, 99.80

Benjamin Marshall studied under portrait painter Lemuel Francis Abbott, but his own portraits were more of horses and people in scenes of horse racing, foxhunting, coaching, and the like. Marshall allegedly claimed he painted such subjects because "I discover many a man who will pay me fifty guineas for painting his horse, who thinks ten guineas too much for painting his wife."

Marshall depicts the hunter Noble being ridden by an unnamed servant. The horse's grey coat stands out against a rough, primordial landscape. Noble has "the look of eagles" and surveys a hunt taking place in the distance, poised to spring into action. John Scott turned this large canvas into a print with an accompanying description of the horse's pedigree and accomplishments: "The subject of this print . . . is the portrait of a famous hunter, well known in Kent. He was got by Noble [Derby winner in 1786], a son of Highflyer, out of nearly, or quite, a thoroughbred mare. He is famous for having carried a gentleman, 17 st. [238 lbs] for a number of years, up to the fleetest of hounds, and in a country where the hills are tremendous. His master, to find out all his perfections, has ridden him as a pleasure horse in the summer, and raced him in the autumn."[1]

Paintings such as this prove that portraits of horses were not only reserved for racehorses and that pedigree mattered in a hunting horse, too. At this point in the history of foxhunting, hunters were normally three-quarters or seven-eighths thoroughbred to provide enough speed and endurance, as well as strength, to carry a rider over long distances.

1. "Noble," *The Sporting Magazine* 26, no. 206 (April 1810), 1.

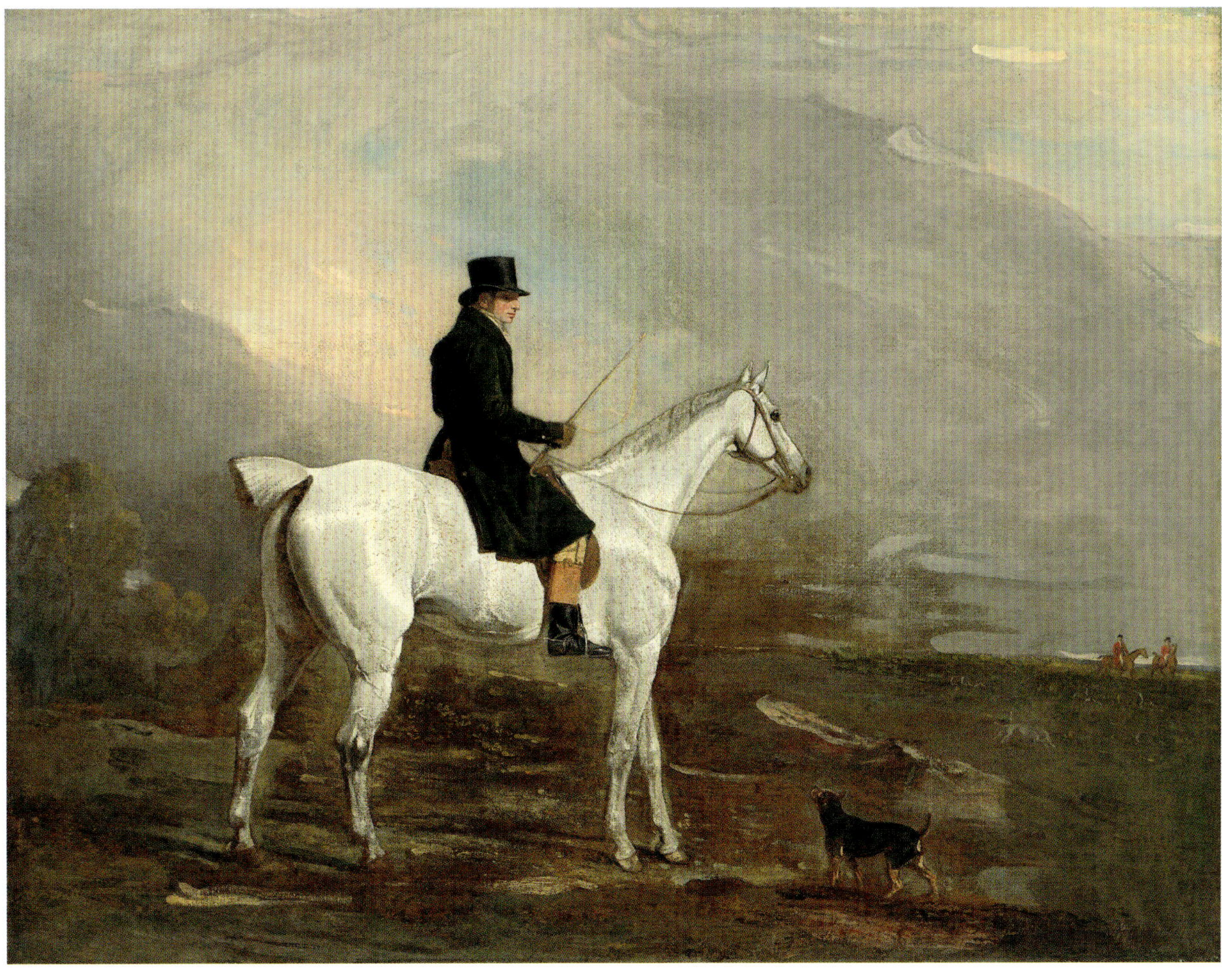

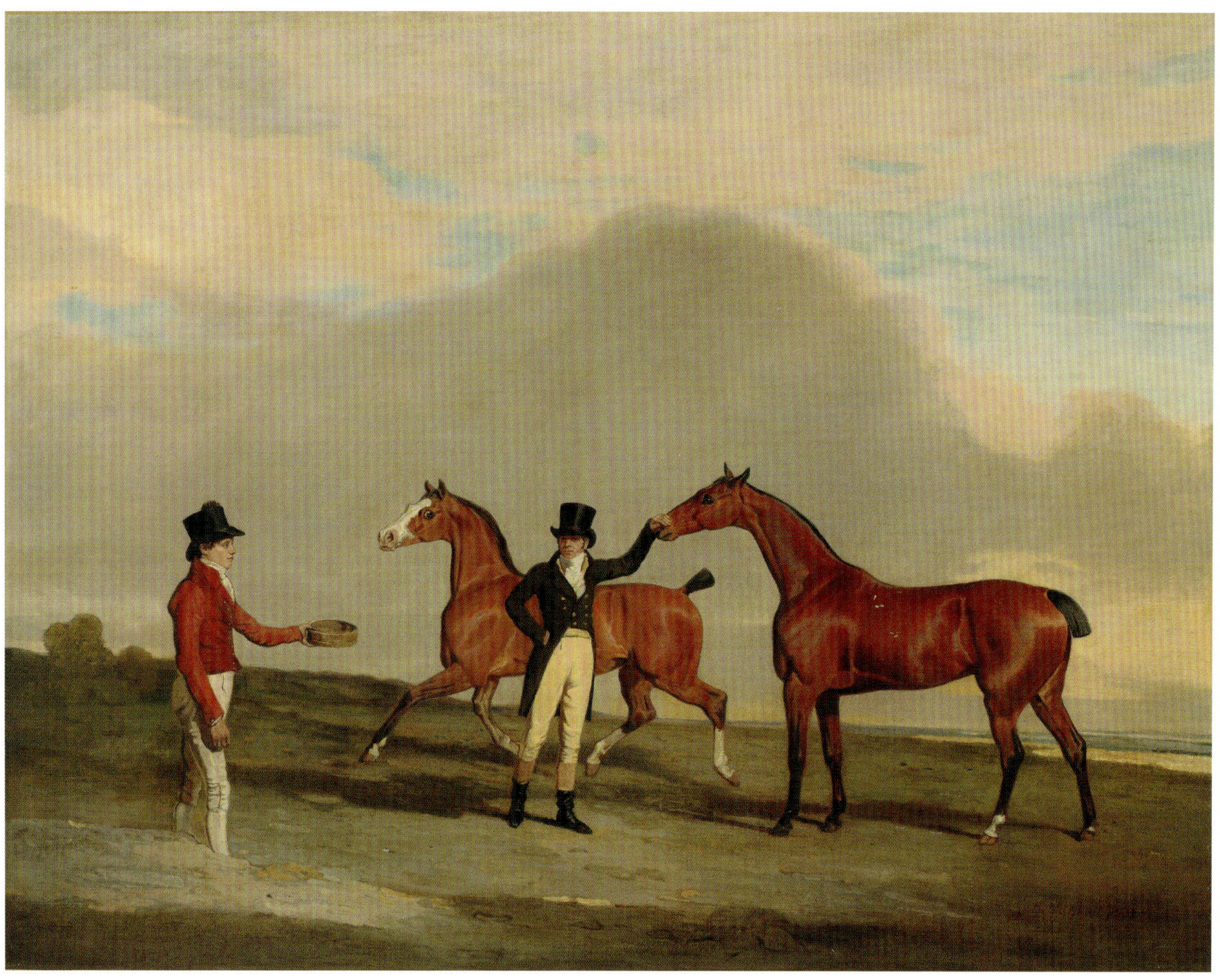

15 Benjamin Marshall (English, 1768–1835)

A Man, Groom, and Two Hunters, Called "Henry Legard with His Favourite Hunters," ca. 1825

Oil on canvas, 40 x 50 in., Paul Mellon Collection, 85.507

Though a fashionably dressed gentleman stands resolute in the center of this composition, our gaze soon tracks everything orbiting around him: the hunter he steadies with his hand, the second hunter looking backward as he trots past, and the groom at left offering a sieve.

Depicting the horses in different stances has allowed Marshall to focus on different attributes, such as the conformation of the standing hunter and the nimbleness of the moving one. Both horses have their intelligent looking, finely chiseled, noble heads held high, and the trotting horse also has a higher tail carriage, perhaps an indicator of its Middle Eastern heritage.

Long shadows indicate a time of dawn or dusk; less certain is the time of year. With hunts now recognized as arduous, hunters began to receive the same training as racehorses, including more exercise to build up stamina and more grain to provide the energy they needed to perform over long distances. Perhaps this gentleman has come to the field to inspect the progress of his mounts.

The presence of two horses in this painting might be explained by a change in hunting during the first decade of the nineteenth century. Up to this point, it had been commonplace to have multiple hunters—the more days spent hunting, the more hunters were needed. However, the two-horse system of hunting was becoming the norm: a second horse ridden into the field by a lightweight groom could be used as a fresh mount and allow a more thrilling chase to the finish.[1] If this is the case, then the gentleman in the center may be showcasing the two superb mounts he would take with him on his next hunt.

1. David C. Itzkowitz, *Peculiar Privilege: A Social History of English Foxhunting*, 1753–1885, 2nd ed. (Brighton: Edward Everett Root, 2016), 43.

16 Henry Bernard Chalon (English, 1770–1849)

Sir Mark Masterman Sykes's Hounds with Huntsmen, ca. 1820

Oil on canvas, 35 3/4 x 48 1/16 in., Paul Mellon Collection, 99.61

Inscriptions on the frame of this painting identify the participants in this lively hunting scene. In the foreground, from left to right, are the workers who made hunting possible: Foxton (earth stopper), Robert Bower of Welham, Tom Carter (huntsman), and Will Carter (1st Whip), with Tom Carter (2nd Whip) following behind. Beyond are the gentlemen: Lord Middleton, Richard Watt, Digby Legard, Sir Mark Sykes, Rev. John Bower, and Tatton Sykes.[1]

The presence of the earth stopper, immediately recognizable by his shovel, makes this painting particularly noteworthy. Earth stoppers had arguably the least visibility and the most power among participants in the hunt.[2] Since foxes are typically nocturnal, earth stoppers would work at night to fill in their dens or "earths" while they were away hunting, which ensured that the foxes would remain above ground and could be hunted themselves. Over the course of the nineteenth century earth stoppers went from being employed by the hunt and paid for each earth stopped to stopping the earths on a farmer's land for a flat rate. If by chance a fox did go to earth, the fee might have to be forfeited.[2]

1. Cormack, 209
2. Itzkowitz, 97.

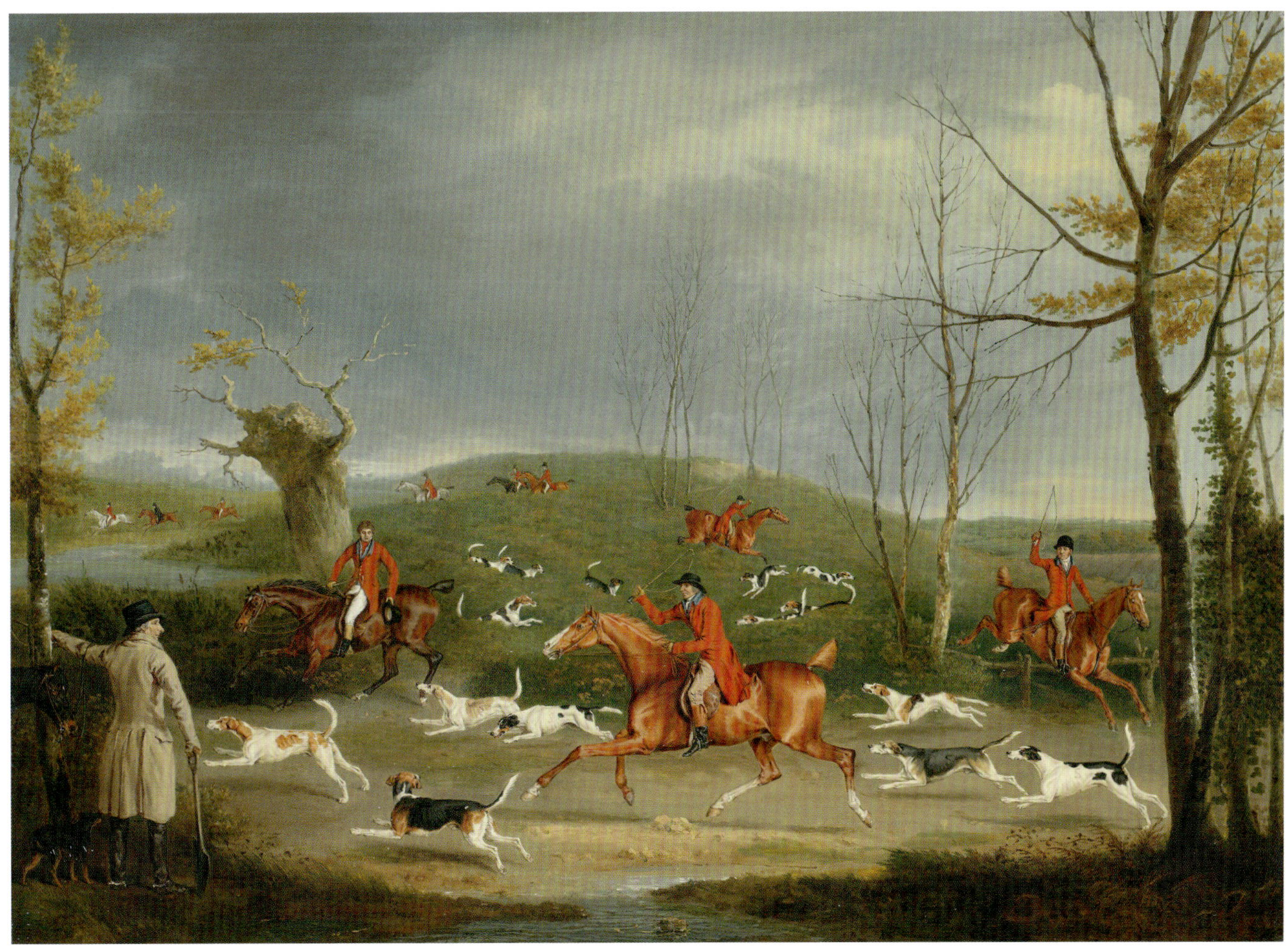

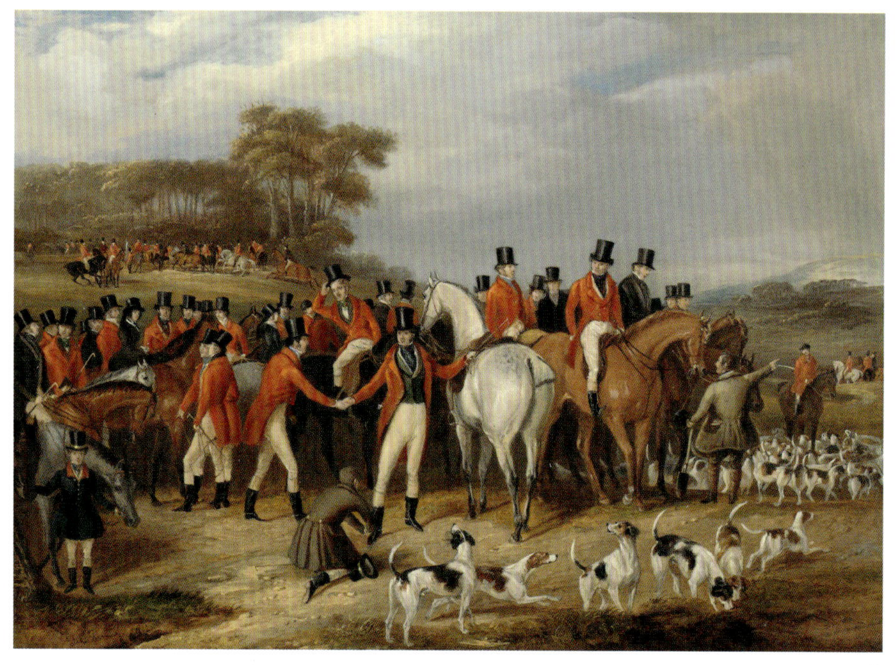

a.

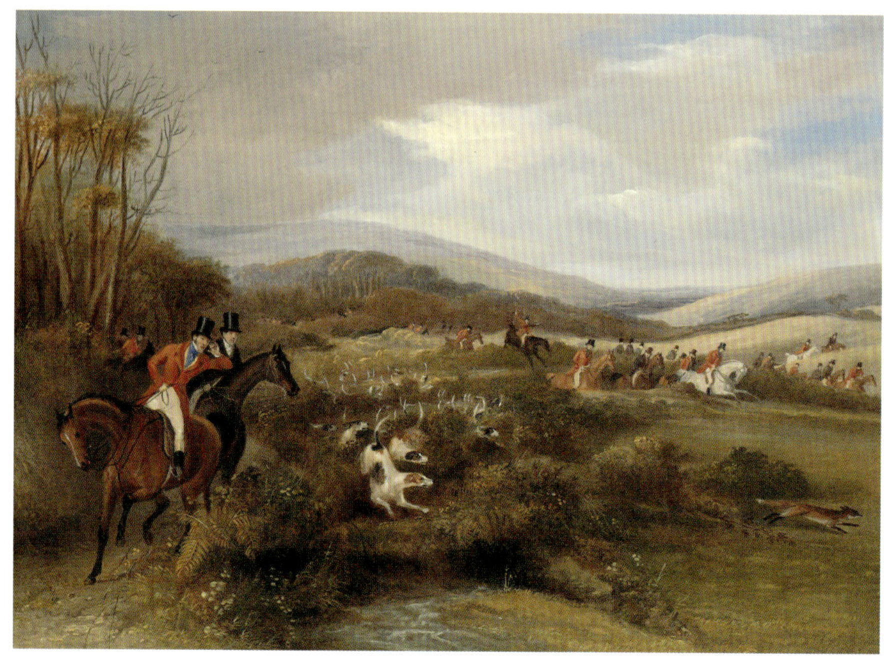

b.

17 Francis Calcraft Turner (English, active 1782, died 1846)

a. *The Marquis of Waterford and Members of the Tipperary Hunt (The Noble Tips): Tipperary Boys,* 1842
Oil on canvas, 17 15/16 x 23 15/16 in., Paul Mellon Collection, 85.484.1

b. *The Marquis of Waterford and Members of the Tipperary Hunt (The Noble Tips): Tipperary Melody,* 1842
Oil on canvas, 18 1/8 x 24 3/16 in., Paul Mellon Collection, 85.484.2

c. *The Marquis of Waterford and Members of the Tipperary Hunt (The Noble Tips): Tipperary Glory,* 1842
Oil on canvas, 18 1/8 x 24 1/8 in., Paul Mellon Collection, 85.484.3

d. *The Marquis of Waterford and Members of the Tipperary Hunt (The Noble Tips): Tipperary "Killing, No Murder,"* 1842
Oil on canvas, 18 1/8 x 24 1/16 in., Paul Mellon Collection, 85.484.4

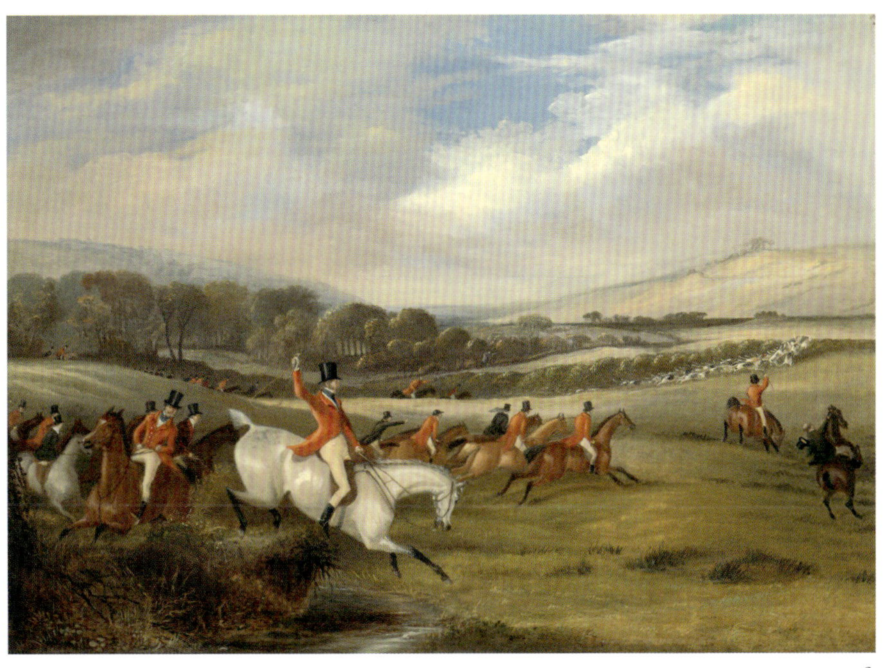

c.

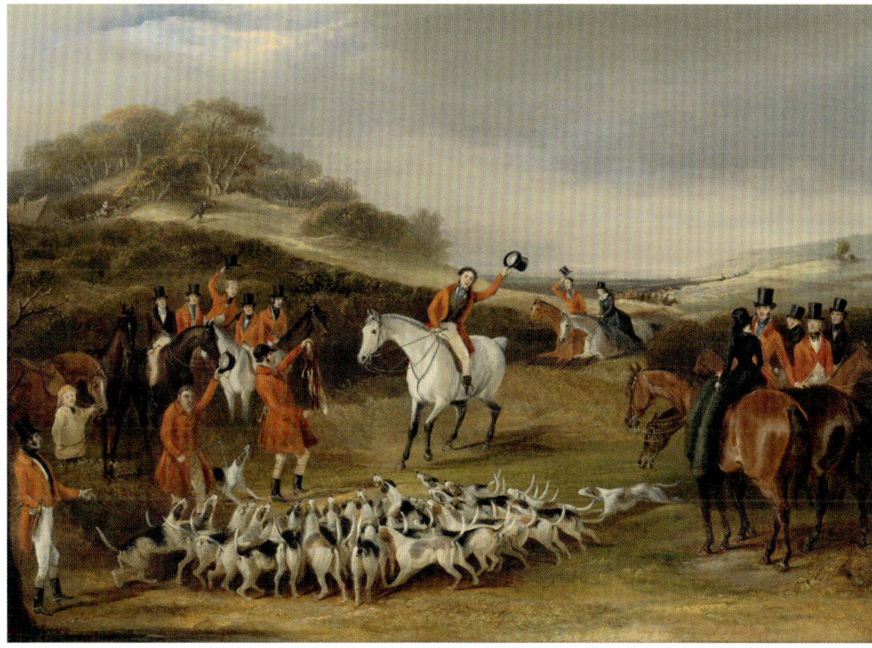

d.

Francis Calcraft Turner lived the life of a sportsman and used his experiences to depict the sporting life, with hunting and racing images being his favorite. In this series Turner portrays Henry de La Poer Beresford, 3rd Marquess of Waterford and Master of the Tipperary Hunt, in four scenes: *Tipperary Boys, Tipperary Melody, Tipperary Glory,* and *Tipperary "Killing, No Murder."*

Though notorious for his destructive behavior and practical jokes, the marquess appears very genial as he is attended by his servant and surrounded by members and participants of the hunt (including an earth stopper with shovel) in the first scene, *Tipperary Boys*.

In the second scene, the hunt is underway and the hounds have been sent to covert, many of them in so deep that only their waving sterns (tails) can be seen. The title *Tipperary Melody* represents the cry of the hounds as they catch the fox's scent, along with the "View Halloo" that comes when the fox is flushed from the covert.

The third scene, *Tipperary Glory,* depicts Waterford as the consummate sportsman in the act of "doing the thing well," or jumping with one hand held aloft above the shoulder.

The last scene, *Tipperary "Killing, No Murder,"* indicates that it was a fair hunt. The fox provided good sport, but in the end the hounds prevailed.[1]

In his memoirs, Mr. Mellon fondly remembers a 1936 foxhunting trip to Ireland, arranged when hunting was suspended in Britain for the period of state mourning after the death of King George V on January 20. Hunting with the Limerick Hounds and the Galway Blazers, he encountered a countryside full of obstacles, so much so that they were described by a local as making one "seasick with leppin"[2]—the feeling one gets from the landscape that unfolds across Turner's panels.

---

1. Cormack, 235.

2. Mellon, 234.

18 Edwin Cooper "of Beccles" (English, 1785–1833)

Waiting at the Meet, 1832

Oil on canvas, 40 x 50 in., Paul Mellon Collection, 85.486

Like Henry Chalon's earlier painting of hounds with huntsmen (cat. no. 16), this canvas by Edwin Cooper portrays the hierarchy of the hunt, with master and servants in the forefront and the gentlemen of the field coming through a gate at upper left.

At the top of this hierarchy is the master of foxhounds, who is probably the gentleman on the light grey horse with the top hat. R. S. Surtees (author of the "Jorrocks" novels) described the ideal qualities needed for this position:

> He should have the boldness of a lion, the cunning of a fox, the shrewdness of an exciseman, the calculation of a general, the decision of a judge, the purse of Squire Plutus, the regularity of a railway, the punctuality of a time-piece, the liberality of a sailor, the patience of Job, the tact of an M. P., the wiliness of a diplomatist, the politeness of a lord, the strength of Hercules, the thirst of a Bacchus, the appetite of a Dando, the digestion of an ostrich, the coolness of a crocodile, the fire-enduring powers of a salamander or of Mons. Chabot, the Fire King, with a slight touch of the eloquence of Cicero, and temper as even as the lines in a copy-book.[1]

Though comical at points, Surtees's quote indicates that to be a successful master of foxhounds was no mean feat.

Under the master of foxhounds, the next most important member of the hunt staff was the huntsman. In this painting, the huntsman is hidden by his dapple grey horse, having perhaps just coupled the nearby hounds to allow the younger one to learn from the older. The two riders wearing green—the livery of an unidentified hunt—may be the first and second whippers-in, or whips, whose job it was to assist the huntsman and keep all of the hounds together as they pursued the fox across the countryside. Gathered around the horses are nine couple (eighteen) hounds, who are waiting for the signal to begin the hunt.

1. Robert Smith Surtees and Henry Thomas Alken, *The Analysis of the Hunting Field* (London: Methuen, 1904), 4–5.

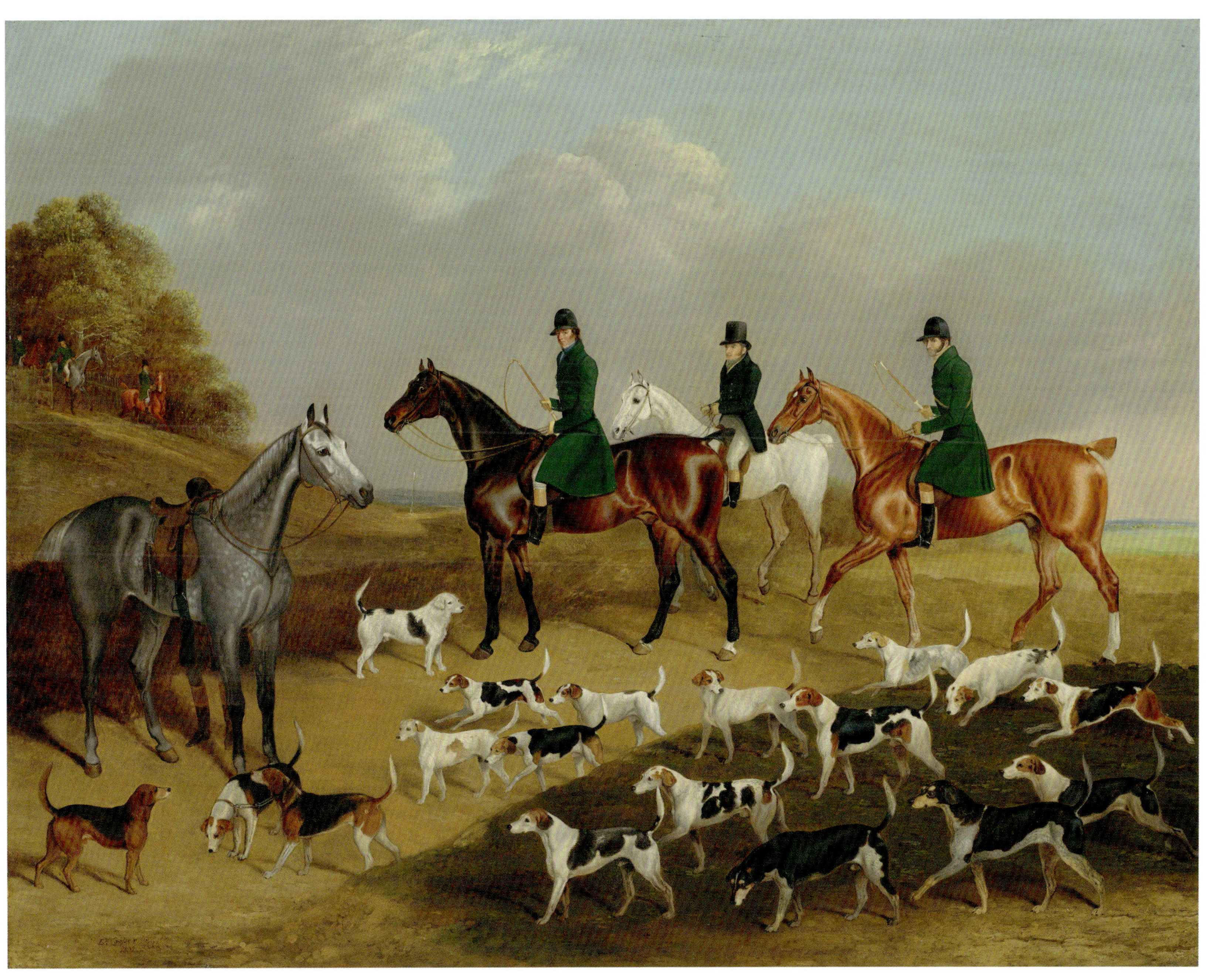

19 Henry Thomas Alken (English, 1785–1851)

a. *Fishing on the River Avon, near Fordingbridge, Hampshire: Trout Fishing at Harper Mill,* 1842

Oil on panel, 6 ¾ x 9 ½ in., Paul Mellon Collection, 85.485.1

b. *Fishing on the River Avon, near Fordingbridge, Hampshire: Fishing for Pike,* 1842

Oil on panel, 6 ¾ x 9 ½ in., Paul Mellon Collection, 85.485.2

Four generations of the Alken family included artists, but Henry Thomas Alken was the most well known. Taught by his father, he painted and then engraved most of his own work, specializing in hunting, racing, and other sporting genres. In these two scenes, Alken captures anglers along the Hampshire Avon, a famous river for trout fishing in England.

In the mid-nineteenth century, fishing was a less restrictive sport than shooting. Local fishermen could often obtain a permit from a landowner or the warden charged with looking after a stream and stocking it with fish, which were categorized as "game" or "coarse." Fish thought to demand more acumen from the fishermen pursuing them were termed game fish and included such species as trout, salmon, and char.

Coarse was an alternate spelling of "course," a term used in the textile industry for ordinary cloth, which could be considered inferior—like the fish (pike, tench, and carp) that had also earned the name. In this pair of paintings Alken has treated the viewer to images of both types of fishing.[1]

Trout are easier to find in clear water, especially chalk streams like the River Avon, and just below a water mill is also a likely spot. Dressed in waders and holding a net in his left hand, a gentleman is about to land the trout he's caught using his skill and a simple cane rod.

Standing on the bank of a slow-moving stream—the type of environment associated with coarse fish—our second fisherman is going after pike with bait attached to a circular float.

1. William Knight, "Blurring the Boundaries: Subsistence and Recreational Fisheries in Late-Nineteenth-Century Ontario," *Subsistence under Capitalism: Historical and Contemporary Perspectives*, edited by James Murton, Dean Bavington, and Carly Dokis (Montreal, Kingston, London, Chicago: McGill-Queen's University Press, 2016), 64–65.

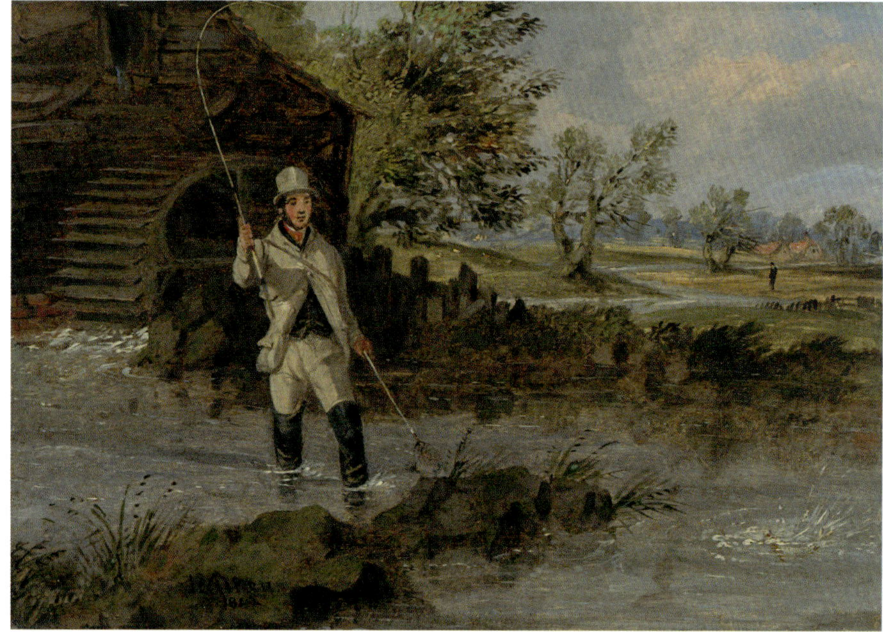

a.

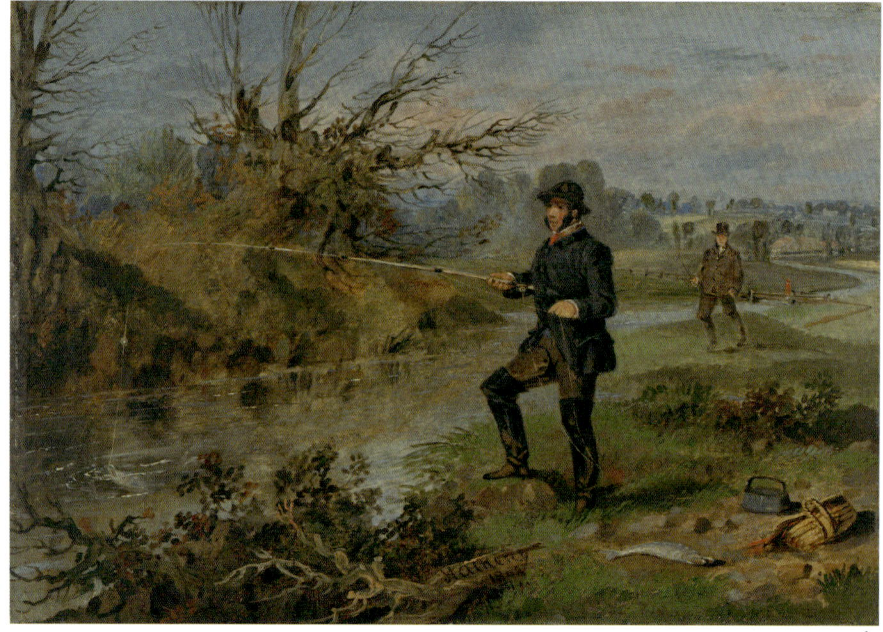

b.

20 John Frederick Herring, Sr. (English, 1795–1865)

a. *Hunting Scenes: A Hunting Morn,* ca. 1840

Oil on canvas, 30 1/8 x 50 1/4 in., Paul Mellon Collection, 85.491.1

b. *Hunting Scenes: Streaming Off,* ca. 1840

Oil on canvas, 30 3/8 x 50 3/8 in., Paul Mellon Collection, 85.491.2

These evocative hunting paintings, almost as richly textured as the Victorian novels of the time, contrast the quiet moments before setting out with the excitement of the chase.

In the first image, Herring has lavishly recreated the sparkling effects of autumn's early morning light upon the cobblestone courtyard and its inhabitants. The hunting staff have gathered the hounds and seem ready to begin the day's activities. However, not all the riders have appeared. The side-saddle on the chestnut horse in the center of the painting signals that a woman will accompany them. Although women were rarely seen in the hunting field in the first half of the nineteenth century, their numbers began to increase around mid-century when this type of saddle—first used in France around 1830—was introduced in England. An extra pommel, or "leaping head," rested across the top of a woman's left thigh and allowed her to jump obstacles with more assurance.[1]

In the second image, the season has convincingly changed to winter. The hounds have led the hunt over fences and into a ploughed field. The rider in the lower right is "doing the thing well" with his hand raised (cat. nos. 17.c and 58.i). In the background to the left a farmer pauses his ploughing to gaze at the hunt, though he is too far away for us to see if he is enjoying the spectacle. His presence reminds us that farmers contributed to the hunt by preserving foxes, walking foxhound puppies, and allowing both horses and hounds to run across their fields—to the shock of visitors to the country. The country gentleman did what he could to foster and maintain positive relationships with farmers through the traditional farmers' dinner as well as occasional presents of game and other small gestures.[2]

1. Cormack, 195.
2. Itzkowitz, 121.

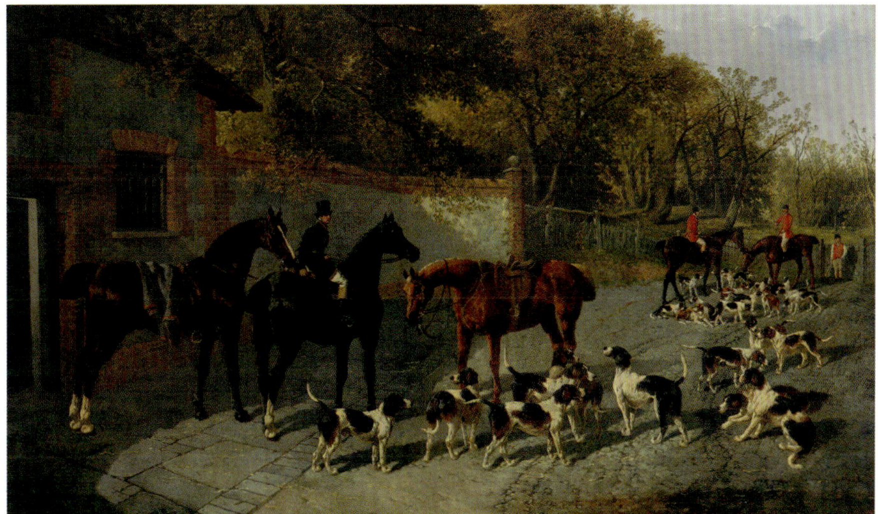

a.

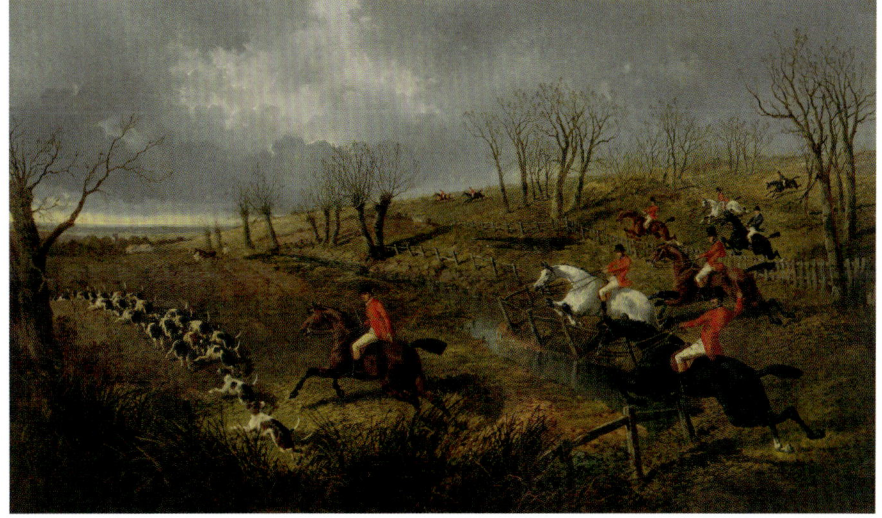

b.

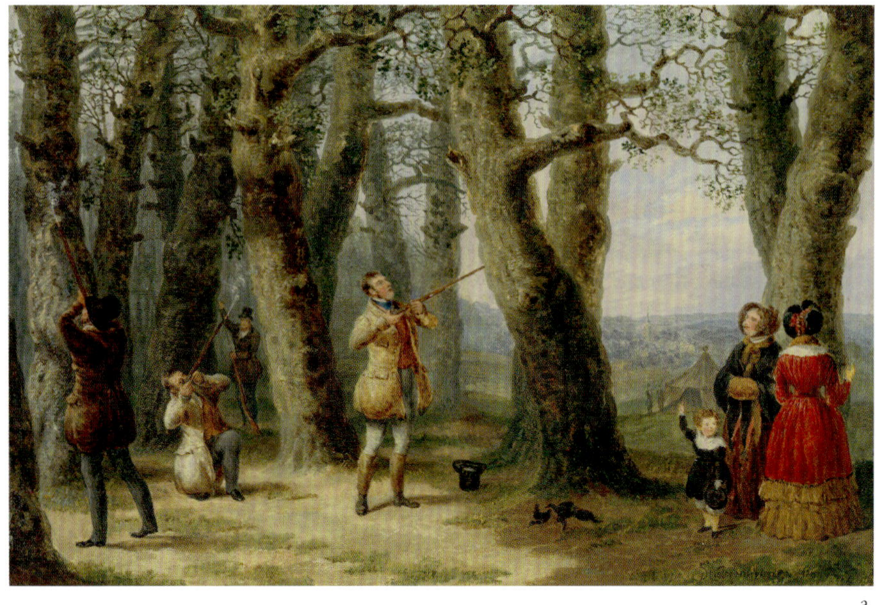

a.

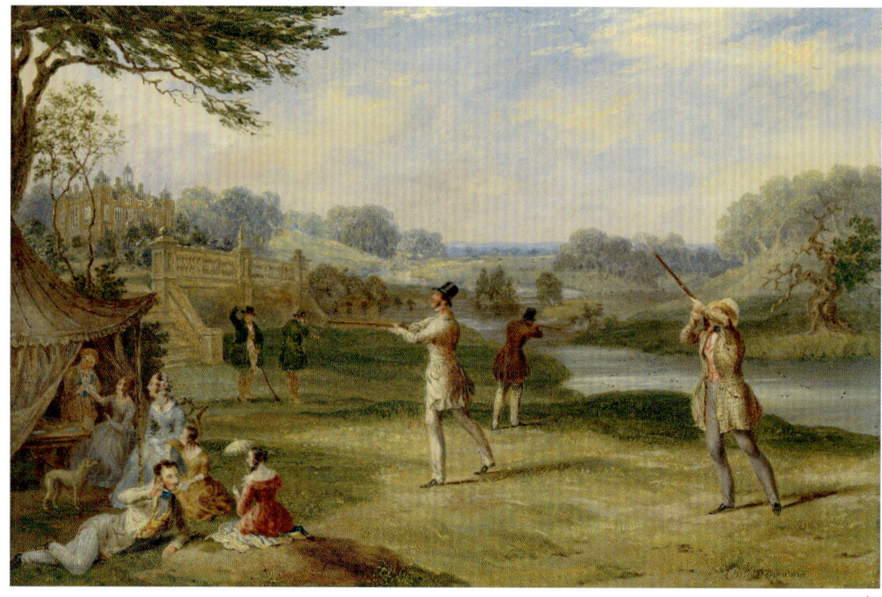

b.

c.

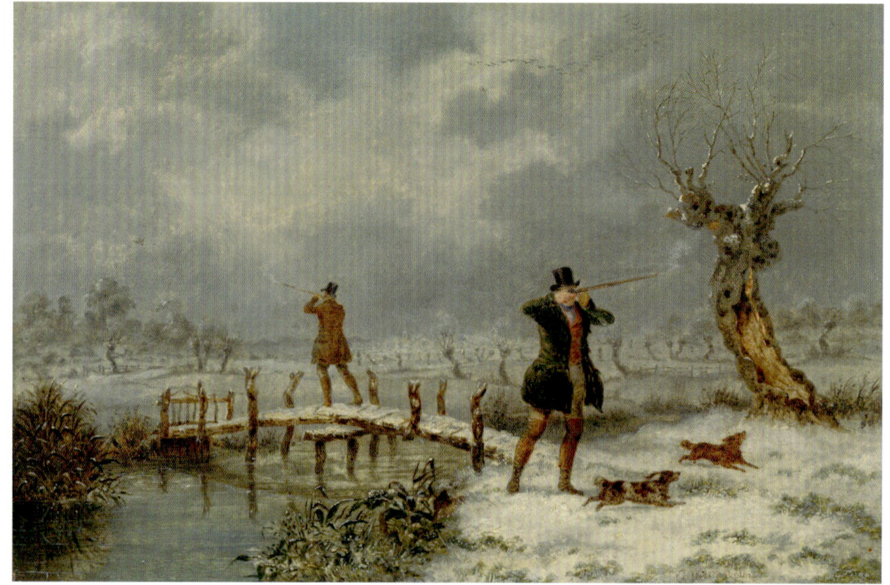

d.

21 Dean Wolstenholme, the Younger (English, 1798–1882)

a. *Shooting in the Four Seasons of the Year: Spring—Rook Shooting in May,* ca. 1850

Oil on panel, 10 3/8 x 14 7/8 in., Paul Mellon Collection, 99.98

b. *Shooting in the Four Seasons of the Year: Summer—A Picnic and Shooting Party,* ca. 1850

Oil on panel, 10 1/2 x 14 15/16 in., Paul Mellon Collection, 99.99

c. *Shooting in the Four Seasons of the Year: Autumn—Pheasant Shooting,* ca. 1850

Oil on panel, 10 1/2 x 14 15/16 in., Paul Mellon Collection, 99.100

d. *Shooting in the Four Seasons of the Year: Winter—Wild Fowling in the Snow,* ca. 1850

Oil on panel, 10 1/2 x 14 3/4 in., Paul Mellon Collection, 99.101

Dean Wolstenholme, the son of a sporting painter and a sportsman himself, portrayed a variety of sports in his art. In this series he uses the traditional theme of the four seasons to showcase the range of shooting activity enjoyed by the British country gentry at different times of year.

In the spring and summer scenes, shooting is depicted as a social affair with families in attendance. In the spring (or May) painting, with a festive tent in the distance, two women and a child stand dangerously close to four gentlemen engaged in shooting rooks. Rooks made their nests in tall trees, which explains why the gentlemen have their attention trained upward beyond the limits of the canvas. The dead rooks on the ground would have been a welcome sight to farmers, since these birds were known for destroying crops.

The summer scene also includes a tent, this time with a great estate in the background. In the foreground, a gentleman enjoys leisurely conversation with a lady while her companions look forward to a picnic lunch. The other gentlemen are engaged in shooting; the one in the brown coat aims at sparrows flying over the stream, but the quarry of the others is not apparent.

The autumn and winter scenes follow the traditional model of shooting with dogs—pointers and a retriever for pheasants in autumn, spaniels in winter for unknown but available quarry. (The Game Act of 1831 made it legal for the wealthiest of landowners to shoot pheasants during the season, which is open from October to February.)

22 Sir Francis Grant, P. R. A. (English, 1803–1878)

The Melton Hunt Going to Draw the Ram's Head Cover, 1839

Oil on canvas, 35 15/16 x 60 in., Paul Mellon Collection, 85.494.1

Sir Francis Grant only turned to painting as a profession after he had spent his inheritance on hunting. After taking a few lessons from John E. Ferneley, Sr. (cat. no. 51), he struck out on his own to create sporting works and portraits for the contacts he cultivated during his own sporting adventures. He became one of only two sporting artists who were elected president of the Royal Academy; the other was Sir Alfred J. Munnings in the twentieth century.[1]

The hunt in the title of this painting is actually none other than the fashionable Quorn Hunt, one of three famous hunts that converged upon the town of Melton Mowbray—the epicenter of English foxhunting. The group is moving off toward the hill in the distance, which is probably the Ram's Head Cover.

Included within this complex painting are thirty-six portraits, some featuring the field's most famous figures. The 3rd Marquess of Waterford (whose exploits are also featured in cat. nos. 17a–d) is depicted on a gray horse, jumping an obstacle in the back right. The inclusion of such a large and well-known party following the hunt captures a highpoint in foxhunting's history and amply conveys the popularity of the hunt at this time.

Hugely admired during its exhibition at the Royal Academy in 1839, this picture was promptly purchased at a high price by Arthur Wellesley, 1st Duke of Wellington, the elder statesman and hero of the Napoleonic Wars.

---

1. Cormack, 452.

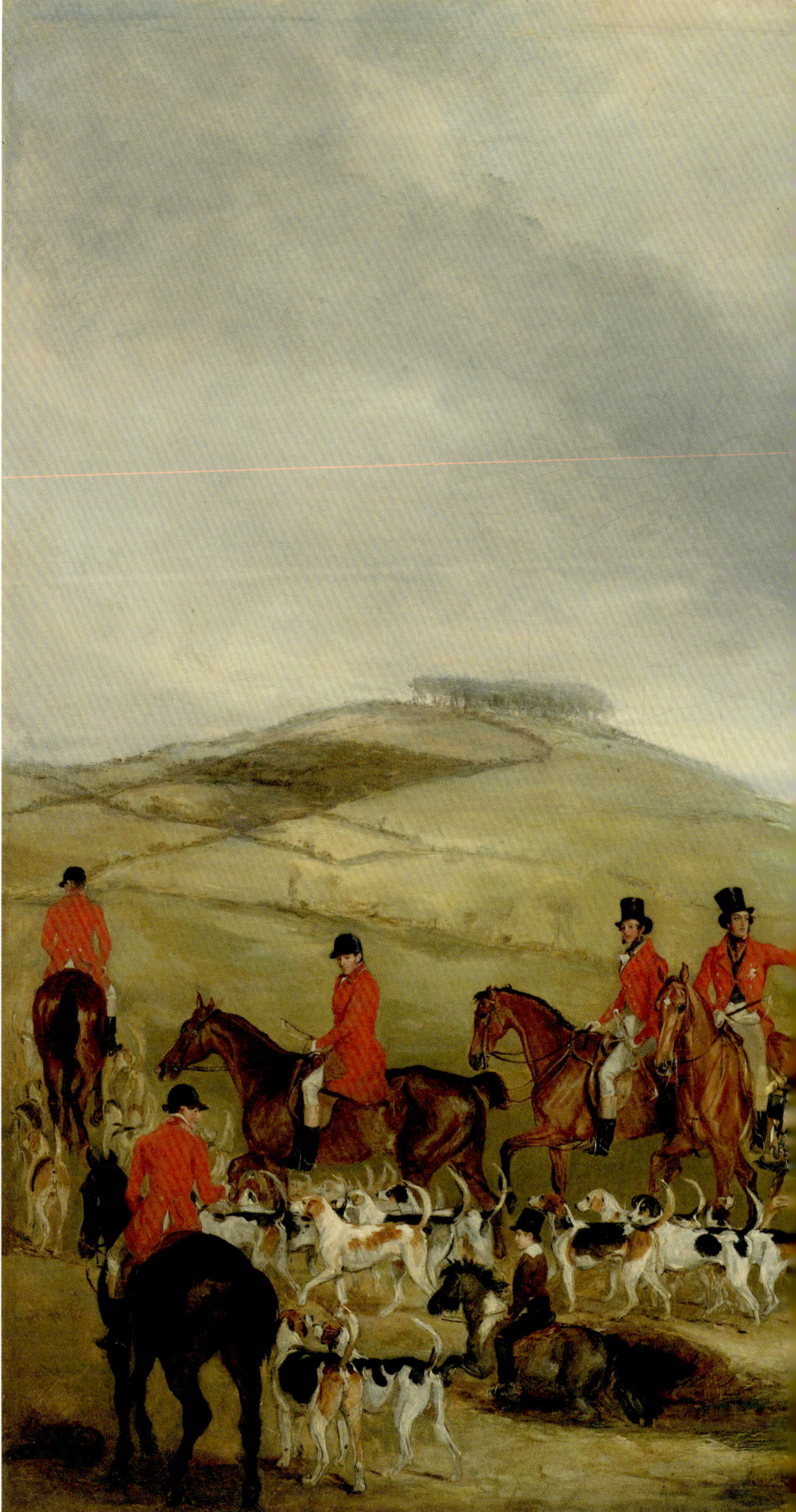

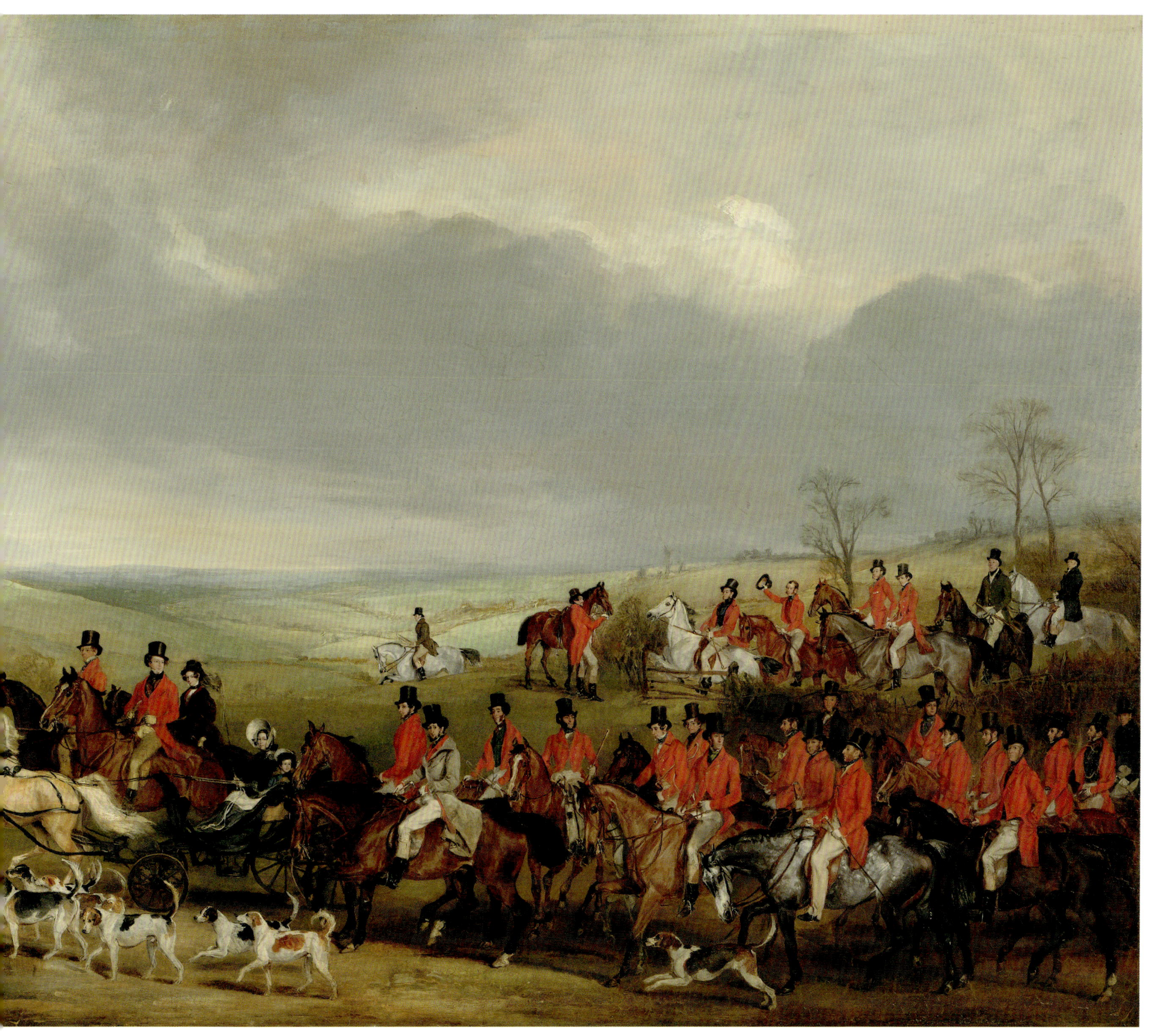

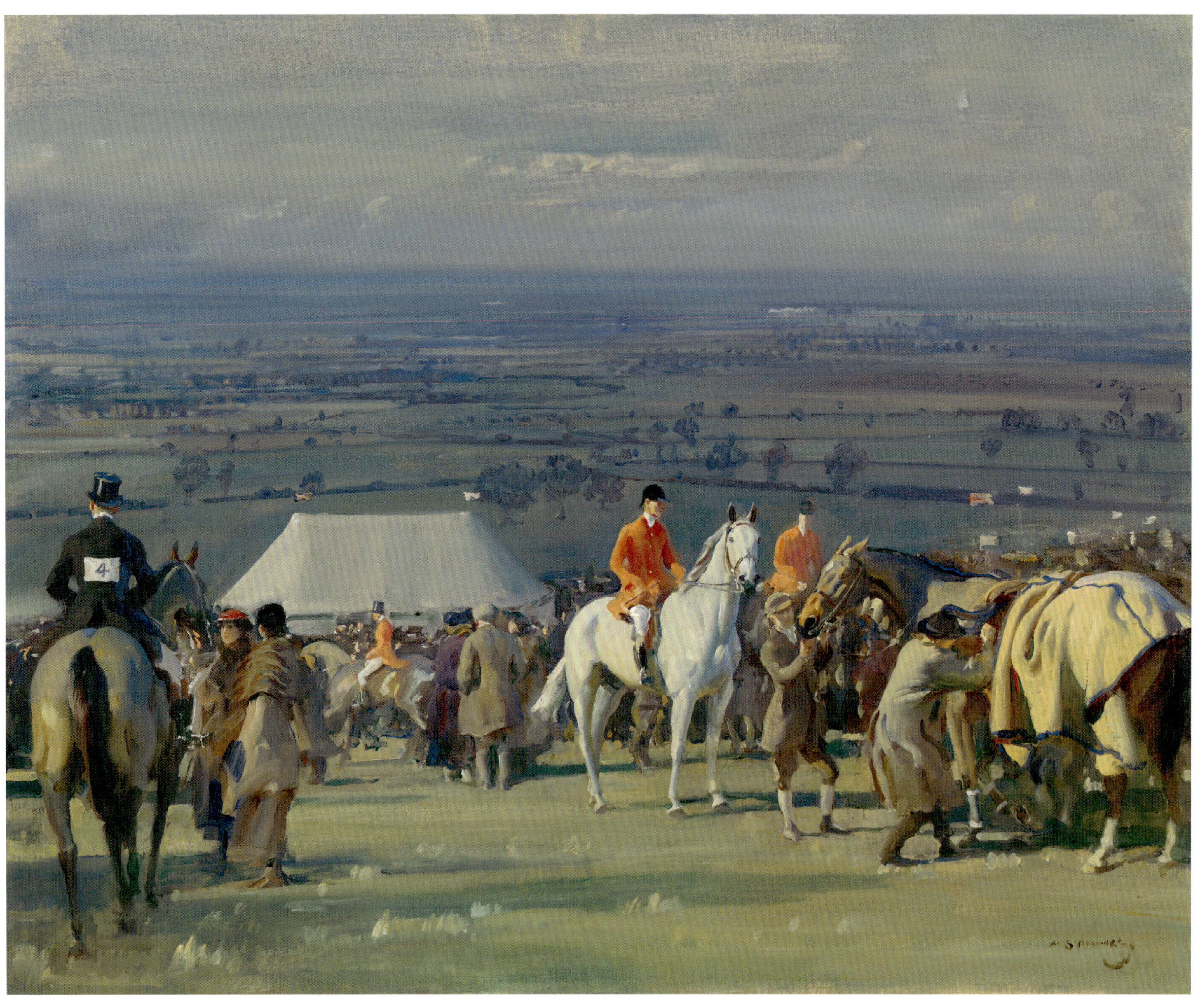

23 Sir Alfred J. Munnings, P. R. A. (English, 1878–1959)

The Belvoir Point-to-Point Meeting on Barrowby Hill, Painted on Woolsthorpe, 1920–21

Oil on canvas, 25 x 30 in., Paul Mellon Collection, 99.83

Sir Alfred J. Munnings was the second of two sporting artists to be elected president of the Royal Academy; the other was Sir Francis Grant (cat. no. 22), during the nineteenth century. Munnings was a passionate horseman and made a comfortable career out of creating paintings, mainly country and sporting images, for wealthy patrons—Mr. Mellon included. While at Cambridge, Mr. Mellon had begun collecting Munnings prints, and in 1932 he commissioned Munnings to paint a portrait of him on his hunter Dublin.[1] In his memoirs, Mr. Mellon describes the process of working with Munnings:

> We traveled down together from London to Mr. Honour's stables to take a look at the horse. I, who was still pretty reserved, said little on the journey, whereas Munnings, apart from being older, was a great extrovert and far from bashful. He was very amusing company. Looking back, I recall that I was probably a little overawed by my bohemian travelling companion and think that I could have taken greater advantage of the meeting if I had been more relaxed. . . . I received a photograph of the finished picture before Munnings had it delivered. Looking at it, I thought the bushy willow tree on the left was a little disturbing and wrote to Munnings asking whether he could do something to make it slightly less prominent. Sometime later I got a blast back saying in the first place, the tree wasn't a willow, it was a pollarded oak, and second, he had no intention of changing anything whatsoever. So that was that.[2]

This encounter did not dampen Mr. Mellon's enthusiasm for Munnings's art, and in 1951 he acquired *The Belvoir Point-to-Point Meeting on Barrowby Hill, Painted on Woolsthorpe*.

In 1920, Maj. "Tommy" Bouch, master of the famous Belvoir Hunt, invited Munnings to paint in the nearby village of Woolsthorpe with the promise, "You shall have all the models you need, horses, hounds, men—all day and every day." Over the winter, Munnings made many paintings and sketches. Back in his studio, he produced this portrayal of a point-to-point—a race across the countryside, not unlike a steeplechase—laid out by a hunt for hunting horses and their amateur riders.[3]

1. Mellon, 229, 265.
2. Mellon, 229.
3. Cormack, 159.

IN MOTION

IN MOTION begins with John Wootton's monumental and classicizing depictions of imported Middle Eastern and African stallions. Crossbreeding the newcomers with English horses produced the modern thoroughbred, which became a primary agent of social and environmental change in Britain.

The thoroughbred's speed and stamina were first recognized at the racecourse, with Newmarket becoming the early center of horseracing. Races gradually transformed from long, grueling heats to shorter sprints—which showcased the thoroughbred's speed to its fullest extent. A number of classic races were created in the late eighteenth century—the St. Leger (1776), the Oaks (1779), and the Derby (1780)—and are still run to this day. However, the speed of the thoroughbred would not be confined to "the Sport of Kings" for long.

Since it was not difficult to imagine that a faster horse could make for a more exciting hunt, thoroughbreds, or predominantly thoroughbred horses, quickly appeared in the hunting field—and also on England's roads, pulling coaches such as the Royal Mail. Along with the mending of deeply rutted roads—which, when wet, turned into muddy quagmires—and the creation of new ones, faster horses significantly cut the transportation time of people and goods from place to place. Just how dramatic was this change? The four-and-a-half-day journey from Manchester to London (187 miles), became reduced to just one day, and the average speed of two miles per hour climbed to between ten and twelve miles per hour. Although the rapid expansion of the railroads after 1830 quickly led to the demise of the vast coach network, coaching survived in the smaller, privatized world of the amateur gentleman driver.

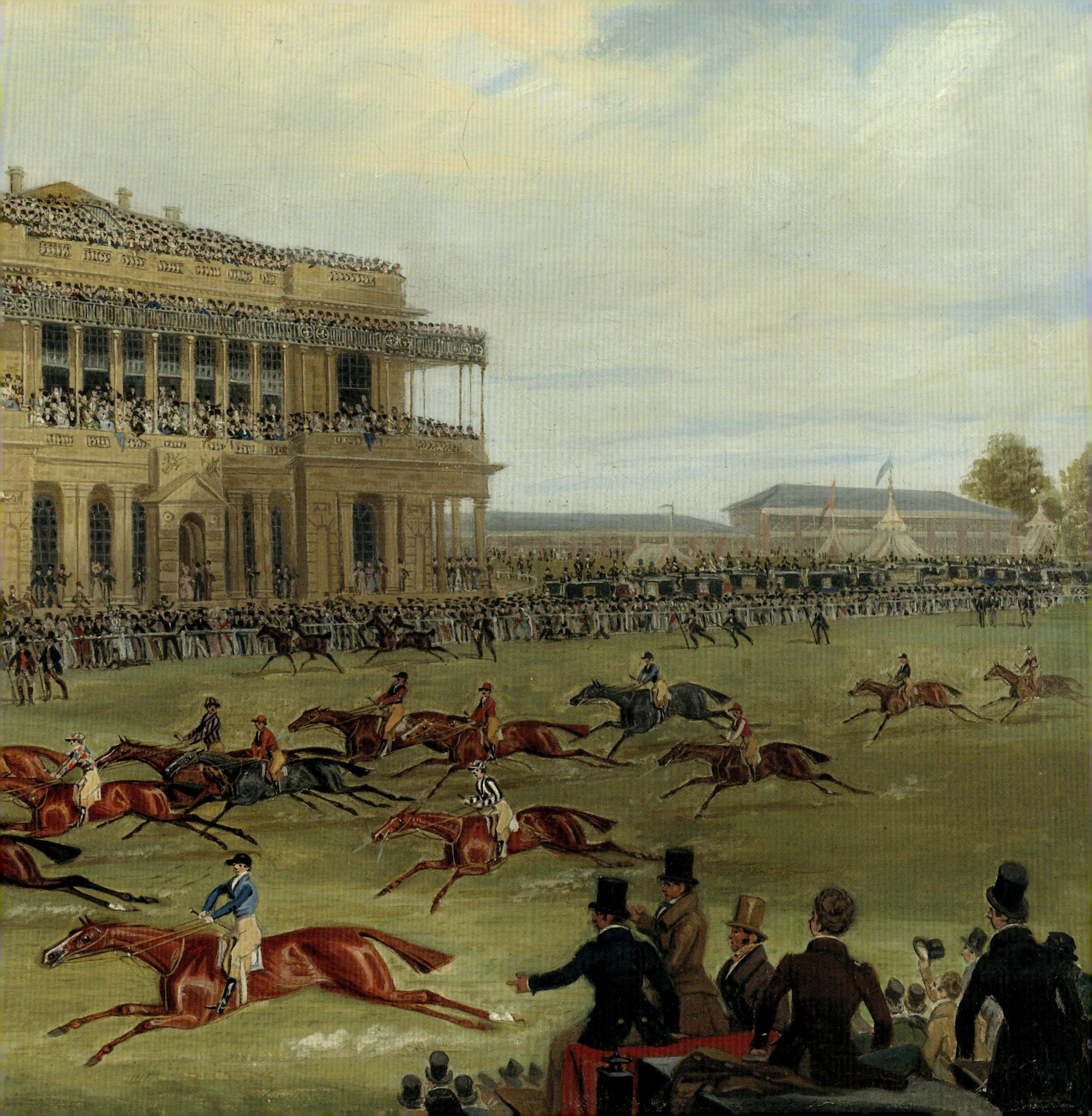

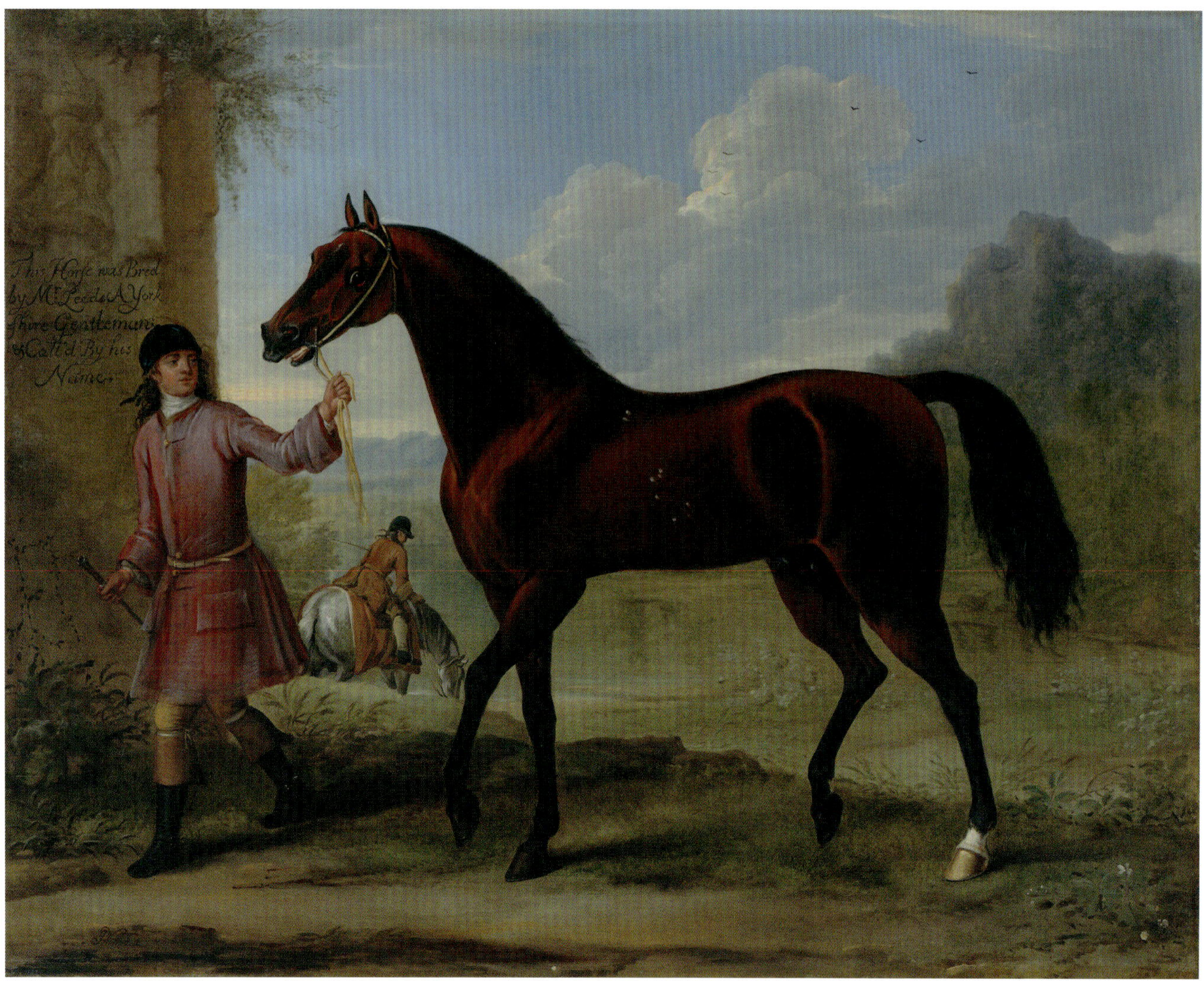

24 John Wootton (English, ca. 1682–1765)

A Bay Horse, Possibly Leedes, Led by a Groom, ca. 1715

Oil on canvas, 39 x 49 in., Paul Mellon Collection, 85.458

John Wootton was born circa 1682 in Snitterfield, Warwickshire (some five miles from Stratford upon Avon). He studied art under the Dutch artist Jan Wyck, who was a specialist in topographical, hunting, and battle scenes.[1] Wootton pursued similar themes, but his adaptability to different subjects allowed him to become one of England's premier sporting artists.

Wootton's artistic career overlapped with the development of the thoroughbred breed from Turk, Barb, and Arabian stallions—among them the Byerley Turk (in the 1680s), the Darley Arabian (1704), and the Godolphin Arabian (1729)—brought to England in the seventeenth and eighteenth centuries to improve the native stock of horses, especially in terms of speed and endurance. The Leedes in this painting was the son of another one of these stallions, the Leedes Arabian. Despite Wootton's flat paint application, Leedes has the delicate features, conformation, and long flowing tail of his foreign predecessors. Wootton subtly alludes to Leedes's long lineage by including ruins and a groom in the pose of a statue from the Piazza del Quirinale in Rome, one of the most famous antique sculptures with equine subject matter.[2]

1. Cormack, 457.
2. Cormack, 129.

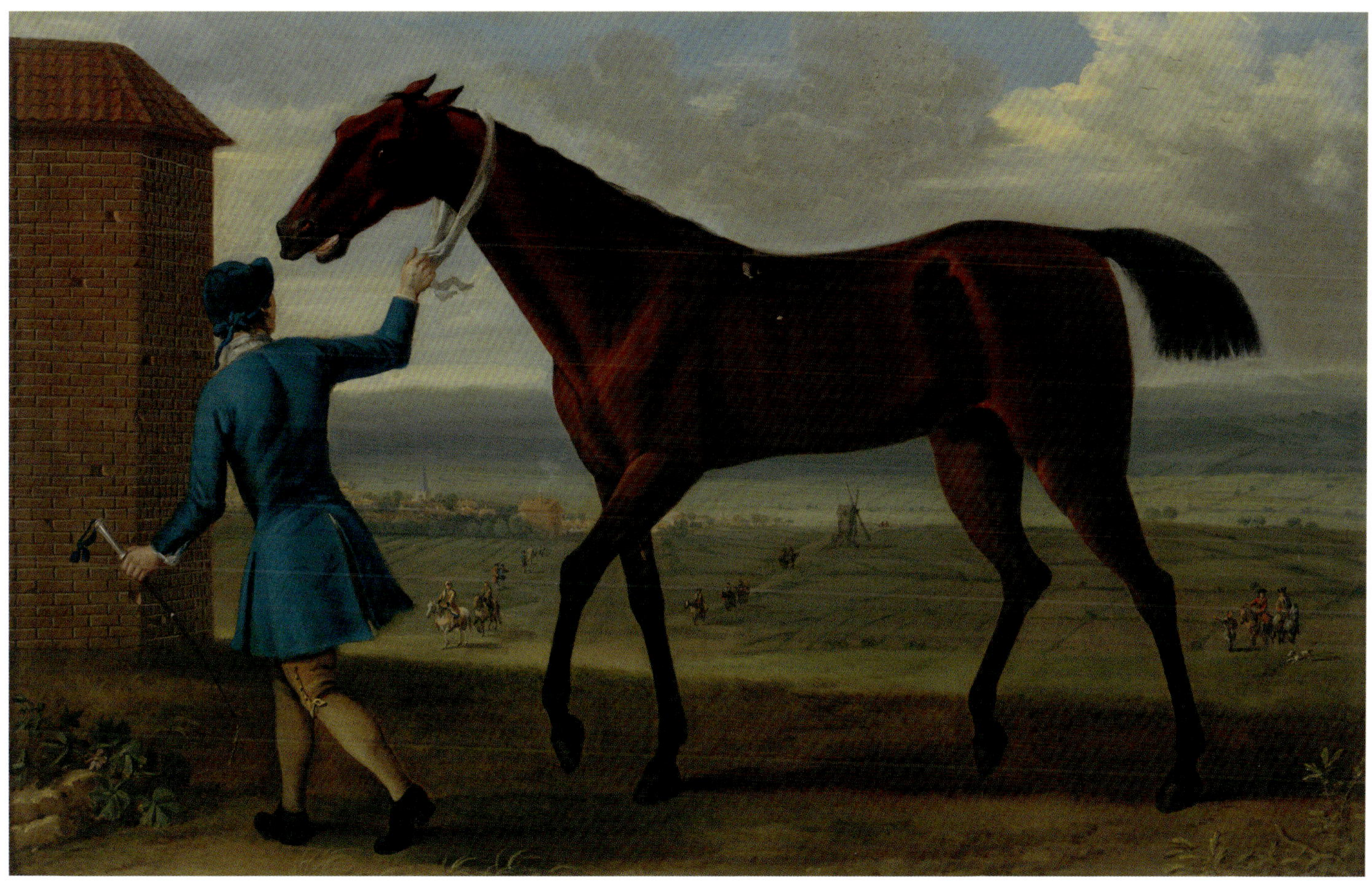

25 John Wootton (English ca. 1682–1765)

A Bay Horse Led towards a Rubbing-Down House at Newmarket, ca. 1715

Oil on canvas, 30 x 47 in., Paul Mellon Collection, 85.457

This painting and the previous one (cat. no. 24) demonstrate the flexibility and naturalism of Wootton's horse portraiture. Although the poses of the horses are similar, there are slight but significant differences in their physiques. Here the horse is not named, but there can be little doubt that he is an early thoroughbred; further removed than Leedes from an Arabian ancestor, he is a "leggier, longer-backed, more raking [fast moving] sort of horse than the short-coupled Arabian."[1] Indeed, with longer legs and back than Leedes, he seems to tower over his groom. His taut muscles are a sign of strenuous training.

Racehorses trained and competed at Newmarket, the "home of racing," even before the earliest documented record of a match in 1619. To ensure that spectators would recognize the Newmarket landscape, Wootton included one of Newmarket's rubbing-down houses, where grooms would use straw or cloth to remove sweat from horses after their grueling runs.

Seventeenth- and eighteenth-century races in England were usually several miles long (the Long Course at Newmarket was six miles), not under two miles like the sprints of today. Another difference between then and now is that racehorses would compete in several heats a day—not just in a single race—and horses were also generally older than two or three years.

1. Landry, 165.

26 John Wootton (English, ca. 1682–1765)

A Nobleman Arriving to Inspect Racehorses at Newmarket, ca. 1732–35

Oil on canvas, 26 ½ x 46 ⅛ in., Paul Mellon Collection, 85.459

Located approximately sixty-five miles north of London, Newmarket and the surrounding area have been inhabited since ancient times. King James I brought the town into prominence for its horseracing and hunting beginning in 1604, and after the Restoration of the monarchy in 1660, King Charles II had the royal racehorses installed there.

Horses were also trained at Newmarket, as is evident in this view of some eighteenth-century training practices. Like the three horses at left, a horse in training would wear a combination of blankets and hoods similar to ones observed in the Ottoman Empire;[1] the idea was to enhance sweating so that the horse would be lean enough to race. The gray horse in the center has had his wraps removed and is receiving a thorough rubdown; after all the sweat from the workout was gone, the horse would be covered again. The trainer, perhaps in charge of all the horses, stands in the middle foreground overseeing things.

As horses were exercised frequently, the rubbing-down house was a busy place; Newmarket had four such buildings in the eighteenth century. At right a nobleman has come to inspect the horses. If, as some have speculated, this man is Lord Portmore—superintendent of the royal racehorses—then we are most likely looking at the rubbing-down house that was reserved for use of the king and nobles.

1. Landry, 133.

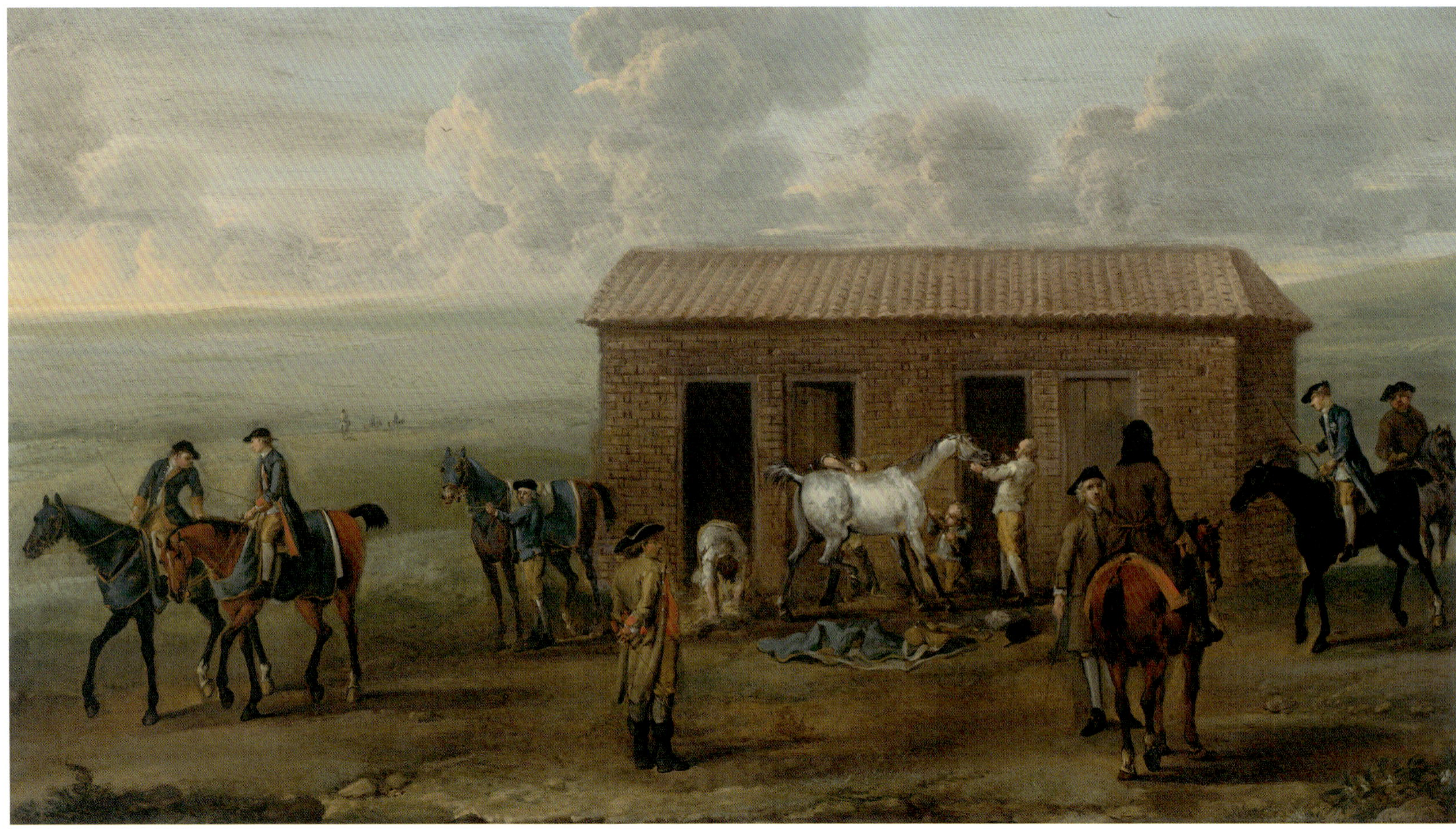

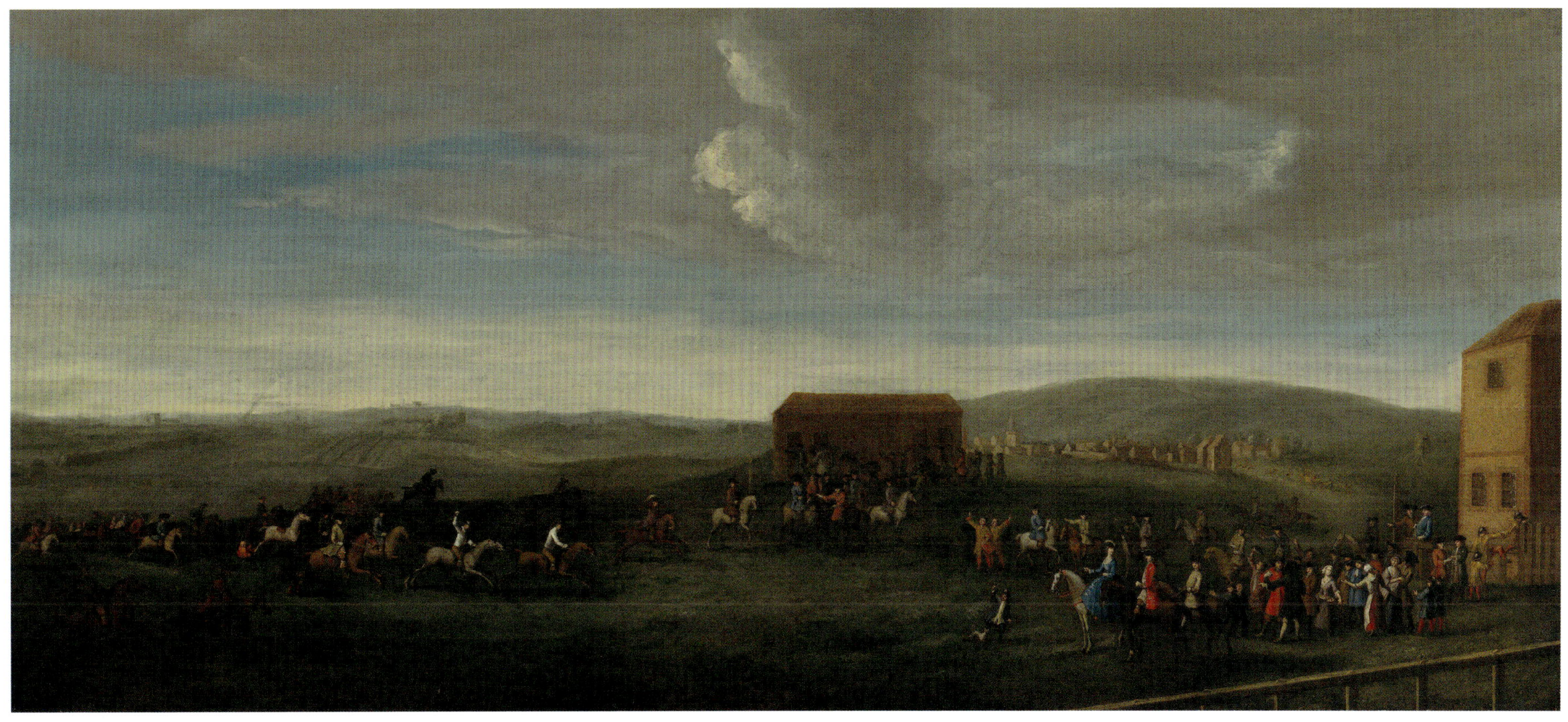

27 Peter Tillemans (Dutch, worked in England, 1684–1734)

View of a Horse-Match over the Long Course at Newmarket, from the Starting Post to the Stand, ca. 1717–23

Oil on canvas, 23 ½ x 50 ¼ in., Paul Mellon Collection, 99.96

Dutch by birth, Peter Tillemans came to England in 1708. Much like fellow artist John Wootton, Tillemans is remembered for working in more genres than just sporting art.

In contrast to works that focus upon a particular horse or location, this painting provides a panorama of the countryside around Newmarket. At the far left, Tillemans has depicted a gap in the Devil's Dyck, or Ditch, an approximately seven-mile-long Anglo-Saxon fortification that runs in an almost straight line between the towns of Woodditton and Reach. The gap remains a part of Newmarket racing as it is located just under a mile and a half away from today's finish line. In the seventeenth and eighteenth centuries, it was a part of the Long Course (a six-mile race), the Round Course (three miles, six furlongs), and the Beacon Course (four miles, one furlong).[1]

Amid much activity a match race is taking place between a bay and a grey horse (their jockeys wear white shirts). These horses are about to run in front of the same royal rubbing-down house that appeared prominently in Wootton's *A Nobleman Arriving to Inspect Racehorses at Newmarket* (cat. no. 26). Spectators have gathered to watch as they close in upon the finishing post set in front of the stand at the extreme right of the canvas. Given the distances of these courses, it is not surprising that some spectators chose to follow the entirety of the race on horseback.

1. Cormack, 131.

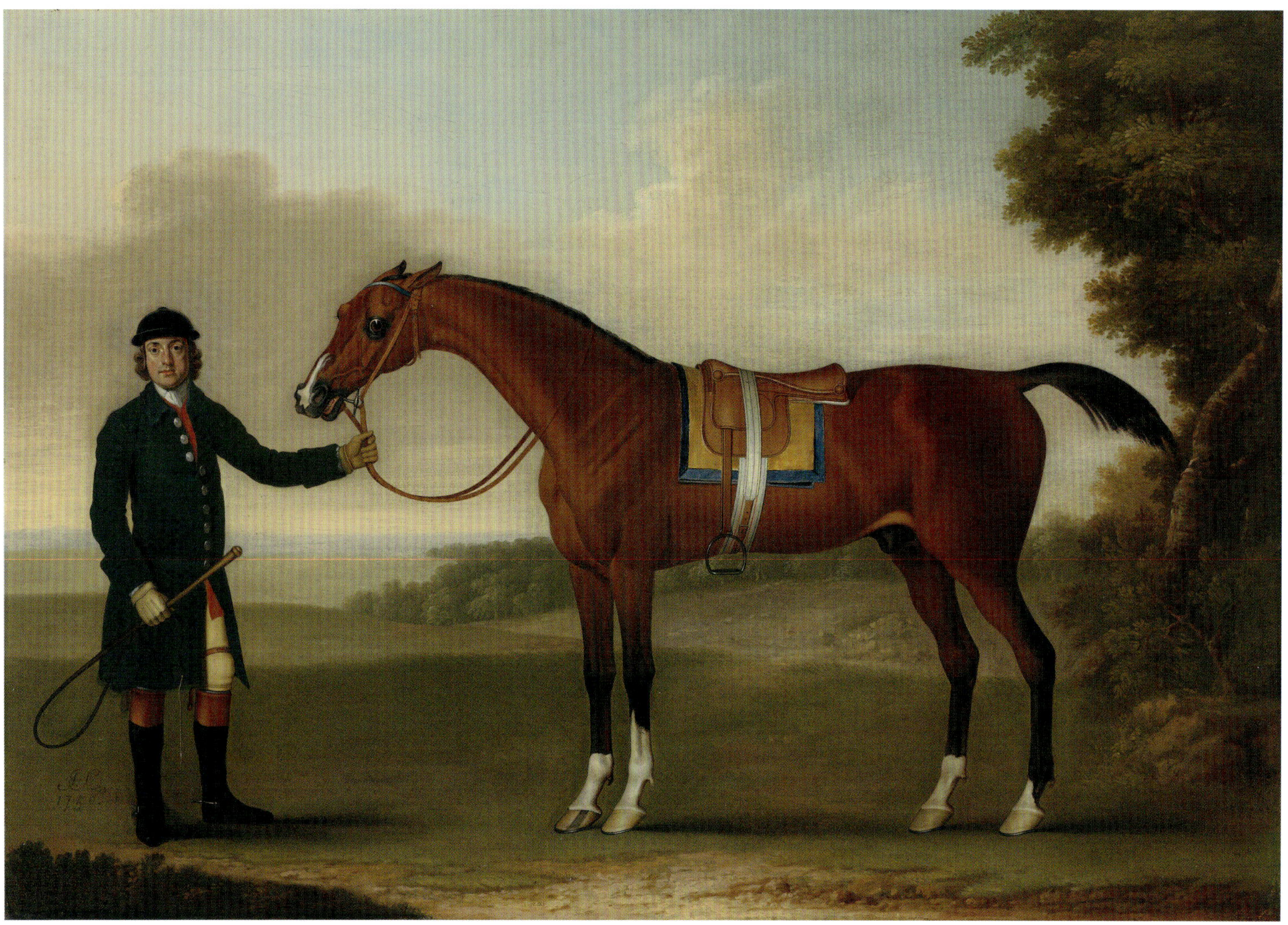

28 James Seymour (English, 1702–1752)

Flying Childers, 1750

Oil on canvas, 30 x 40 in., Paul Mellon Collection, 86.152

This particular painting, produced two years before Seymour's death, is a posthumous portrait of Flying Childers, the first great British racehorse. Childers, as he was first called (the "Flying" epithet came later), was born in 1714. His sire was the Darley Arabian, remembered as one of the three ancestors of thoroughbreds, and his dam was Betty Leedes, granddaughter of the Leedes Arabian and niece of Leedes, who was depicted in the earlier Wootton painting (cat. no. 24).

Childers was sold to William Cavendish, the 2nd Duke of Devonshire, in 1719 and began racing in 1721. He never lost. The sensationalism surrounding him and his speed earned him the title "Flying." He raced until 1723, after which he was put out to stud, dying in 1741.

Retrospective portraits of famous racehorses were not uncommon. Seymour has adopted the standard pose for horse portraits and uses the horse's profile to convey all of the horse's distinctive physical features. Die-hard racing fans would have been able to recognize Flying Childers immediately thanks to Seymour's meticulous recreation of the horse's markings: the white snip on his nose; two white socks on his right side, the front one with a striped hoof; the half-stocking on the front left leg; and a half-pastern on the left rear leg. All of these details, coupled with the nondescript groom dressed in the Duke of Devonshire's colors, would have left no trace of doubt in anyone's mind that this horse was Flying Childers.

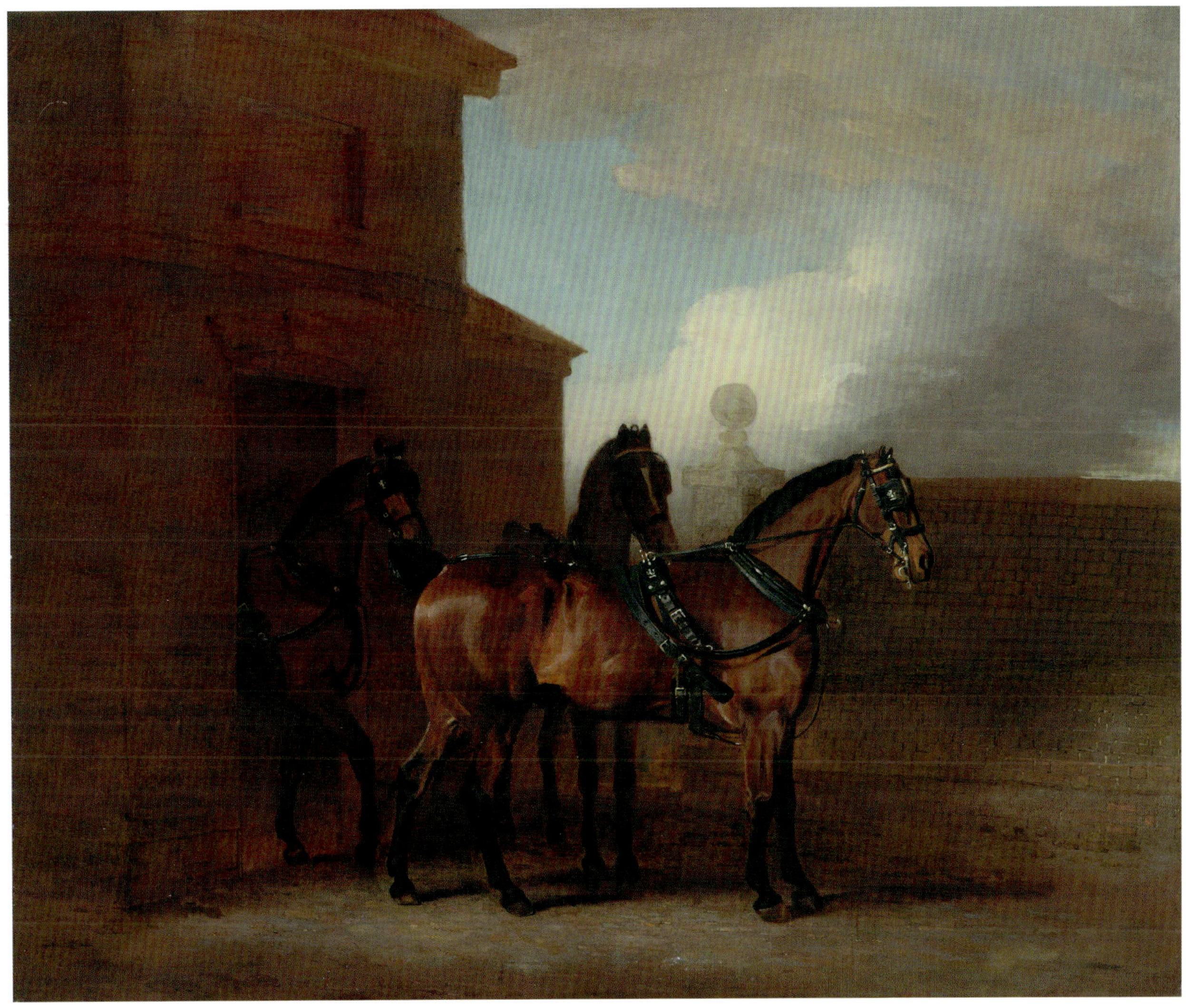

29 Benjamin Marshall (English, 1768–1835)

David, the Property of Henry Villebois, Esq., with Two Other Coach Horses, 1802

Oil on canvas, 33 ½ x 39 in., Paul Mellon Collection, 85.476

Henry Villebois (1778–1847) was a country gentleman and amateur coaching enthusiast. His lifetime overlapped with the rise and fall of the coaching system across the United Kingdom. Though coaching had previously been the province of royalty, which included the Royal Mail service, coachmanship became a fashionable amusement when the quality of roads had improved overall.

In 1807 Villebois founded the Benson Driving Club; like other similar clubs it held meetings in public places so that participants could show off their well-matched horses and fashionably painted coaches. Marshall has created an entire scene around David, one of Villebois's carriage horses. The plasticity with which Marshall rendered David is not matched in the rest of the canvas—perhaps because of Marshall's well-known tendency to use thin layers of paint, some of which may have come off with overcleaning.

That Villebois had latched onto something fashionable is without question. This original painting was turned into a popular print, about which a contemporary critic wrote that "it represents one of our highest and most fashionable forms of the Coach Horse, trimmed with respect to tail and mane, and harnessed in the prevailing style of the gay and splendid metropolis. . . . The Coach Horses of former days were comparatively Dray Horses; those of the present wear the semblance of Hunters and Racers." Interestingly, in the print, the back wall has been turned into a coach house that includes a private drag.[1]

1. Cormack, 259.

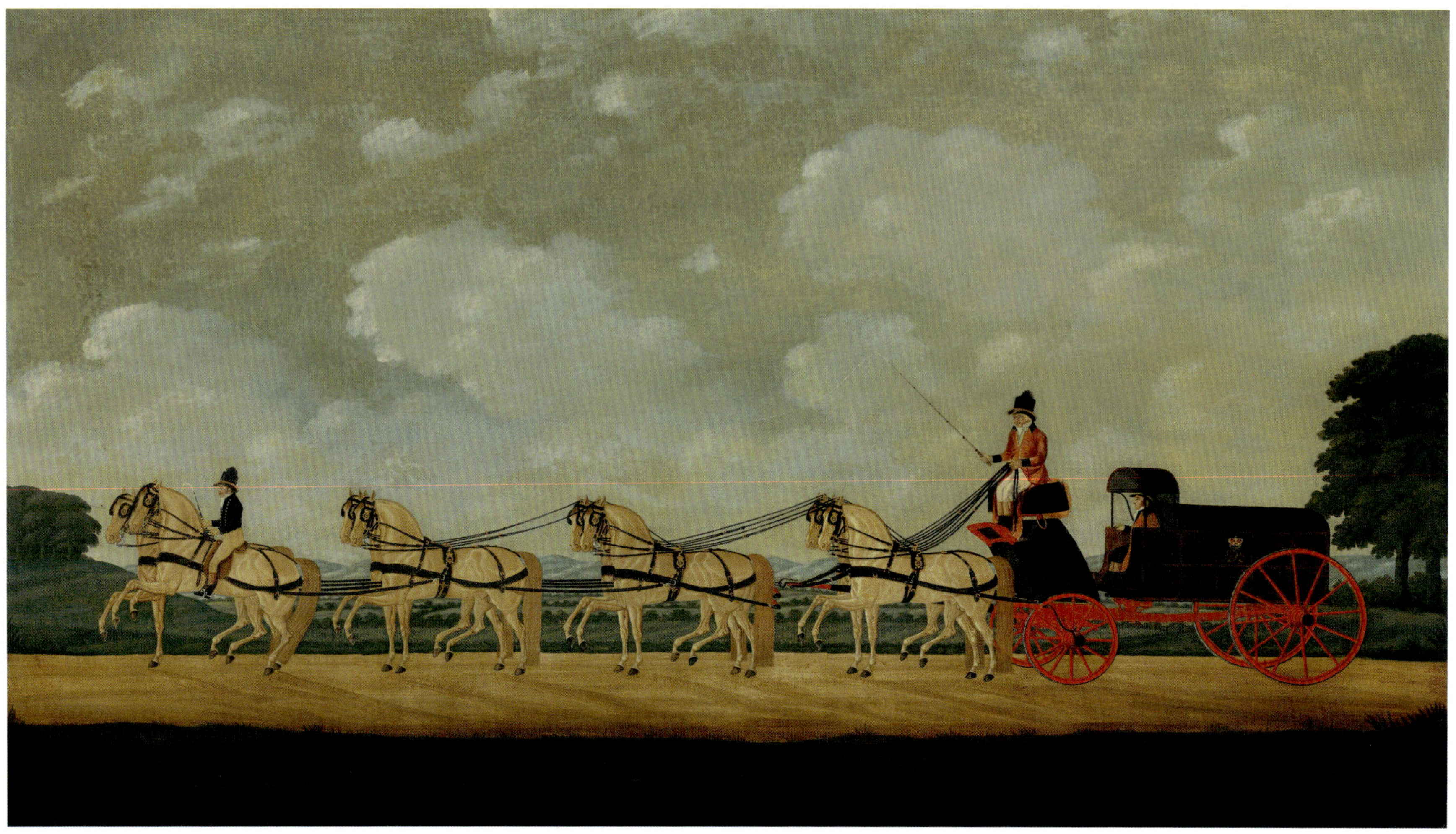

30 John Cordrey (English, active 1765–1825)

The Royal Foregon Pulled by a Team of Eight Hanoverian Creams, 1812

Oil on canvas, 20 13/16 x 36 in., Paul Mellon Collection, 86.153

A foregon, or baggage wagon, preceded the royal family when they traveled. This one is being pulled by a team of eight horses; a postilion on the left lead horse directs the first two horses, and the coachman controls the rear six horses.

Hanoverian Creams, as their name suggests, were specially bred in Hanover to have the color of cream, or buttermilk. The horses in this painting have long flowing tails during a time when docking was deemed fashionable. Though depicted as dainty, they had the build of a light draft horse; in addition to being strong, they were calm, obedient, and hard-working. Cordrey's naïve style, in which the horses in the foreground are shown in strict profile, nevertheless conveys the formality and precision characterizing the royal retinue.

Hanoverian Creams were brought to England when George I ascended the English throne and were used by royal families for more than two hundred years until George V sold them all: after World War I he could not justify the use of German horses to pull English royal carriages. Windsor Greys have been used ever since, and despite having once existed across the globe, no true Hanoverian Cream horses remain.

31 Richard Barrett Davis (English, 1782–1854)

Portraits of Old Carriage-Horses in His Late Majesty's Stud at Windsor, 1820

Oil on canvas, 39 ½ x 49 ¾ in., Paul Mellon Collection, 85.482

The three dark-bay horses depicted here belonged to King George III. Though the king had died on January 29, 1820, the daily routine continued at the royal stables. Grooms are in the process of taking the horses out of their stalls, removing their blankets (and discarding them on the stable floor), and harnessing them for some daily exercise. The quiet and deliberate atmosphere within the stable befits the recent death of the horses' owner.

Davis may have juxtaposed the dark coats of the horses with the light-colored walls of the stable to recall George III's history with the Hanoverian Creams. Like his forebears (cat. no. 30), he admired them and selected one to be his official charger. However, when Napoleon invaded Hanover in 1803, took the Hanoverian Creams from their stud, and used eight of these stallions for his coronation carriage, it proved to be an affront that could not be brushed off. George III swore that his beloved horses would never pull his state carriage while Napoleon was in power. True to his word, he used black horses until 1815, which may be another reason why Cordrey depicted the Hanoverian Creams pulling the royal foregon, or baggage wagon, instead.

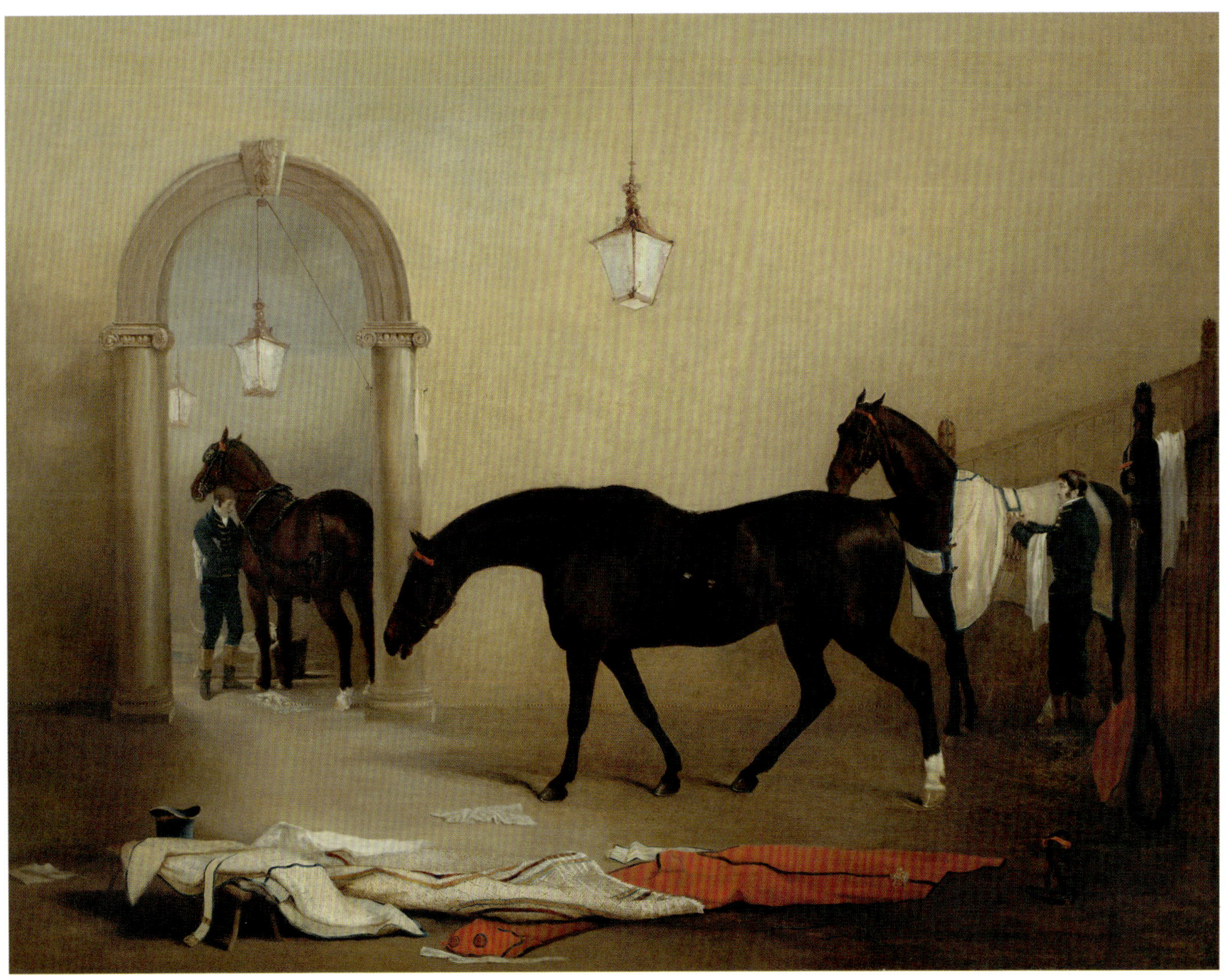

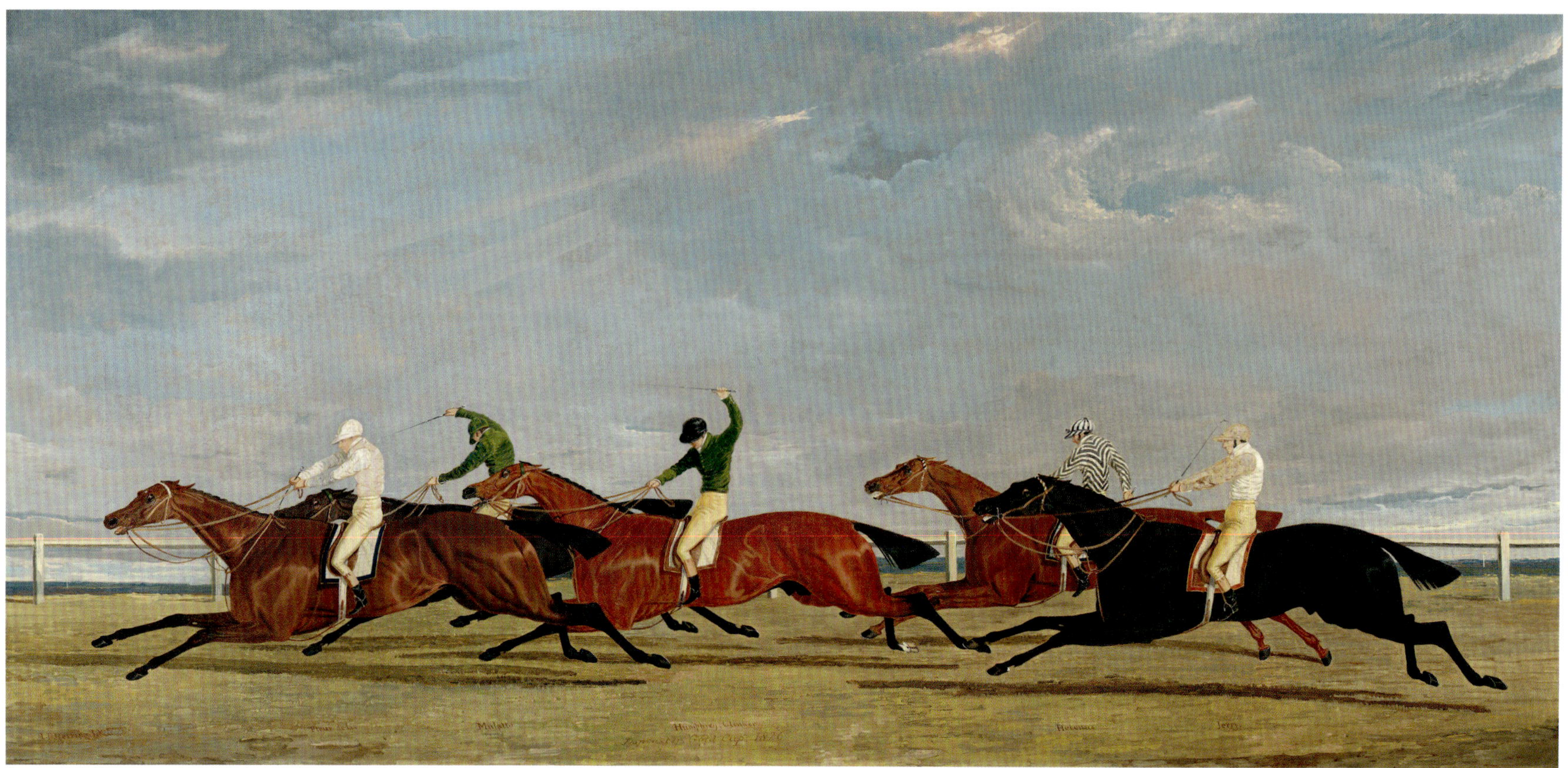

32 John Frederick Herring, Sr. (English, 1795–1865)
The Final Lengths of the Race for the Doncaster Gold Cup, 1826

Oil on canvas, 17 ¾ x 35 ¾ in., Paul Mellon Collection, 99.79

As a former coach driver who also painted coach panels and inn signs, John Frederick Herring, Sr., brought a unique perspective to the sporting art he created.[1] He was frequently commissioned to paint winners of horse races, especially at the Doncaster Racecourse, and other sporting art scenes. Paintings made by this self-taught artist were typically engraved, elevating his popularity.

This particular painting recreates the final lengths of the Doncaster Gold Cup race of 1826. This race, also known as simply the Doncaster Cup, was first run in 1766 and consisted of four-mile heats, which was typical for racing in the eighteenth century. In 1825, the year before this painting was completed, the race was shortened drastically to two miles and five furlongs. This distance has continued to dwindle over time and is now two miles and two furlongs. The substantial shortening of the course must have made the race seem faster, a quality that Herring successfully recreates in his painting.

The racehorses he portrays are (from left to right) Fleur-de-Lis, Mulatto, Humphrey Clinker, Helenus, and Jerry. They are shown moving at top speed in the conventional "flying gallop" manner, with their legs raised both fore and aft like rocking horses. More accurate depictions of a horse galloping would come after the publication of Eadweard Muybridge's studies of horses in motion in the 1880s.

If the finish of this race was indeed as close as Herring depicts (the horses finished in the order they are shown), it becomes easier to see why Muybridge predicted that "in the near future . . . no race of any importance will be undertaken without the assistance of photography to determine the winner of what might otherwise be a so-called 'dead-heat.'"[2]

1. Cormack, 452.

2. Eadweard Muybridge, "A Dead Heat," *Nature* 26 (May 25, 1882), 81.

33 James Pollard (English, 1792–1867)

Mr. J. F. Sharp's Private Drag outside the Roebuck Inn, Turnham Green, 1824

Oil on canvas, 19 7/8 x 30 1/4 in., Paul Mellon Collection, 99.85

This meticulously rendered painting reveals much about the state of coaching in early nineteenth-century Britain. Though the Roebuck Inn was a familiar stop on the main road west out of London, Mr. J. F. Sharp's identity remains unknown. Indeed, all that Pollard includes of him is a cape draped over the box seat, indicating that he may have stopped in for a drink and left his servants to watch over his belongings, coach, and horses: a valet or postboy standing on the back of the coach and an ostler (caretaker of horses) behind the horses at right. The figure standing below Mr. Sharp's cape appears to be another driver since he is holding a whip.[1]

Mr. Sharp's "drag"—a slang term used for any smart and well-made coach in the pre-railway era—has red wheels, a maroon body, and black top. This restrained color scheme is similar to that of the Royal Mail Coaches but does not include a coat of arms emblazoned on the sides.

This particular painting also illustrates a reason why other paintings such as Marshall's *David, the Property of Henry Villebois, Esq., with Two Other Coach Horses* (cat. no. 29) depict only three matching horses, instead of four. Usually a light-colored horse was chosen as the "off-leader" (off = right, leader = front); since carriages were driving on the left side of the road, the light-colored horse would be more visible in the dark and thus more easily avoided by other drivers.

1. Cormack, 270–71.

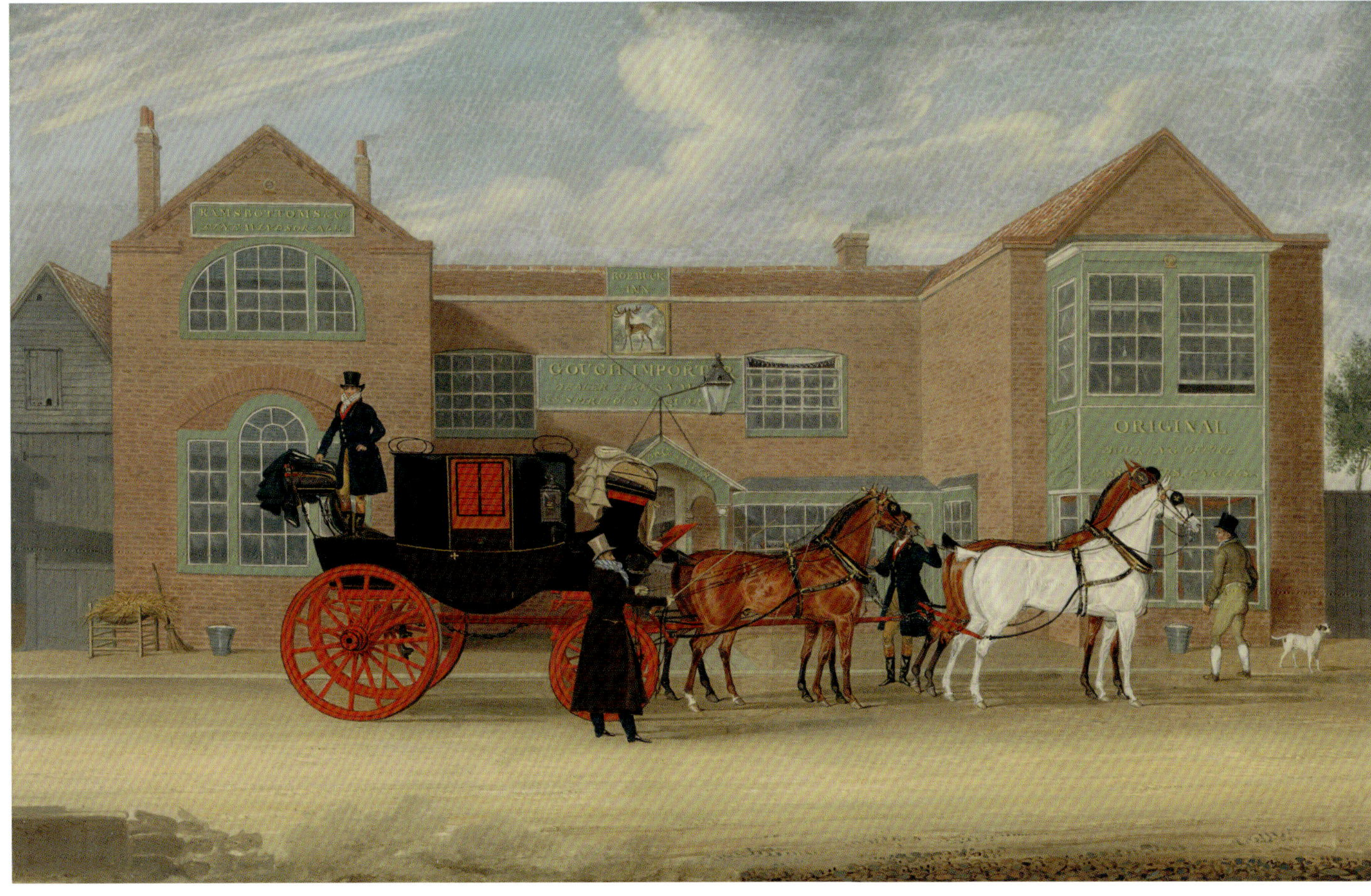

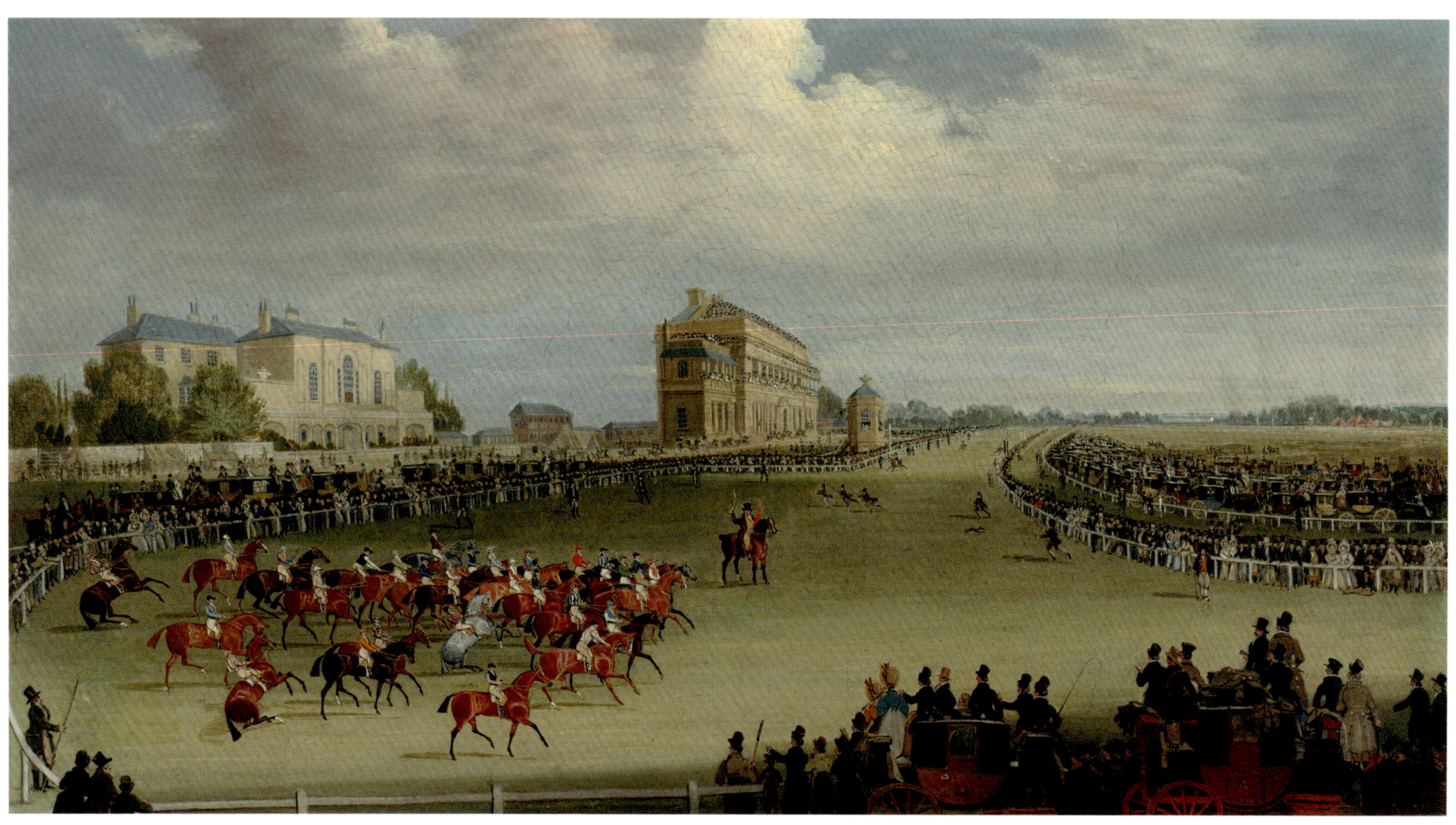

a.

34 James Pollard (English, 1792–1867)

a. *Doncaster Races, 1831: Horses Starting for the St. Leger,* 1831

Oil on canvas, 14 ½ x 25 ½ in., Paul Mellon Collection, 85.489.1

b. *Doncaster Races, 1830: Passing the Judges' Stand,* 1831

Oil on canvas, 14 ½ x 25 ½ in., Paul Mellon Collection, 85.489.2

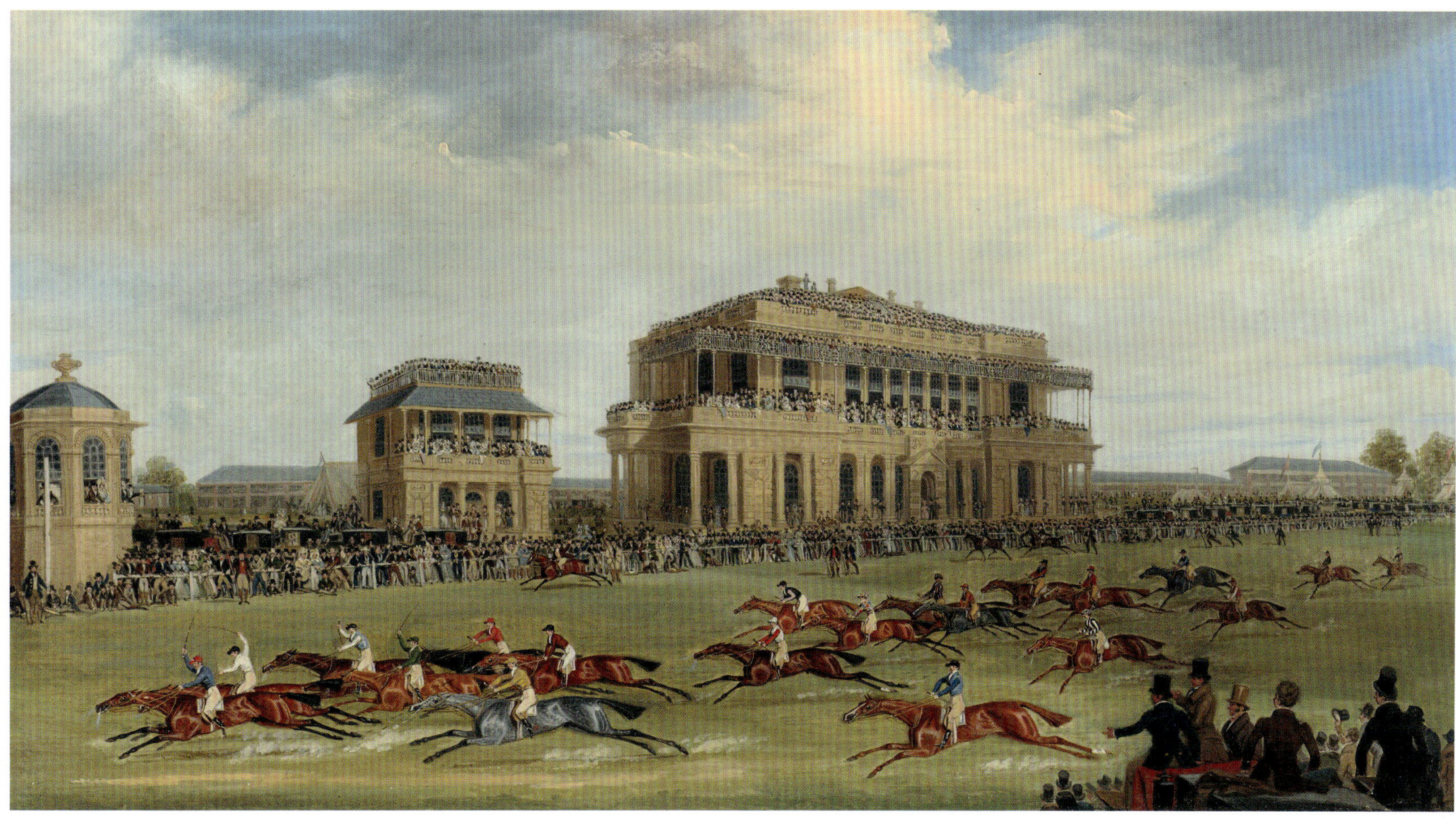

b.

James Pollard was a sportsman as well as a sporting artist who produced paintings and engravings that documented all types of sport. Though he is best remembered for his carefully crafted coaching scenes (cat. no. 33), these two oils depict the St. Leger race at the Doncaster Racecourse.

The St. Leger race was established in 1776, ten years after the creation of the Doncaster Gold Cup. Taking place in the autumn, at just over one and three-quarter miles long, the St. Leger is a grueling test for racehorses at the end of the racing season. The paintings depict the beginning of the 1831 race and the conclusion of the 1830 race won by Birmingham, on the far left, followed by Priam, Emancipation, Pedestrian, and Brunswicker (the horses and jockeys are all identifiable through contemporary records).

Pollard highlights two other features distinctive to early racing. For one, races had walk-up starts. In the first painting, twenty-eight horses wait for the rider in the middle of the composition to drop his arm, signifying the start of the race. The same rider would use the red flag in his other hand to indicate a false start. Secondly, the track is turf, not dirt. This is still a key difference between English and American horseracing.

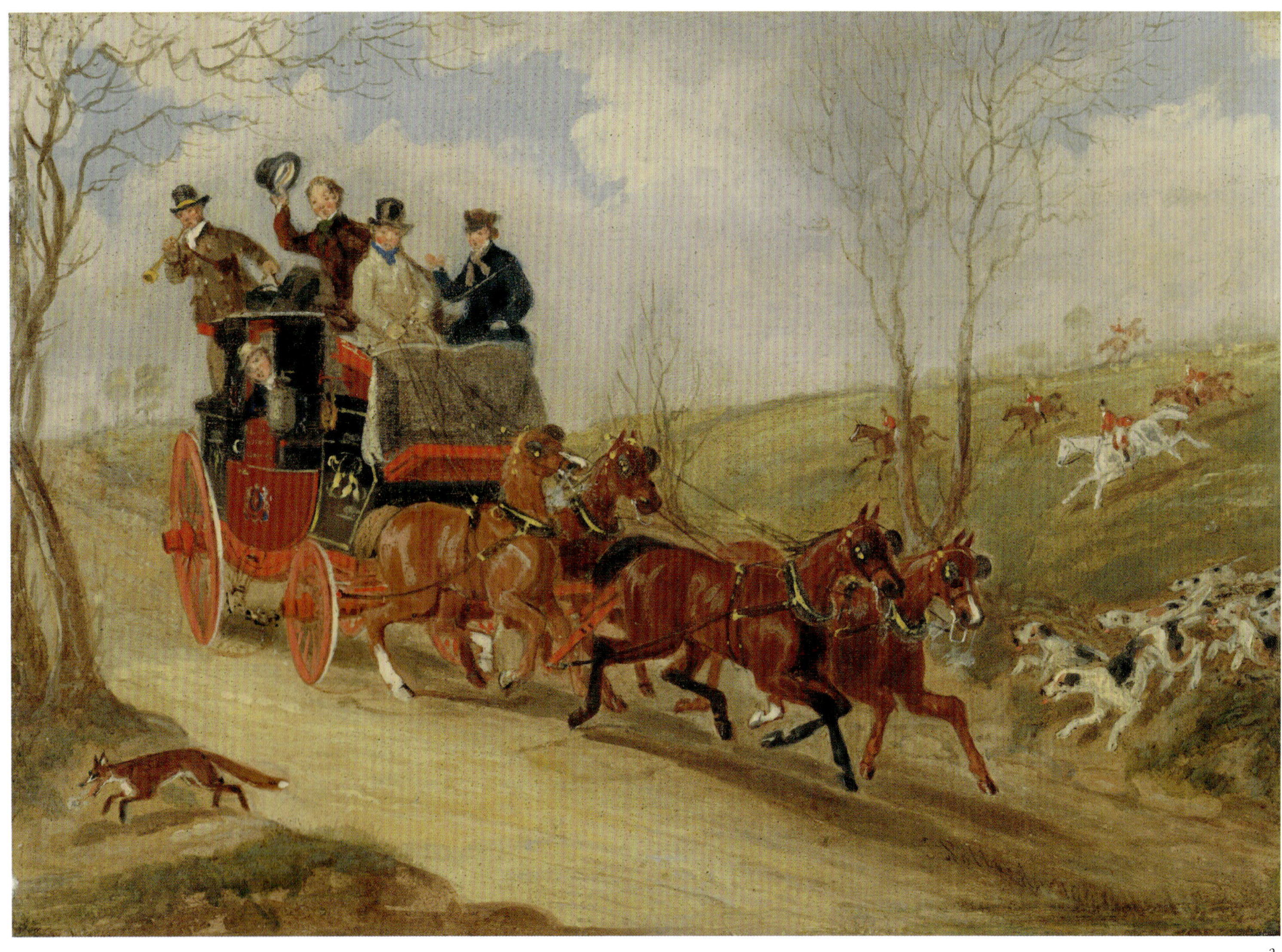

a.

35 James Pollard (English, 1792–1867)

a. *Coaching Incident: Royal Mail Coach Interrupting a Fox Chase,* 1843

Oil on panel, 8 1/2 x 11 3/4 in., Paul Mellon Collection, 99.86

b. *Coaching Incident: A Railway Train Overtaking the Hull-London Royal Mail Coach,* 1843

Oil on panel, 8 3/4 x 11 3/4 in., Paul Mellon Collection, 99.87

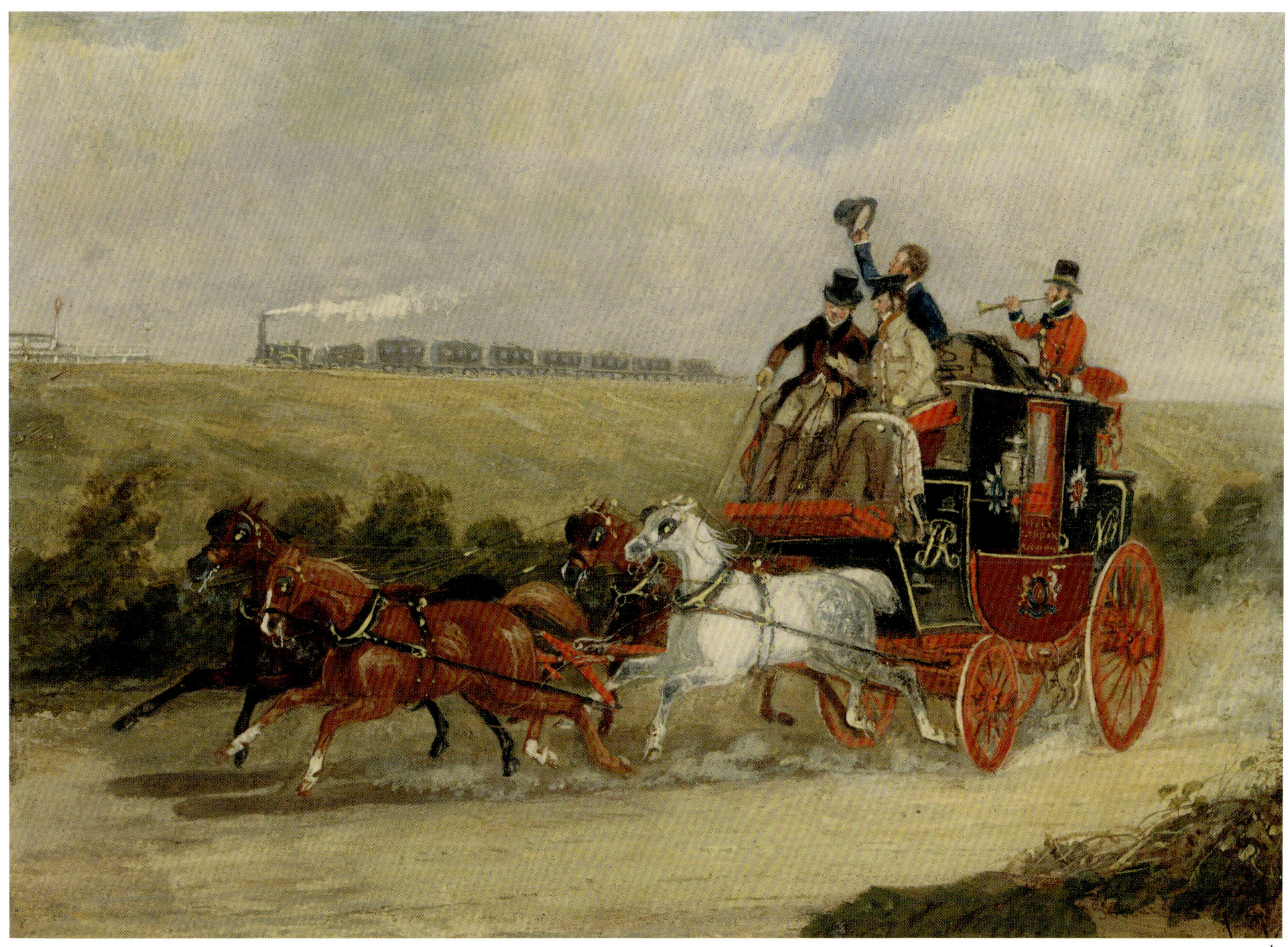

b.

The "coaching incidents" depicted in this pair of paintings appear to parallel each other, yet together they tell a story that begins with humor but ends on a poignant note.

In the first painting, thanks to the sudden appearance of a Royal Mail Coach, a fox seems to have escaped a pack of hounds while capturing the attention of all the coach's passengers—even the guard is blowing his horn.

In the second painting, another speeding Royal Mail Coach throws up lots of dust in its wake. Coach horses could only average speeds of ten miles an hour if they were changed every ten to fifteen miles. Even though ostlers could make the switch in about two minutes, coaches were nowhere near fast enough to derail the ascendancy of trains like the one in the distance, which at this time was capable of sustained speeds of up to forty miles per hour. The network of railways that would ultimately replace coaches spread across England in the 1830s and 1840s. The last mail coach would retire before the end of the 1840s.

36 Charles Hancock (English, 1802–1877)

Gentlemen's Carriages: A Gentleman Driving a Bay Horse to a Tilbury Gig, ca. 1820–30

Oil on canvas, 25 1/8 x 30 1/8 in., Paul Mellon Collection, 99.74

Although Charles Hancock's beginnings as an artist are obscure, he is known to have shown at the Royal Academy. His repertoire consisted largely of sporting subjects: racing, hunting, and coaching scenes with portraits of horses and the occasional human being.

"Gig" is a term used for any two-wheeled carriage driven by a single horse. In this particular image, a fashionable gentleman sits atop a Tilbury gig, recognizable by its cutaway body. Designed by the London firm of Tilbury, it was cost-effective and easy to steer, and its seven-spring suspension made it well suited to riding on rough roads. By 1825 gigs were the most common carriages to be driven by gentlemen in both the city and the country.[1]

Hancock successfully portrays the elegance of the wealthy owner's horse and conveyance, ennobling the scene with the classical archway at left.

1. Hugh McCausland, *The English Carriage* (London: Batchworth, 1948), 45–56.

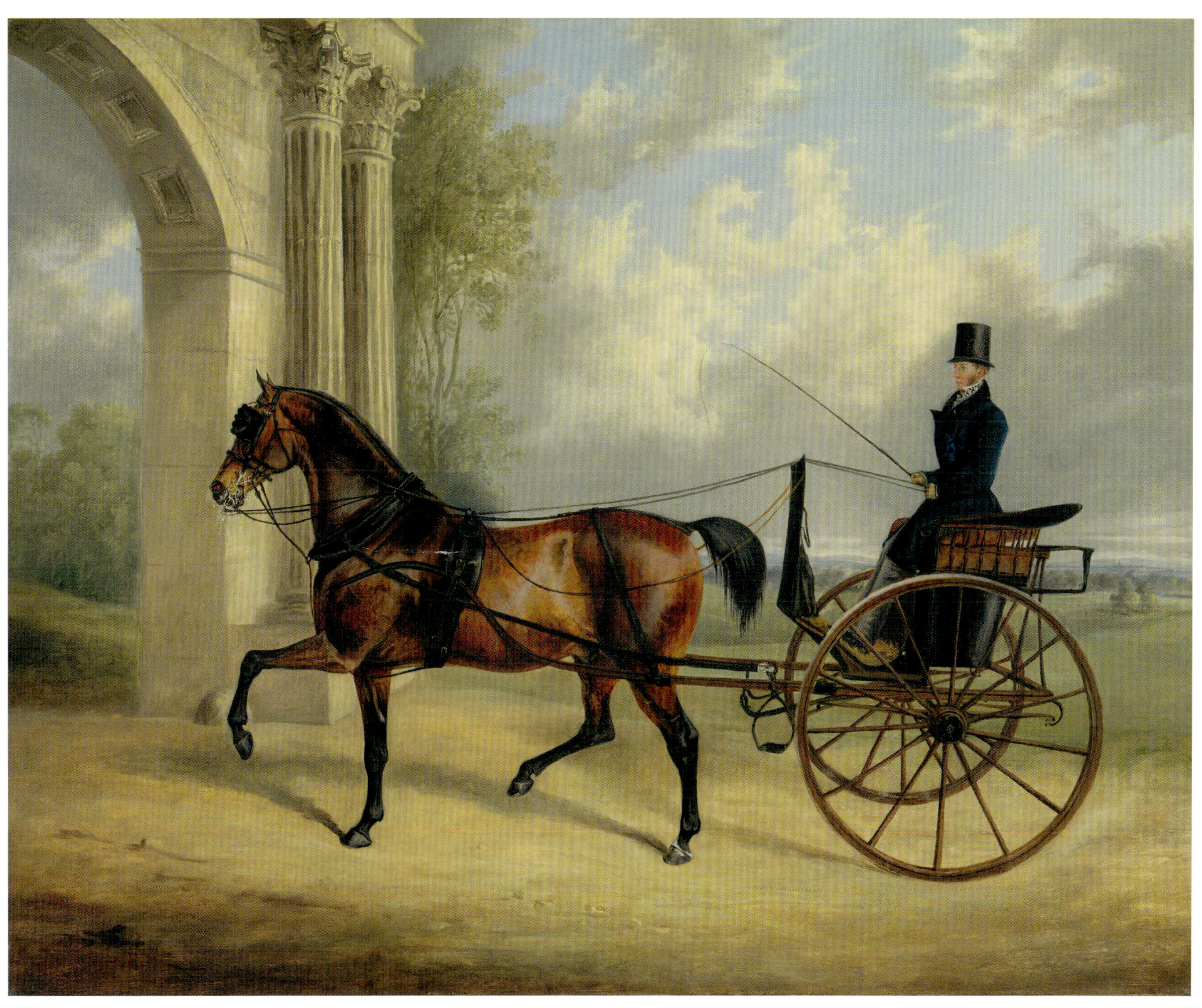

37 Charles Cooper Henderson (English, 1803–1877)

Charles Cooper Henderson had the opportunity to become a lawyer after studying at Winchester and qualifying for the bar. However, he turned his back on that profession to become an artist and is known for his coaching scenes.

Coaching only flourished in England after roads, coaches, and horses all improved. Thomas Telford and John Loudon McAdam took care of the roads; Royal Mail Coaches were streamlined to move faster and enlarged (in addition to the driver and the Royal Mail guard, they could carry seven passengers, four inside and three outside—one next to the driver, and two on the roof); and horses were bred for increased speed and endurance.

These images were produced during the heyday of coaching, which lasted from approximately 1815 to 1840. Henderson reveals some of the trials and challenges that could befall the Royal Mail Coach—which is easily identified with its distinctive red wheels, maroon body, black top, and guard dressed in the red Royal Mail livery with its blue collar.

In the first image, the Birmingham–London Royal Mail coach has stopped because the near-wheeler (near = left; wheeler = rear horse) has fallen. The Royal Mail guard descends from his seat in the back to assist.

The second painting provides a contrast to the first as the Dover–London Royal Mail's team of four is moving at top speed—despite a law that made it illegal for four horses to be galloping at the same time and with an extra passenger on the roof! Safety issues arising from competition between coaches had led Parliament to enact the law, but proprietors of coaches then trained one horse to trot as fast as the other three galloped. In this image the "Parliamentary Horse," as these fast trotters were called, is the near-wheeler.

The third image shows the Hull–London Royal Mail outside a blacksmith's shop, where it has been forced to stop because of a lame off-wheeler (off = right). An ostler has arrived to switch out the horse so the coach can resume its journey.

The nocturnal setting of the fourth image testifies to the importance of prompt mail delivery. Every evening at 8 pm, London mail coaches set out from the General Post Office of Martins-Le-Grand. Traveling through the night, they only stopped to switch out their horses—tolls were not required. To avoid slowing down, the Royal Mail guard would sound his horn as they approached toll gates. The toll taker would have to open the gate at any time of day or night or face a fine of forty shillings.[1]

1. Cormack, 265–67.

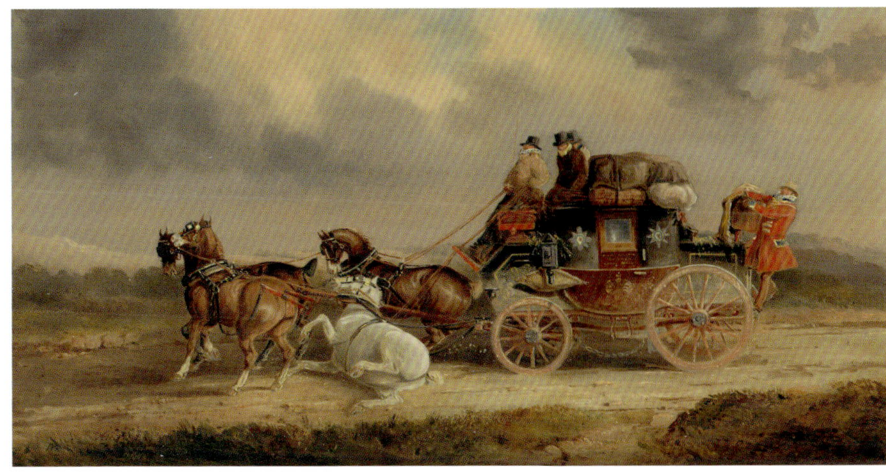

a. *Mail Coach Incidents: The Birmingham–London Royal Mail,* ca. 1820–30

Oil on canvas, 13 x 24 in., Paul Mellon Collection, 99.75

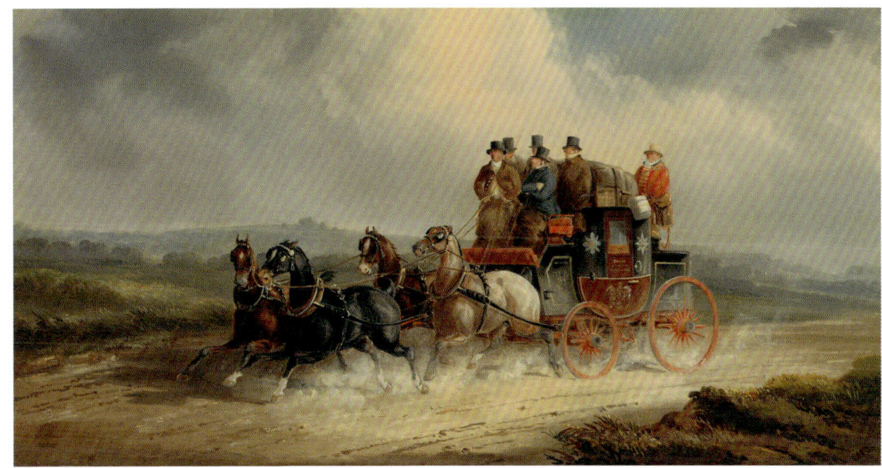

b. *Mail Coach Incidents: The Dover–London Royal Mail,* ca. 1820–30

Oil on canvas, 13 x 24 in., Paul Mellon Collection, 99.76

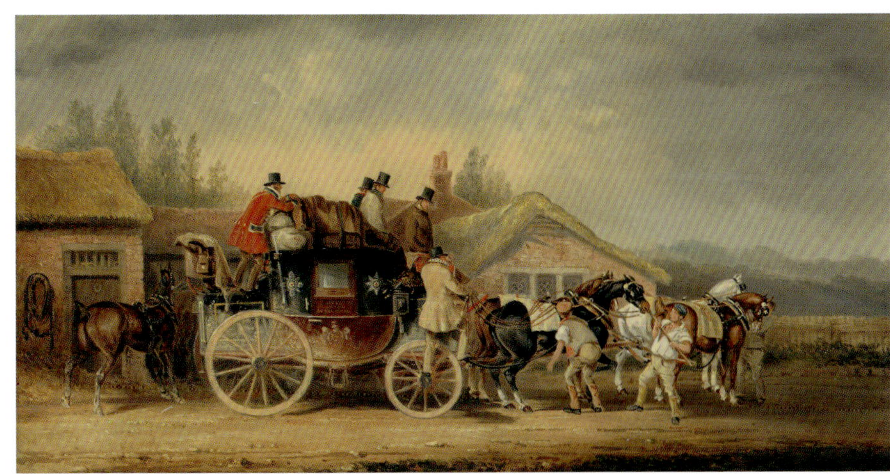

c. *Mail Coach Incidents: The Hull–London Royal Mail Outside a Country Blacksmith's Shop,* ca. 1820–30

Oil on canvas, 12 ¾ x 24 in., Paul Mellon Collection, 99.77

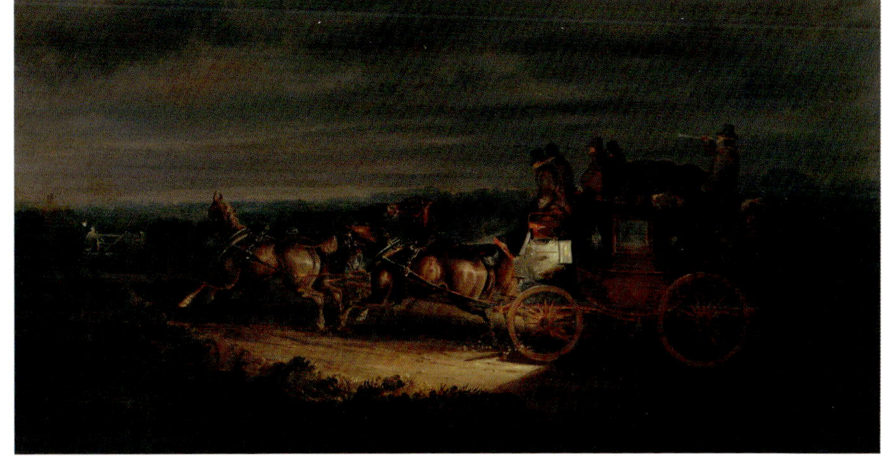

d. *Mail Coach Incidents: The Wells–London Royal Mail by Night,* ca. 1820–30

Oil on canvas, 12 ¾ x 24 in., Paul Mellon Collection, 99.78

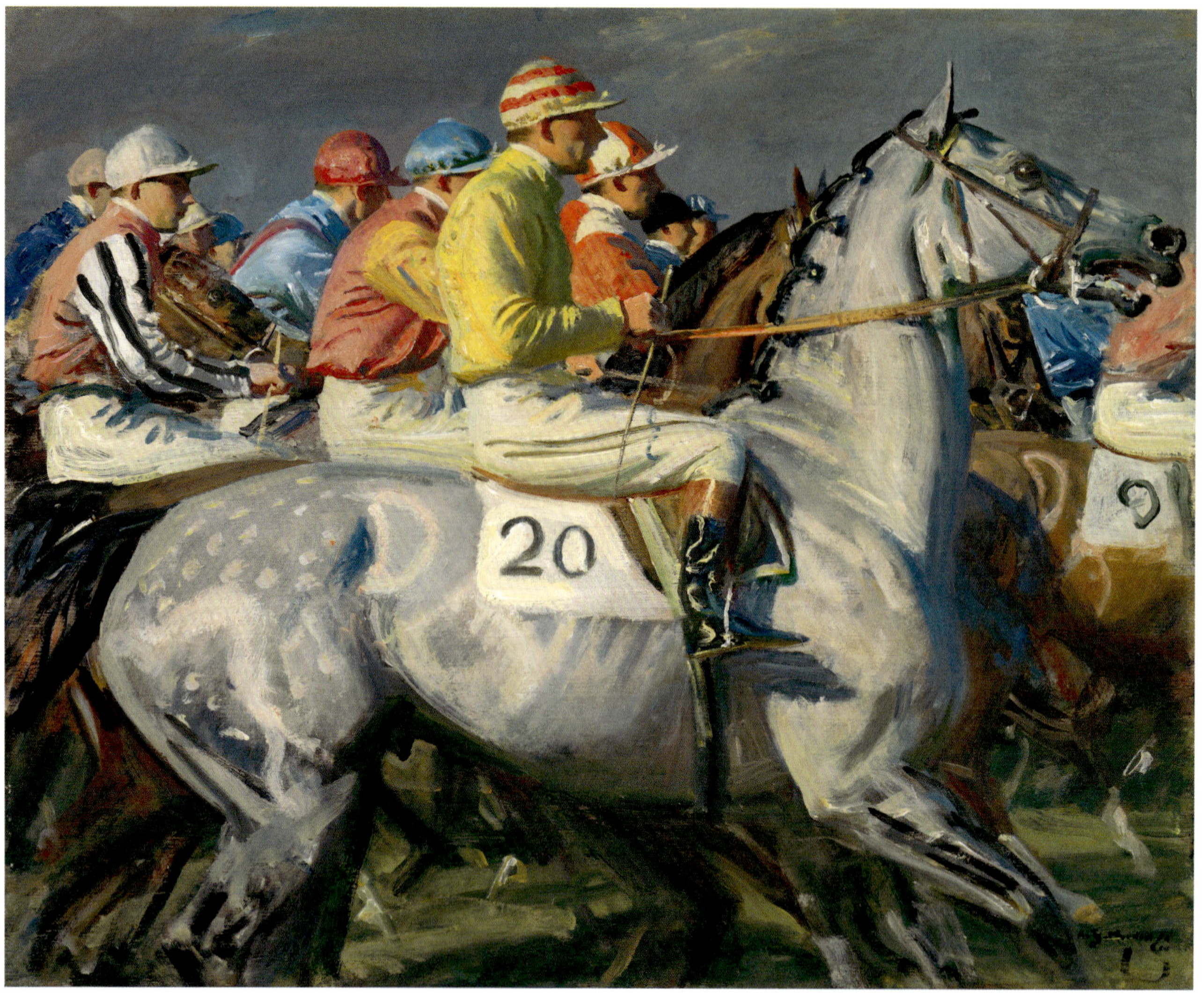

38 Sir Alfred J. Munnings, P. R. A. (English, 1878–1959)

Linin' 'em Up, Newmarket, ca. 1940–53

Oil on panel, 19 ¾ x 23 ½ in., Paul Mellon Collection, 96.24

In the last twenty years of his life, Munnings painted many variations on the theme of jockeys lining up and getting ready for the start of a race (starting gates would only be adopted in English racing in the 1960s).[1] According to Munnings, "Each start was a fresh picture for me; as they have been, meeting after meeting, year after year."[2]

The close-up vantage point and cropping of the scene give the work a sense of immediacy. Though not created specifically for Mr. Mellon, its connection to his racing sensibilities cannot be overlooked. In his words, "There are the same elements in racing that attract me as in hunting, although it is more its aesthetic quality. . . . It is the colour, the movement, the speed, the excitement, the competition, the skill of riding, the cleverness of the horses, and the primitive element of luck. . . . But it is mostly the love of the horse, the well-kept, well-trained, beautifully moving horse, the horse as an object of art."[3]

1. Cormack, 155.

2. Alfred J. Munnings, *The Finish* (Museum Press, 1952, 216–17.)

3. Mellon, 152.

39 Sir Alfred J. Munnings, P. R. A. (English, 1878–1959)

After the Race, Cheltenham Saddling Paddock, ca. 1946

Oil on canvas, 40 ¾ x 63 ¾ in., Paul Mellon Collection, 99.84

This painting by Munnings came into Mr. Mellon's possession in 1967. The steeplechase (racing over fences, or hurdles) first began in 1834 at Cheltenham Racecourse, and Munnings's painting illustrates his own description of the aftermath of such a race: "Many horses are returning after a steeplechase. With extended nostrils and quivering tails, they come to stand; the jockeys dropping the reins, dismount and unsaddle, and all too soon the steaming horses are led away and the scene is ended."[1]

Mr. Mellon's attraction to this work can perhaps be explained by a speech he gave at the dinner of the "Ye Anciente Fraternite of York Gimcracks" after his horse, Mill Reef, won the Gimcrack Stakes in 1970. By this time, Mr. Mellon was well known as a racing and hunting enthusiast and one of the greatest living art collectors.

In his speech he mentioned that over the years he had come to admire the racecourses at York, Goodwood, Sandown, and Cheltenham—the location of this painting. He also reminisced about his earliest experiences at the turf, saying, "I still hark back to those long, soft, eminently green gallops stretching to the horizon in the slanting afternoon sun, and the late October sunlight on the warm yellow stone of the old, high stands at Newmarket—the bright colours of the silks flashing by, the sheen of the horse's coats . . ."[2]

1. Munnings, 284–5.

2. Mellon, 265.

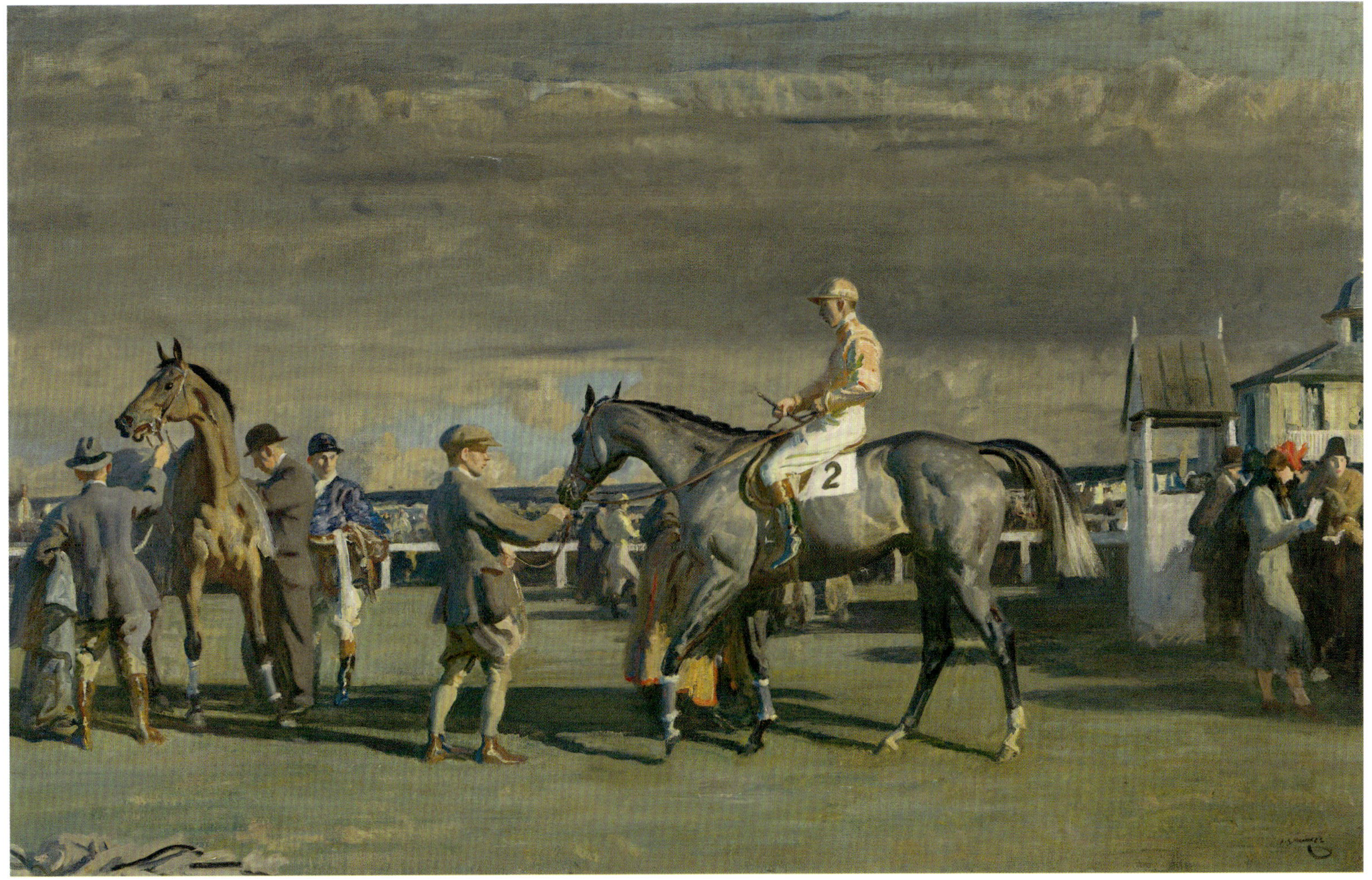

ANIMAL, MAN, COUNTRY

As access to the British countryside evolved, so too did the relationships of humans and animals to each other and to their environment. Despite the very straightforward, if not blunt, styles used in the portraits and landscapes discussed in this section, these works can be understood as highly complex representations of historically charged subjects.

The animals chosen as subjects range from the greatly esteemed to the overlooked, and from the exotic to the everyday. Depictions of rare animals, especially George Garrard's *A Barbary Antelope and a Black Swan* (1811) and Abraham Cooper's *The Wapati or North American Deer* (1818), were commissioned to record natural history. Paintings such as Thomas Weaver's *Two Durham Oxen* (1827) celebrate the success of specialized breeding practices, while Thomas Gooch's *A Gentleman with His Horse and Dogs* (1780) and John Frederick Herring, Sr.'s *Thomas Dawson and His Family* (1842) highlight changes in the treatment of animals.

The idealized countryside depicted in Pieter Angellis's *A Game of Skittles* (1727) is balanced with George Morland's *Paying the Ostler* (1792) and *Pigs and Piglets in a Sty* (ca. 1800), which are less romanticized versions of country living.

It is not surprising that Mr. Mellon collected such a wide array of country images. When he was a child, his father owned houses in the city, with interludes at rented houses in the country, in America as well as in England. As an adult, reflecting on the many moves of his childhood, Mr. Mellon bought land in Virginia and set down roots. He would go on to purchase farms and other properties that adjoined his own, amassing 4,000–4,500 acres in the manner of the great English estates and preserving them from development.[1]

1. Mellon, 258.

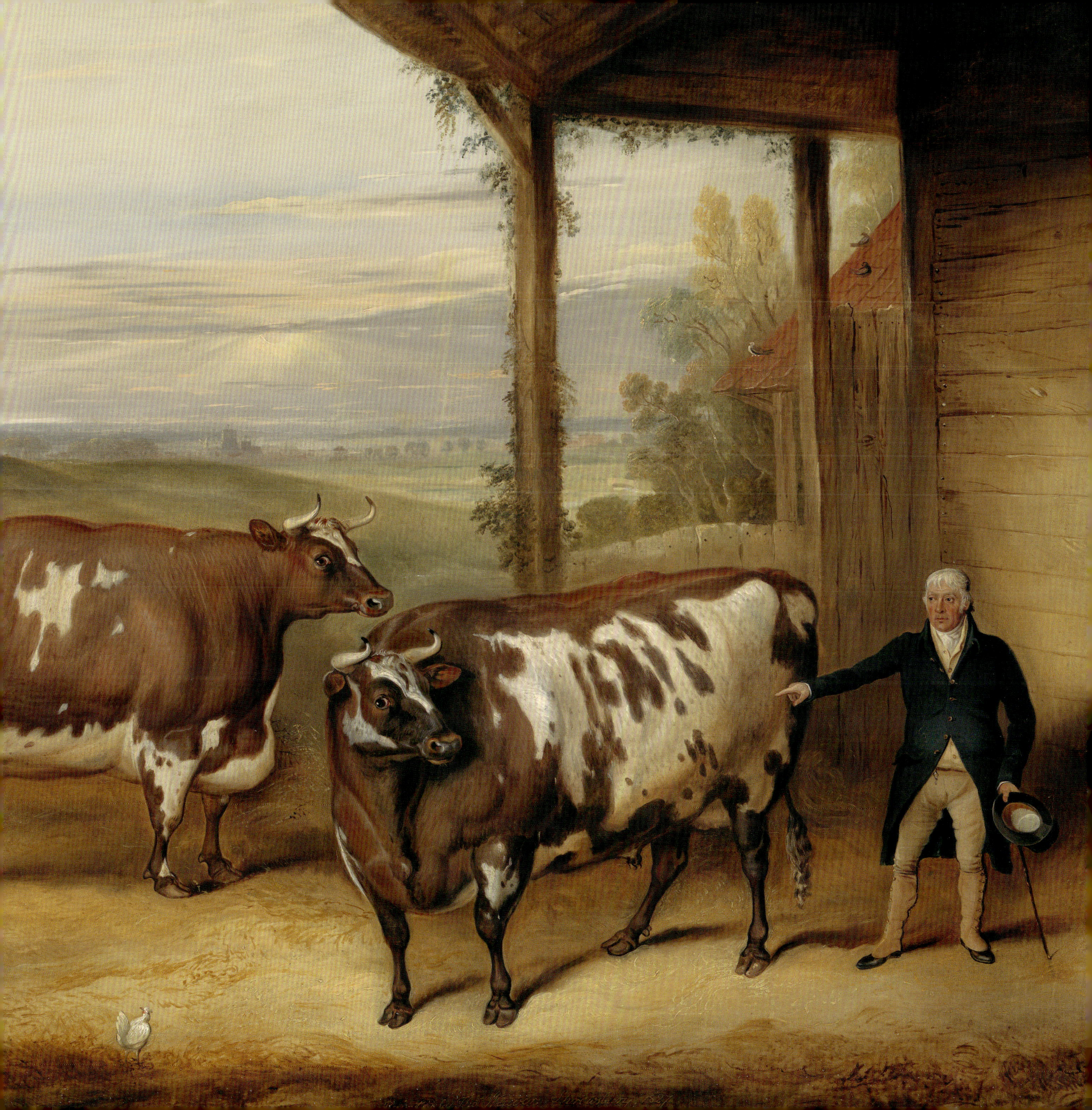

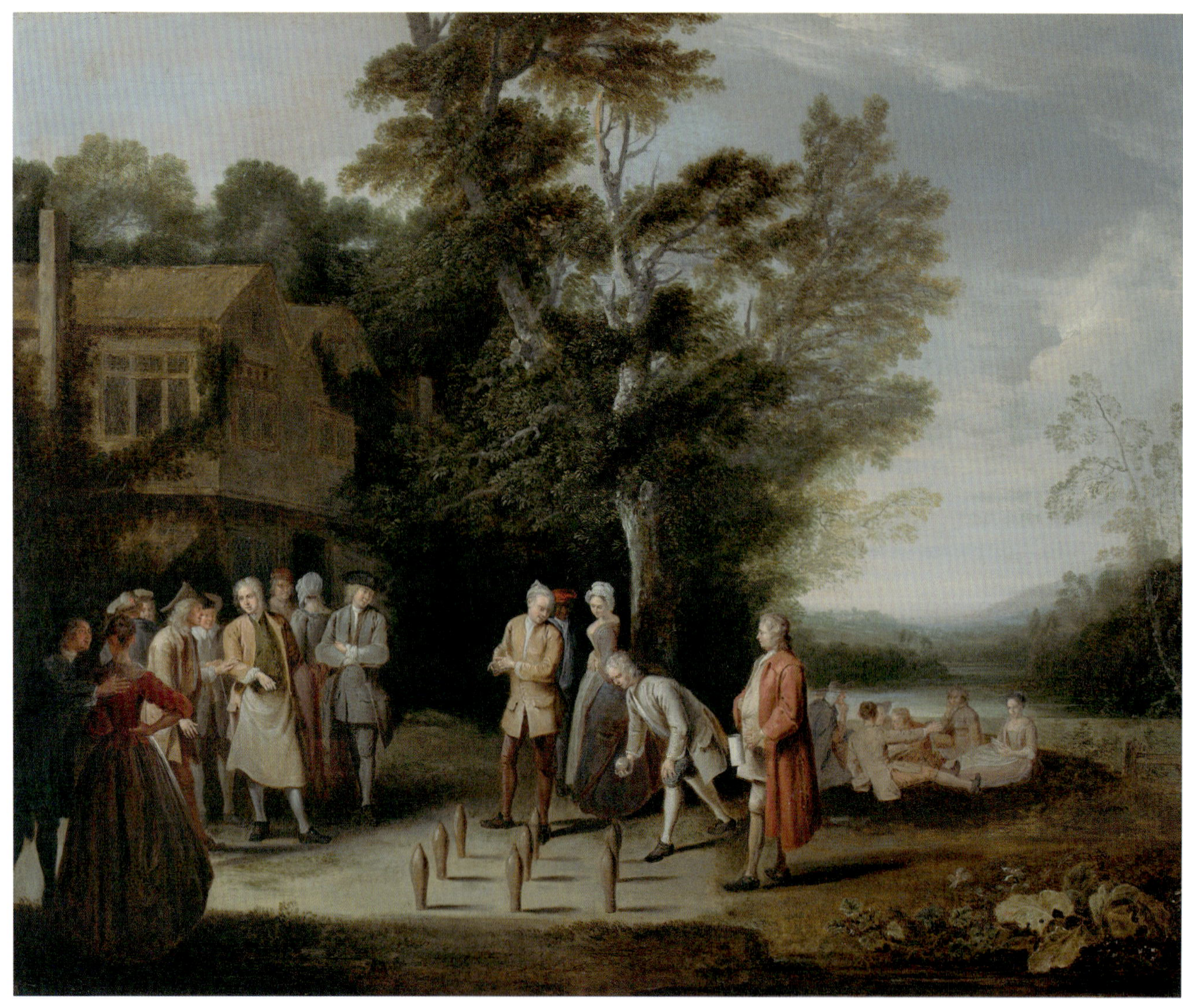

40 Pieter Angellis (French, worked in England, 1685–1734)

A Game of Skittles, 1727

Oil on canvas, 25 x 29 5/16 in., Paul Mellon Collection, 85.460

Born in Dunkirk, France, Pieter Angellis worked on the continent and became a master with the Antwerp Guild in 1715–16. Shortly afterward he moved to London and settled in Covent Garden, where he specialized in country scenes such as this one. Angellis's notion of the rustic ideal was likely indebted to French artists such as Antoine Watteau (1684–1771), who was well known for his *fête-galante,* or images of elegant outdoor entertainment.

As indicated by the man wearing an apron, this scene takes place in front of an inn—the hub of social life in the country—where a number of people have gathered to enjoy some conversation and a game of skittles. Much like bowling today, the object of skittles was to knock down nine pins with a ball in two attempts. Those who succeeded got a bonus throw and could pitch from close range. The beautiful landscape is probably imagined rather than topographically accurate.

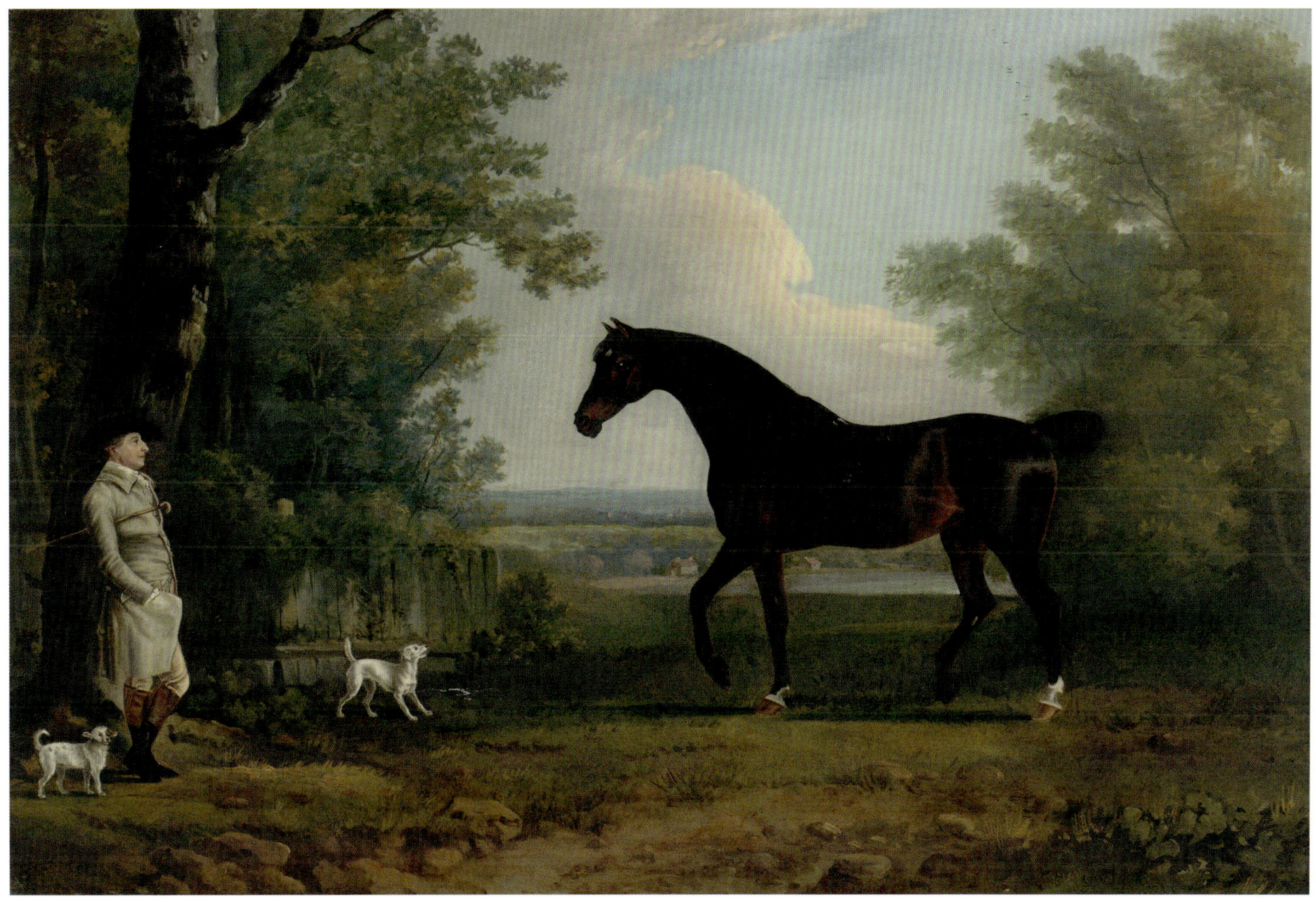

41 Thomas Gooch (English, 1750–1802)
A Gentleman with His Horse and Dogs, 1780

Oil on canvas, 24 ¾ x 36 in., Paul Mellon Collection, 85.466

Very little is known about Thomas Gooch's training and career except that he submitted images of country life to the Royal Academy between 1781 and 1802.[1] In this idyllic image, a lush swath of English countryside forms the backdrop for an unnamed gentleman, his dogs, and his horse. With legs crossed and hands in his pockets, the gentleman is a study in nonchalance as he gazes at his horse, which also seems at ease as it approaches from the right.

Gooch's scene highlights the changing nature of relationships between humans and animals. Once known for their brutal treatment of horses during training, Europeans were gradually learning from their contacts with the Middle East that gentle handling encouraged horses to serve their masters instead of fear them. The willingness of the horse in this painting to approach its owner is a sign that Britain was importing not only horses from the East but new attitudes as well.

1. Cormack, 452.

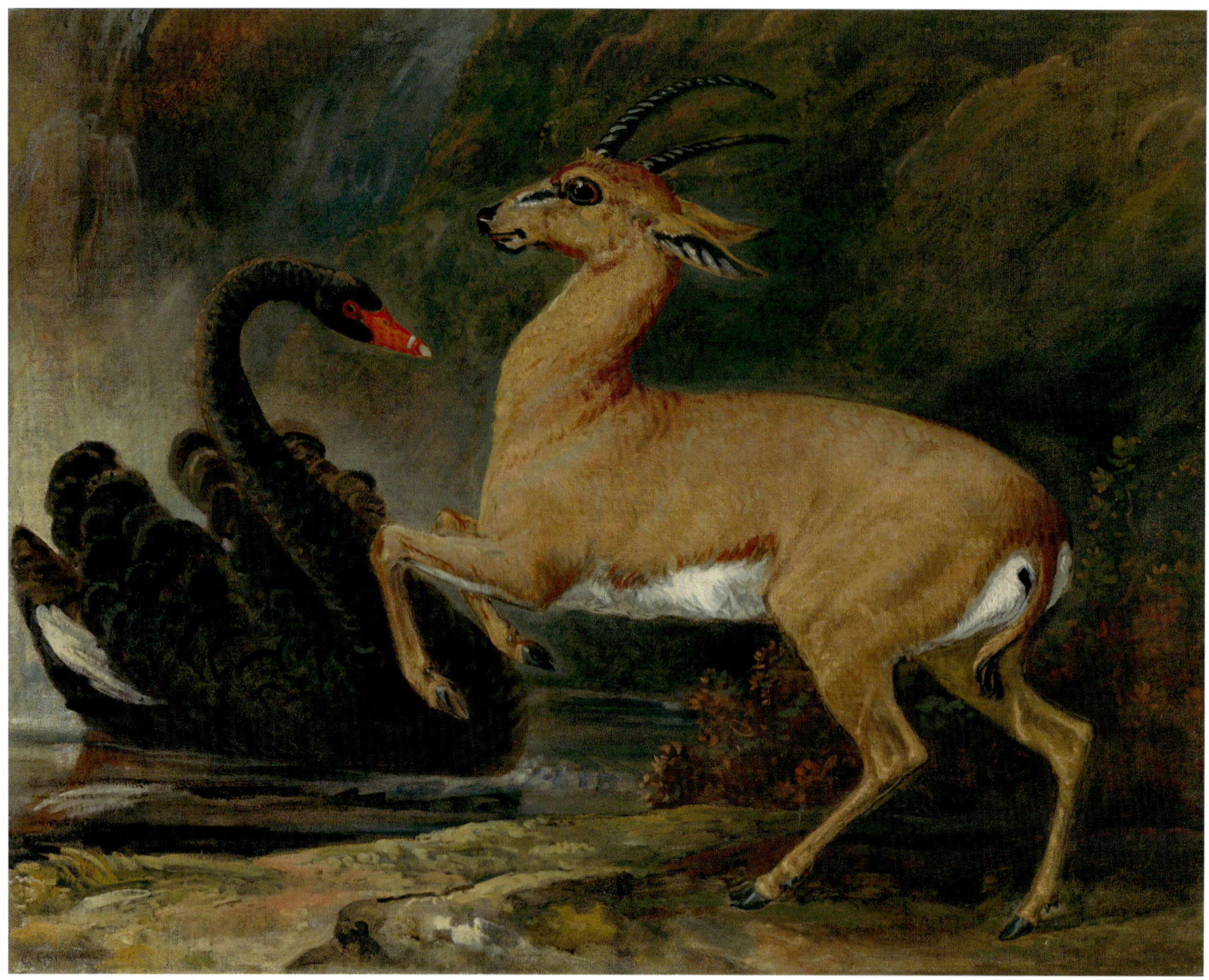

42 George Garrard (English, 1760–1826)
A Barbary Antelope and a Black Swan, 1811

Oil on canvas, 30 x 37 in., Paul Mellon Collection, 85.471

Born in London, George Garrard trained under the animal specialist Sawrey Gilpin and entered the Royal Academy in 1778. In his early career he specialized in horses; later his range expanded to include exotic animals, as exemplified in this work. At the time of its creation, however, this combination of animals would have existed only in a menagerie, or in art.

The Barbary antelope was common to the northern parts of Africa and Mesopotamia. Garrard has included all the animal's distinguishing features: ringed horns, reddish-brown coloring on top separated from a white belly by a dark line, and black markings near the nose and in the ears.

The 1697 discovery of black swans in Australia sent reverberations through the naturalist world. Before then, using the term "black swan" in the West was a way of saying something was impossible—since everyone believed all swans were white. Garrard has accurately documented the bird's red bill, curved neck, and dark plumage.

43 George Morland (English, 1763–1804)

Paying the Ostler, 1792

Oil on canvas, 28 1/8 x 36 3/8 in., Paul Mellon Collection, 86.129

George Morland apprenticed to his father, painter Henry Robert Morland, and first showed his work at the Royal Academy when he was ten. As an adult, Morland lived the life of a sportsman and earned a reputation as a specialist in rural imagery and as a social and artistic renegade.[1]

Before the coming of railroads, the journey from city to country was quite an ordeal. Many inns sprung up along the roads to accommodate weary travelers and their horses. A sign on the side of this inn's stable advertises the availability of single-horse gigs and saddle horses. In the middle of the stable yard a gentleman seems to have just secured a mount, though he perhaps would have preferred a gig like the one traveling away down the road at right—especially given the quality of his saddlehorse. Despite the docked tail (deemed smart at the time), which a groom is hurriedly combing, the horse's short neck and furry ankles are the ultimate indicator of a horse that had not a drop of Eastern blood. Mismatched tack completes the shabby, unpolished look. No wonder the "gentleman" seems to begrudge his payment to the half-hidden ostler.

1. John Barrell, *The Dark Side of the Landscape: The Rural Poor in English Painting, 1730–1840* (Cambridge: Cambridge University Press, 2006).

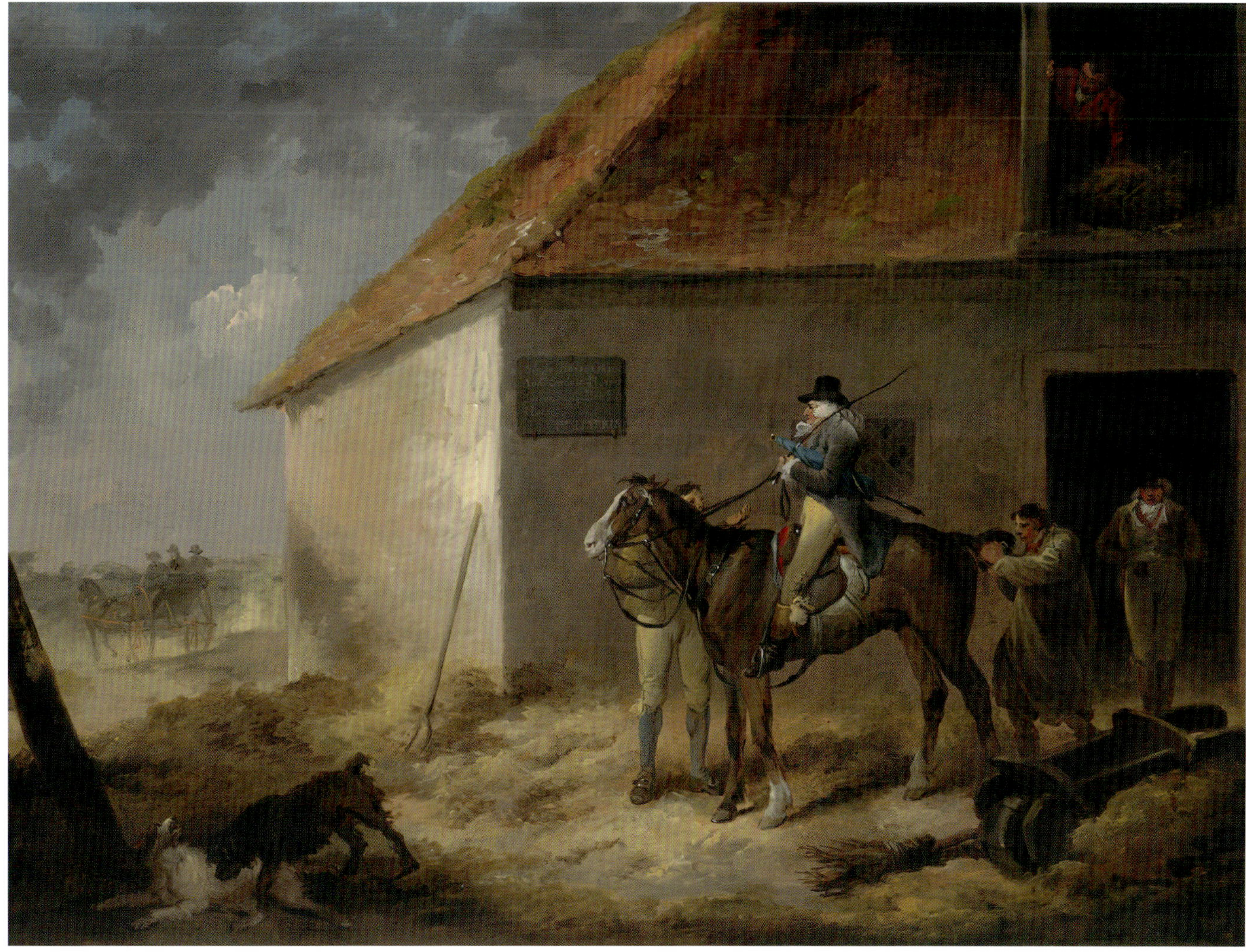

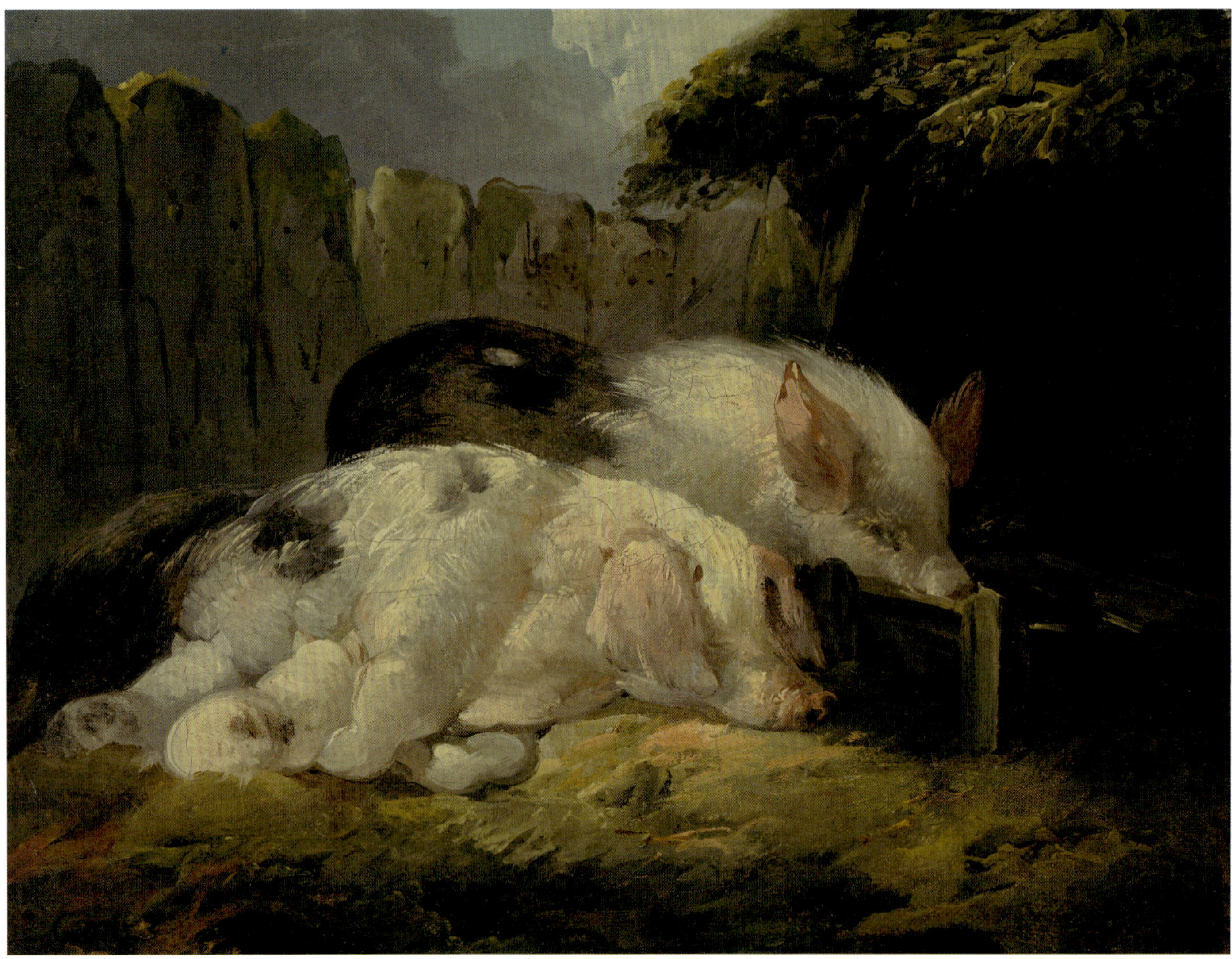

44 George Morland (English, 1763–1804)

Pigs and Piglets in a Sty, ca. 1800

Oil on canvas, 9 ½ × 12 in., Paul Mellon Collection, 85.472

Pigs were a frequent subject for George Morland, who is said to have studied them "as closely as he had studied horses, and painted them no less successfully. . . . He revealed the possibilities of the pig in art as no painter had done before."[1]

In this scene of porcine bliss a sow is resting, suckling her piglets, while the pig behind her focuses on the trough. Morland's loose painterly style was well suited to capturing these subjects up close, emphasizing their thick hair—a characteristic that was to give way to smoother hides as pigs were bred for pork production.[2] At the same time, Morland depicted these pigs from a low vantage point within the muddy sty, perhaps to indicate their humble status within the hierarchy of animals.

1. Sir Walter Gilbey and Edward William Dirom Cuming, *George Morland: His Life and Works* (London: Adam and Charles Black, 1907), 209.

2. Cormack, 109.

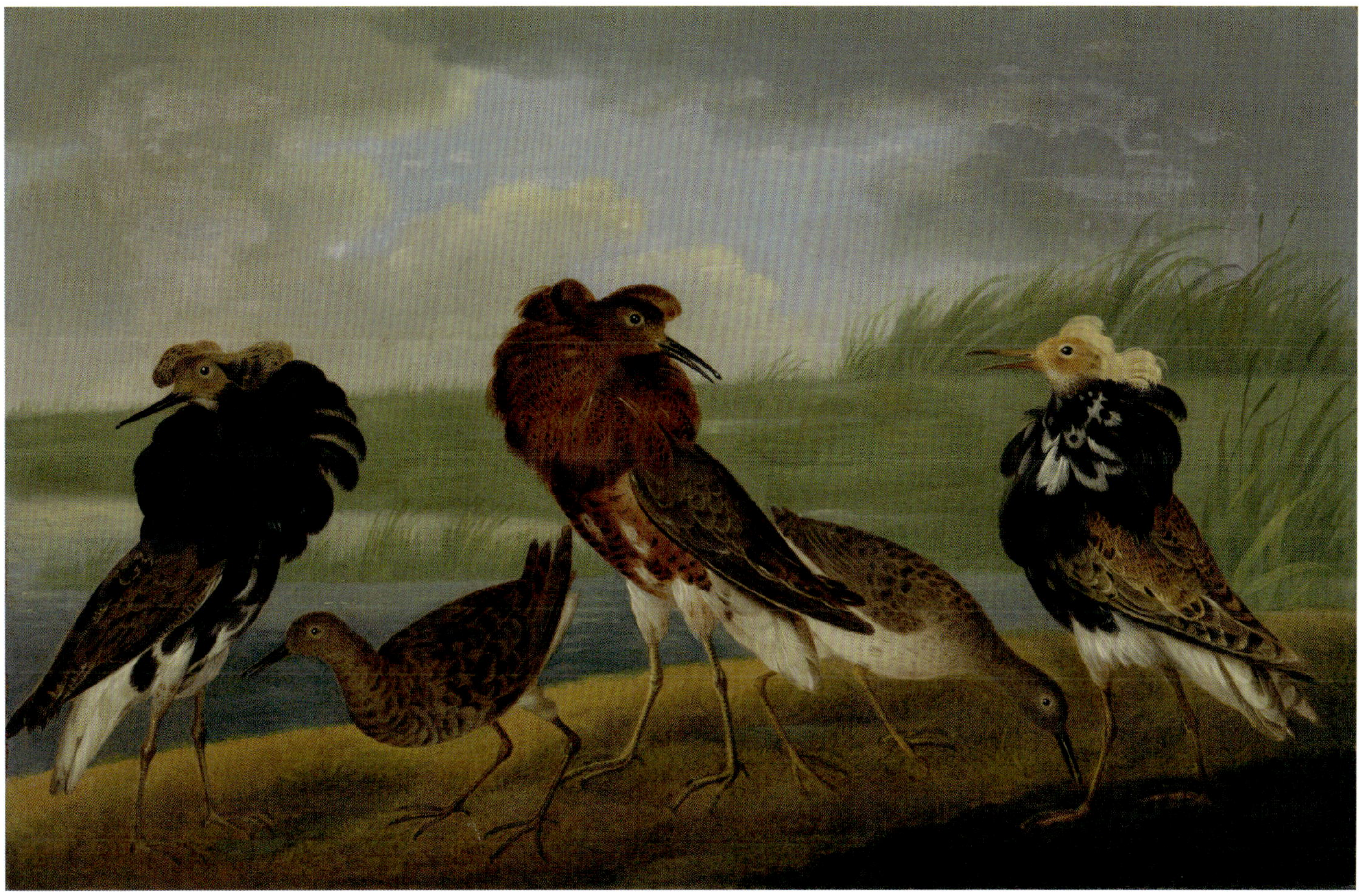

45 James Sillett (English, 1764–1840)

Ruffs and Reeves, 1824

Oil on canvas, 19 x 29 3/8 in., Paul Mellon Collection, 86.151

A native and long-time resident of East Anglia, James Sillett began his career as a heraldic painter. He matured into an artist who specialized in still-lifes and images of game, accented with some landscapes and portraits. He exhibited his works frequently at the Royal Academy.[1] This work, however, was probably commissioned or collected by a local sportsman.

Ruffs and reeves are the male and female members of the species *Philomachus pugnax,* which belongs to the European sandpiper family. These migratory birds come to East Anglia in the spring for their mating season, during which the males develop unique collars of billowy feathers (hence the name "ruff") around their necks and tuffs of feathers on their heads. This display of finery signals their readiness to fight each other for the right to mate.

Sillett has chosen to portray three ruffs and taken great care to emphasize the differences in their plumage. Set between the ruffs are two mottled brown-grey reeves. Sillett furthers the ecological exactitude of this work by setting these birds in a marshy area, which is where these courtship rituals would take place.

The date of this painting coincides with a drastic reduction in the ruff population across England. This decline has been attributed to multiple factors: the transformation of its habitat into arable land, hunting, and the obtaining of specimens by naturalists.[2] Given Sillett's almost life-size depictions of these birds, the careful detailing of the feathers, and the accurateness of the bird's habitat, this canvas may have been acquired by a naturalist who was unable to obtain a taxidermy example.

1. Cormack, 455.

2. Simon Holloway, *The Historical Atlas of Breeding Birds in Britain and Ireland: 1875–1900* (Poyser, 1996), n.p.

46 James Ward (English, 1769–1859)
A Lady's Hack, 1796

Oil on canvas, 18 1/8 x 24 1/8 in., Paul Mellon Collection, 99.97

For foxhunting, hacks were horses that were ridden by men and women to the location where a fox might be found. Once a fox had been flushed, riders would switch to the mounts that would carry them cross-country in pursuit.

Before 1800, women rarely participated in the field. They might accompany the hunt until a fox was found, but then, for reasons of safety, they would either head home or follow at a distance. The side saddle, introduced to England in the fourteenth century by Anne of Bohemia, continued to hold sway until the early twentieth century. Catherine de Medici had invented a second pommel for the side saddle in the sixteenth century, which allowed for more stability while riding. The pommel allowing for jumping would only be invented later, as seen in John Frederick Herring, Sr.'s *Hunting Scenes: A Hunting Morn* (cat. no. 20a), and would allow women to experience all the speed and movement on a horse that had once been monopolized by men.

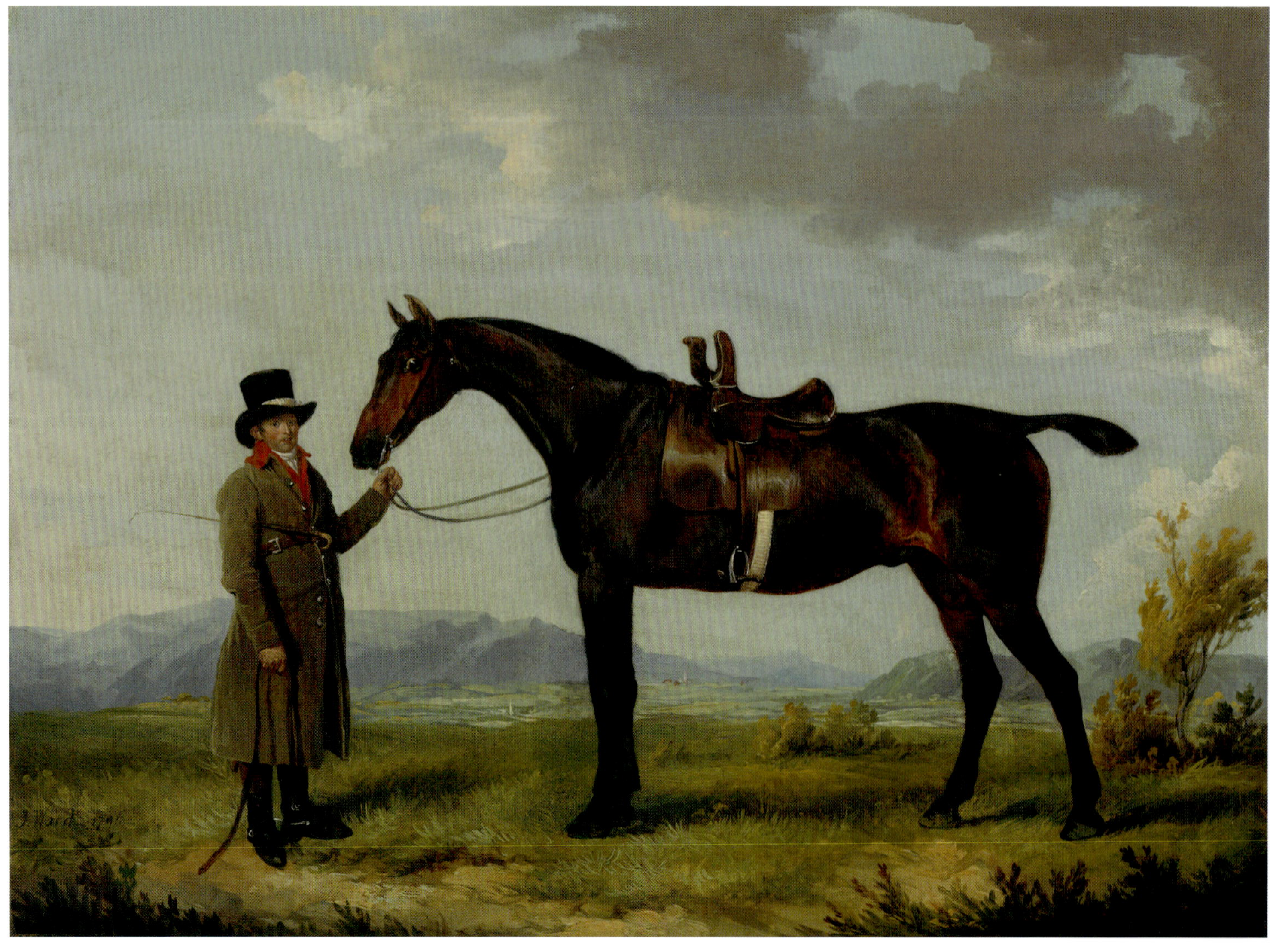

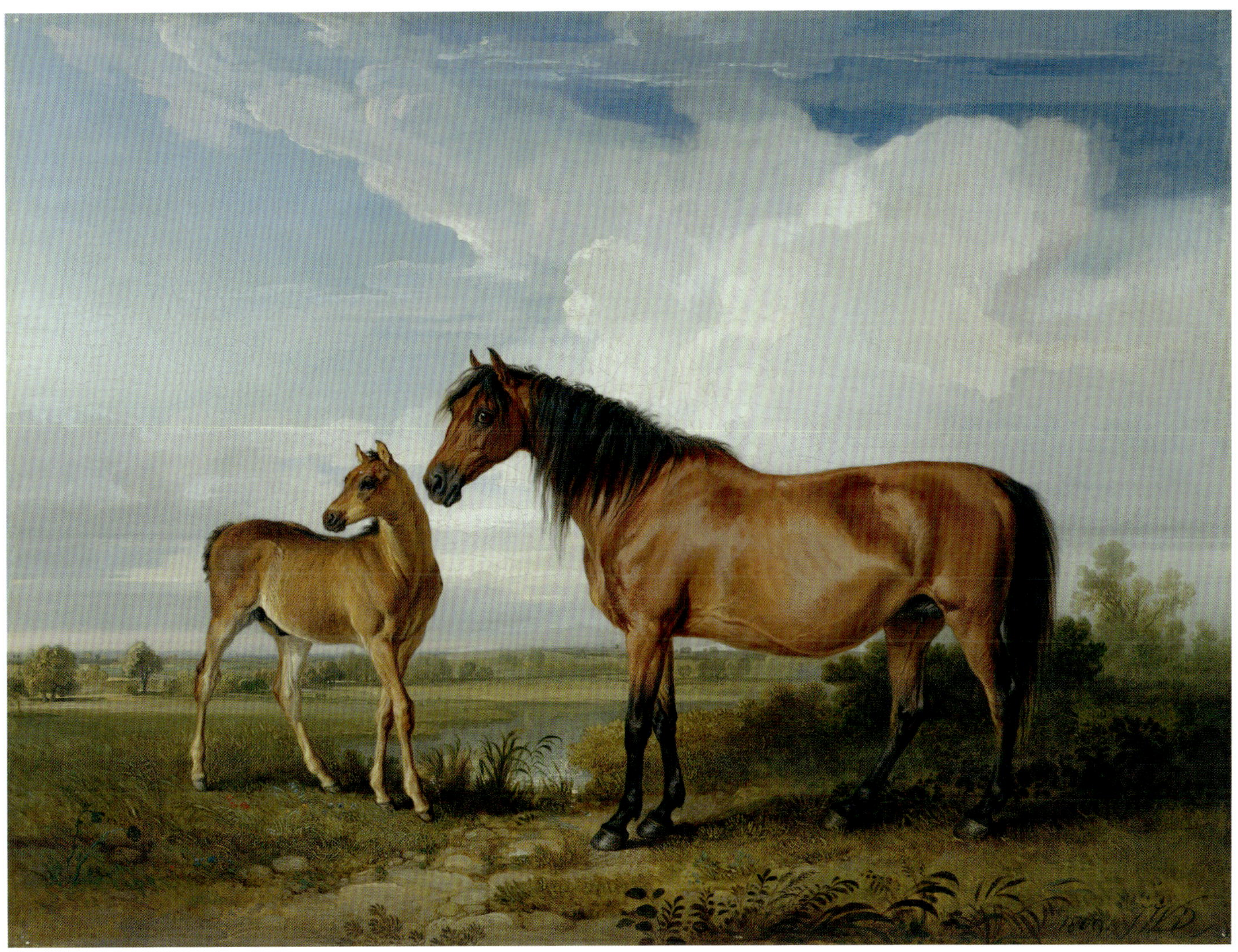

47 James Ward (English, 1769–1859)

Portraits of Granadillo, a Brood Mare, and Skyscraper Colt, the Property of T. Crook, Esq., 1809

Oil on canvas, 27 ⅞ x 35 ¾ in., Paul Mellon Collection, 85.477

This image undoubtedly resonated with Mr. Mellon, who wrote, "I don't think there is anyone who enjoys racing more than I do, or the sight of mares and foals grazing in green fields, or yearlings running wild and throwing themselves about."[1]

Mr. Mellon had begun breeding steeplechasers before his service in World War II, but once he returned home he began to specialize in racehorses. Early on in this enterprise, Mr. Mellon purchased only fillies. As he put it, "it seemed foolish to buy expensive colts when if things didn't work out racing, they would have little value. A well-bred filly, on the other hand, whatever she did on the racetrack, could be a good prospect as a broodmare."[2]

Despite his preference for fillies, Mellon chose a colt with a sterling pedigree when he acquired this pastoral image. The colt's dam, Granadillo (or Granadilla), a fifteen-year-old mare, is shown here; his sire was Skyscraper, winner of the 1789 Epsom Derby; his great-granddam was Hyena (cat. no. 1); and his great-great-great grand-sire was Flying Childers (cat. no. 28).

1. Mellon, 259.

2. Mellon, 251.

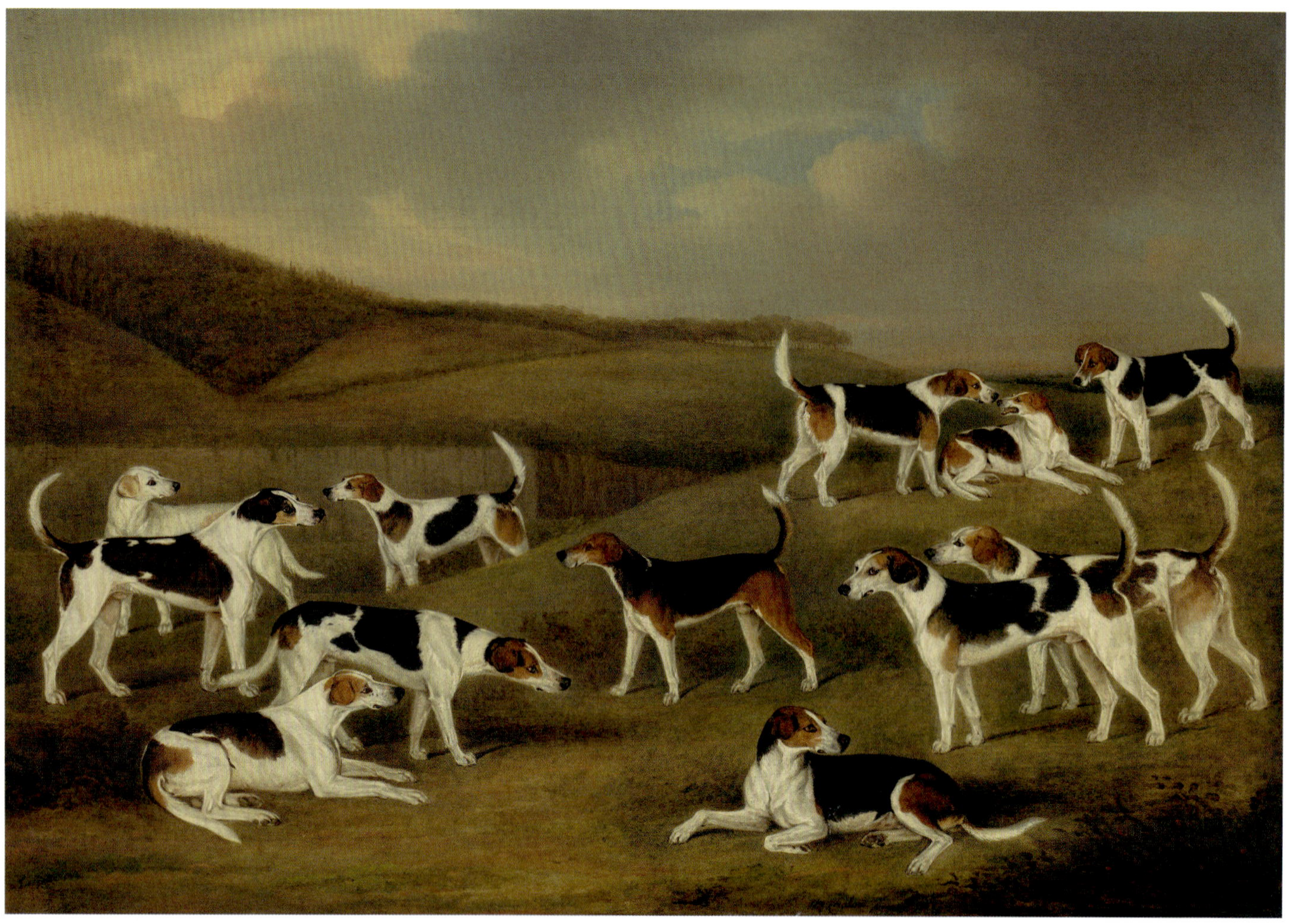

48 Henry Bernard Chalon (English, 1770–1849)

Sir Mark Masterman Sykes's Hounds, 1828

Oil on canvas, 29 ½ x 41 ½ in., Paul Mellon Collection, 93.83

Chalon's canvas glorifies the foxhound, a product of over three-quarters of a century of selective breeding that fused characteristics of hounds from opposite ends of the country. Hounds indigenous to Southern England were heavy and slow but also steady, calm, and patient when following a scent. In contrast, hounds from Northern England were smaller and faster, hunting more with the eye than the nose.[1]

The job of selecting the best characteristics for breeding became the province of gentleman like Hugo Meynell (cat. nos. 10a–d), who had the money and the leisure time for this long-term endeavor. By the end of the eighteenth century, gentlemen interested in hunting foxes were able to create a hound with the necessary speed, stamina, and nose to pursue them.

This monochrome landscape is punctuated by twelve such hounds (six couple). Though Chalon posed the hounds in different positions, he created a very deliberate overall impression of desirable homogeneity: they are almost uniformly colored and have very similar conformation.

1. Raymond Carr, *English Fox Hunting: A History* (London: Weidenfeld and Nicolson, 1986), 36.

49 Thomas Weaver (English, 1774–1843)

Two Durham Oxen, 1827

Oil on canvas, 39 x 49 in., Paul Mellon Collection, 85.478

Thomas Weaver was a self-taught artist who specialized in depictions of prized livestock. His work has the naïve charm of horse-racing images from almost a century before.

Theories of specialized breeding, first applied to racehorses and hounds, were eventually adapted to livestock. These two enormous specimens of Durham oxen were bred and raised by John Bond, the gentleman at right, on his farm, Brancote. The ox at left weighed 2,742 pounds, the one at right 2,437. Weaver accentuated the size of these two animals even more by depicting a few chickens roaming about the stable yard. An inscription included on an engraving made of this work provides pertinent details: "The above oxen were descended from the stock of Edwd. Blount Esqr. of Bellamore, Rear'd and Fed by Mr. John Bond, of Brancott, near Stafford and slaughtered to celebrate the coming of Age of Sir Thomas Aston Clifford Constable Bart. On the 3rd of May 1827."

The background provides a vista of the Staffordshire landscape. Brancote was part of the Tixall estate, which belonged to Sir Thomas (mentioned above). The village of Tixall is two miles east of Stafford, the county town of Staffordshire. Several Stafford landmarks can be identified, including the Stafford "Castle" on its motte (hill) at left, Baswich Church to the immediate right, and St. Mary's Stafford below the setting sun.[1]

1. Cormack, 121.

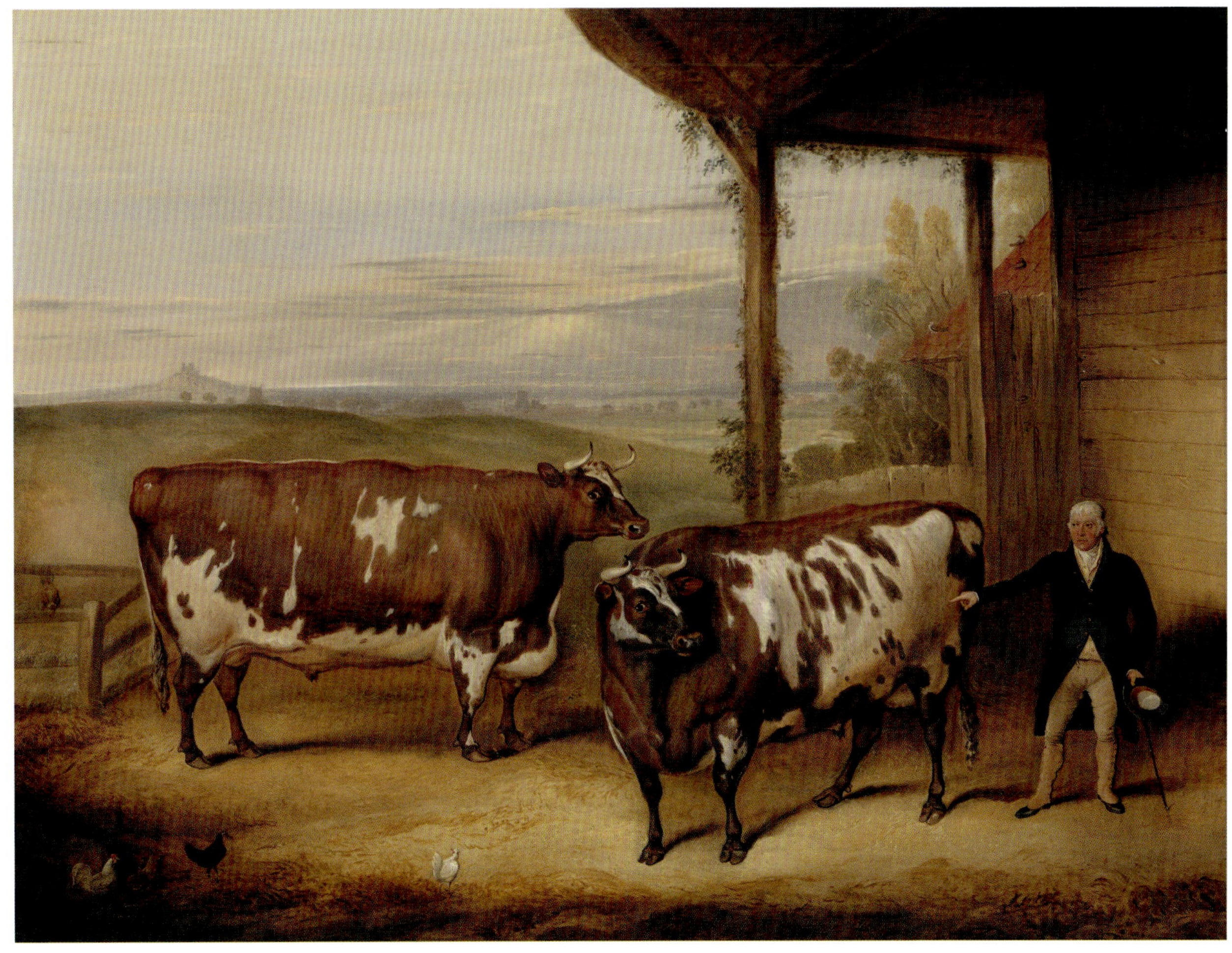

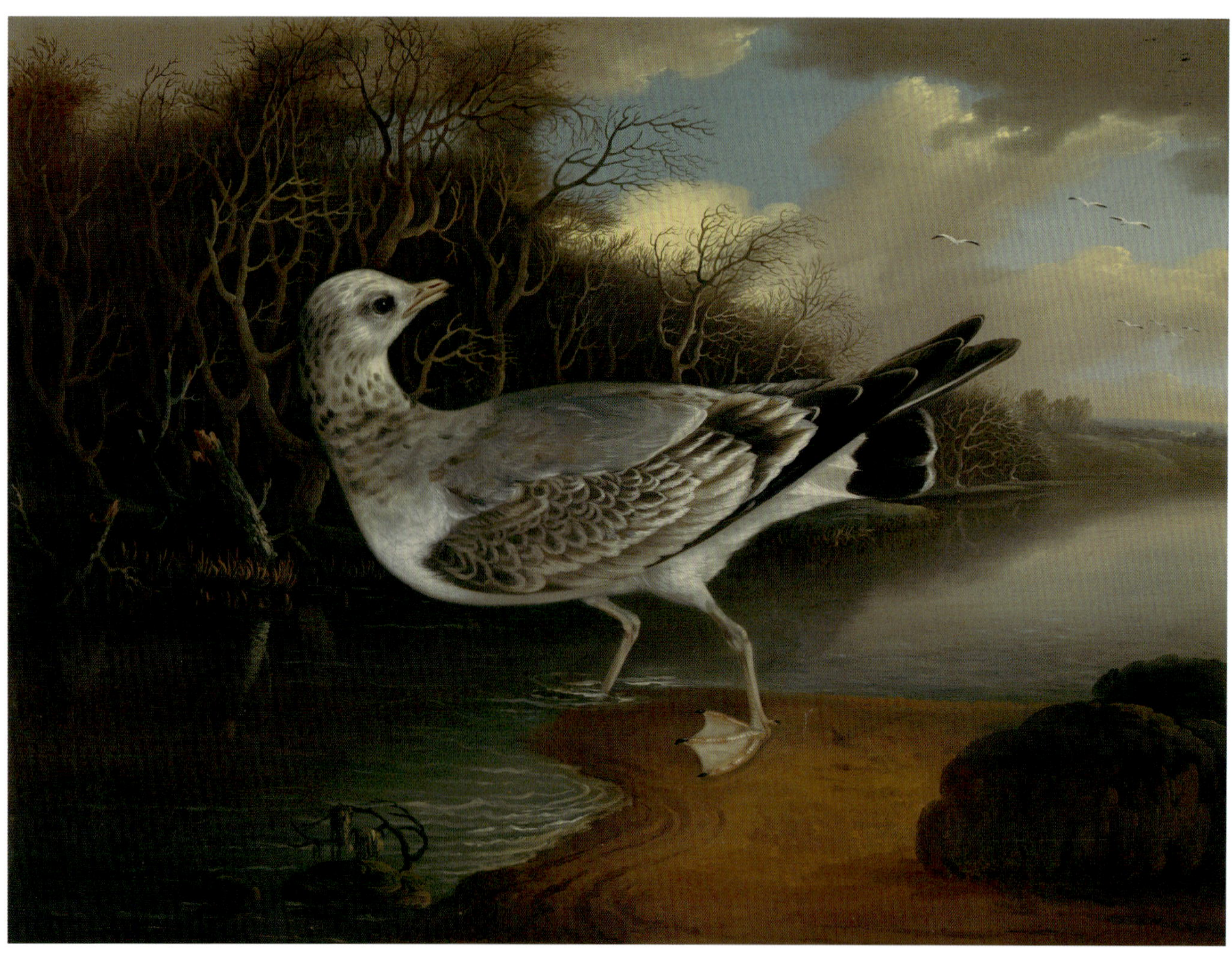

50 Robert Wilkinson Padley (English, ca. 1775–1835)
A Winter Gull, 1812

Oil on canvas, 22 1/4 x 29 in., Paul Mellon Collection, 85.480

Little is known about Robert Wilkinson Padley except that he hailed from Nottinghamshire and exhibited at the Royal Academy in 1815.[1] An inscription tells us that he shot his subject on the river Trent the same year he painted it.

Despite flaws in scale and perspective (which suggest that he was self-taught), Padley pays homage to his former prey through his attention to detail—from the variegated feathers to the scaly legs and feet. The gull's coloring is a sign of his immaturity, and one might read a sense of loss in the backward turn of his head as he seems to watch the other gulls flying away into the distance.

1. Cormack, 115.

51 John E. Ferneley, Sr. (English, 1782–1860)

Filagree and Her Foal, Charlotte West, in a Paddock, 1827

Oil on canvas, 26 x 31 in., Paul Mellon Collection, 99.73

All of the horses in this painting were bred by George Child Villiers, 5th Earl of Jersey, as was Filagree's dam, Web, who was bred to the famous racehorse Soothsayer. The earl, like Mr. Mellon, was an ardent foxhunter, racehorse enthusiast, and breeder at his stud in Middleton Stoney in Oxfordshire.

Filagree, who was foaled in 1815, would go on to become a successful broodmare like her dam. Ferneley included two of her foals in this painting. Lying on the ground directly behind Filagree is Charlotte West, a successful racehorse who was sired by Tramp and the only foal born to Filagree in 1827.

In the background is Filagree's older daughter, Cobweb, who was foaled in 1821 and sired by Phantom. Cobweb also had a distinguished racing career and foaled several winning racehorses.

Mr. Mellon could clearly relate to a painting that showcased three generations of horses bred by the same person, as he had done the same thing for his most successful racehorse, Mill Reef: "One of the greatest racehorses of all time was a true product of Rokeby Farms."[1]

1. Mellon, 268.

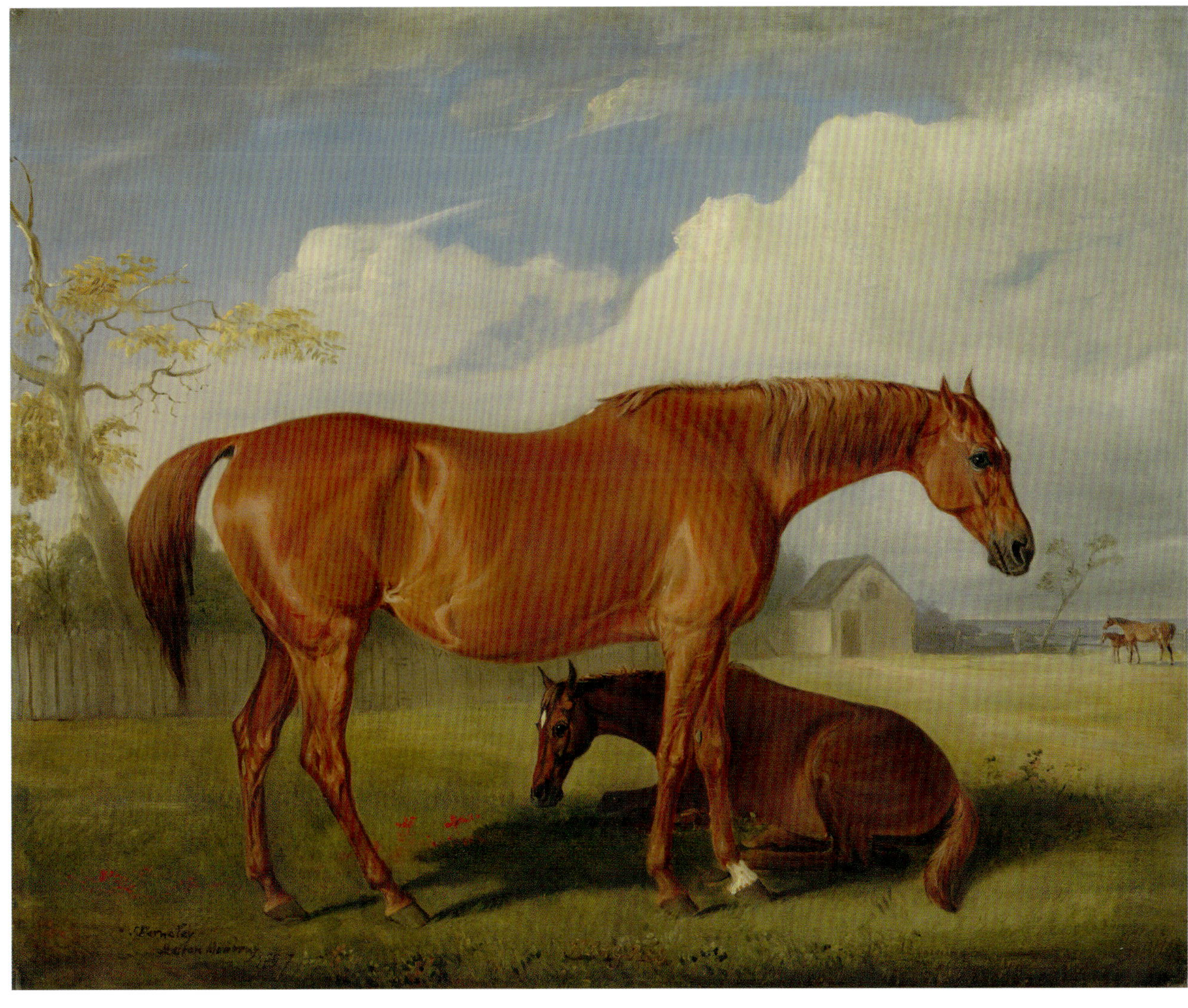

52 Richard Barrett Davis (English, 1782–1854)

Foxhounds in Kennels, 1837

Oil on board, 11 ½ x 15 ¼ in., Paul Mellon Collection, 85.483

Richard Barrett Davis occupied the unique position of being the son of the huntsman to the royal harriers under King George III, and his predilection for drawing was encouraged by the king himself. Davis would go on to create many images of country life and enjoy the patronage of King George IV, William IV, and Queen Victoria.[1]

The title of this painting implies a generalized view of the subject, and Davis seems to have emphasized the way hounds live peacefully among each other when relieved of the responsibility for chasing foxes. At the same time, he also showcases the conformation of the hounds in the foreground and grants individuality to each hound that goes beyond the markings of its coat—even more so than Chalon's painting of Sir Masterman Syke's hounds (cat. no. 48).

That each of these dogs comes across as an individual underlines the unusual set of skills needed by a huntsman, who was the primary caretaker of hounds:

> He bred them, selected them, often fed them, nursed them, trained them and hunted them. He was expected to know each of the up to 150 hounds in his care by name, to know their idiosyncrasies, and the extent to which they could be depended upon in the field. He often was able to tell one hound from another merely by their voices when they were hidden from his view in drawing a covert, and the good huntsman could, on the basis of this knowledge, decide whether or not the hounds had actually found a fox.[2]

1. Cormack, 223.
2. Itzkowitz, 94.

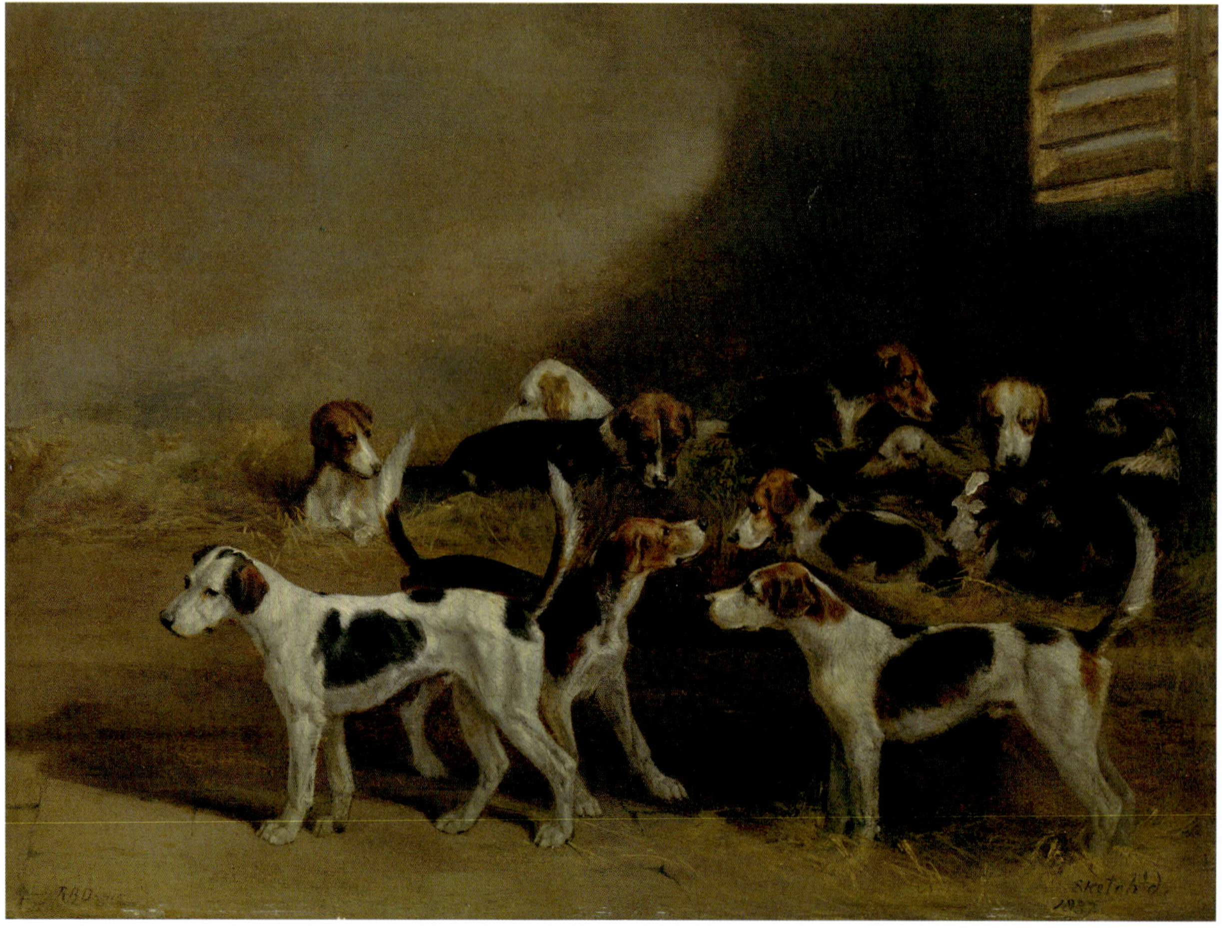

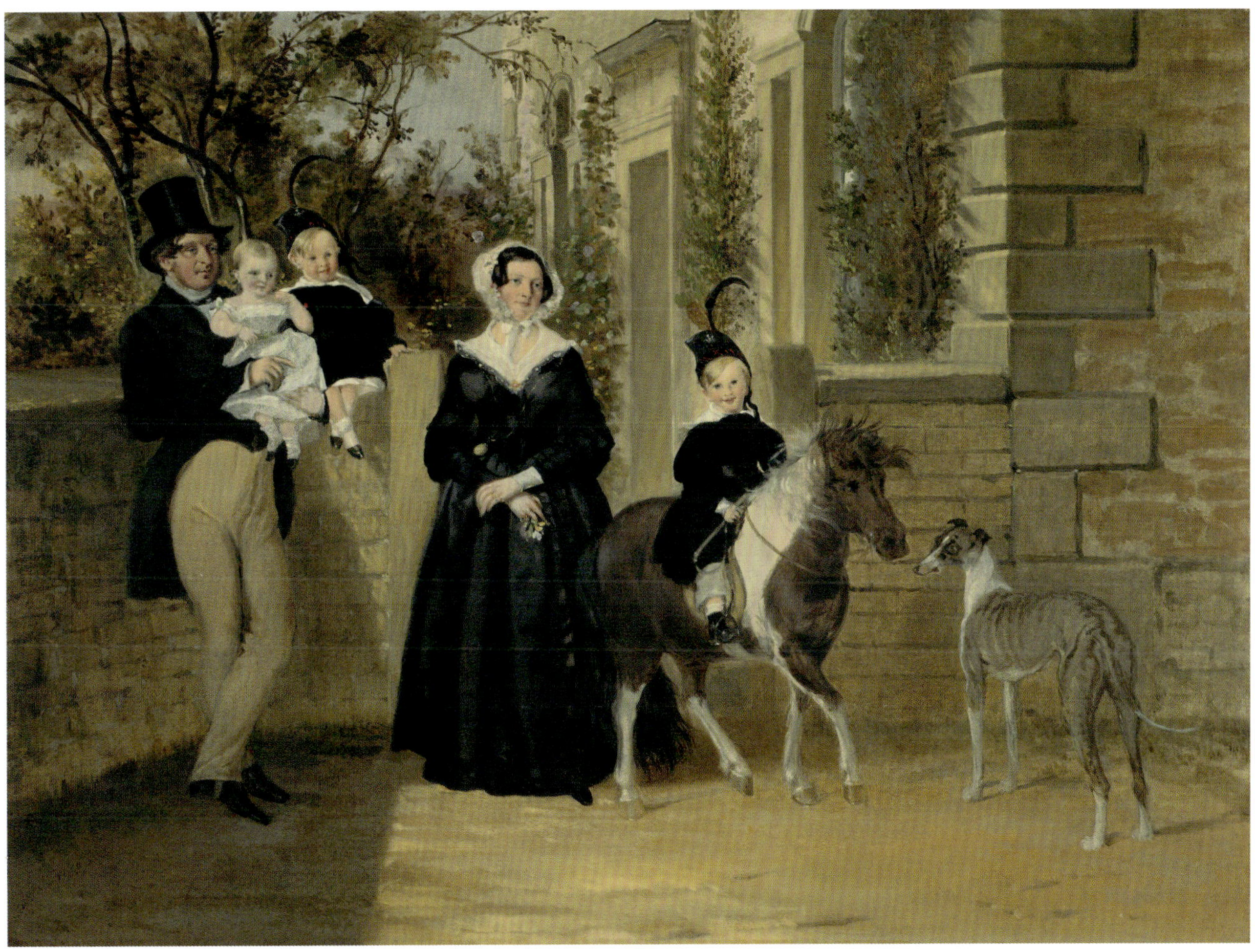

53 John Frederick Herring, Sr. (English, 1795–1865)

Thomas Dawson and His Family, 1842

Oil on canvas, 19 x 25 in., Paul Mellon Collection, 85.492

This work's importance lies in its rare depiction of a racehorse trainer, Thomas Dawson (1809–1880), despite the fact that he is shown away from the track. Dawson's prosperity is reflected in the façade of his house (in Tupgill, Middleham, Yorkshire) and his family: his wife, Grant Watt (nee Sutherland), and his three children.

Dawson came from a line of successful horse trainers that formed a sort of Scottish dynasty (hence the Glengarry bonnets on the boys). His father, George, trained for Lord Eglinton. His brother Matthew trained for Lords Falmouth, Portland, Hastings, and Roseberry, while his brother John trained for Prince Batthyany. And a cousin, also named George, trained for the Duke of Rutland. Together, the family could claim to have trained the winners of over fifty classic races.[1]

Dawson distinguished himself from his family by being the first to do away with sweating as a training technique. He earned renown for developing training regimes to suit the individual needs of each horse under his care. His method was soon copied as it became evident that Dawson's horses were better tempered and had fewer injuries.

1. Cormack, 157.

54 Abraham Cooper (English, 1787–1868)

The Wapati or North American Deer, 1818

Oil on canvas, 10 7/8 x 14 1/8 in., Paul Mellon Collection, 85.487

The largely self-taught son of a tobacconist, Abraham Cooper was encouraged by Benjamin Marshall to pursue his art. Cooper would go on to paint race-horses and hunters, sporting dogs and show dogs, and exotic animals such as these deer.

The opportunity to document the "Wapati" (*Cervus canadensis*) came after a German naturalist captured these specimens in Upper Missouri. After being shown in Baltimore, Philadelphia, and New York, they were brought to England and kept in the Royal Mews menagerie, where Cooper was able to study them.

Cooper's painting depicts stags and does in different poses. In the foreground, a stag stands with his body in profile, but Cooper shows his head full on in order to demonstrate the breadth of his antlers. In contrast, the doe next to him is foreshortened and placed so that we see both the profile of her head and the unique markings around her rump and hind legs. In the background, a stag lies down and a doe grazes.

Accompanying John Scott's print of Cooper's painting was the following text:

> The color of these animals is, in the winter, on the body of a peculiar dunnish hue; the neck and legs are dark brown; the rump is a pale yellowish white, the colour extending about six or seven inches from the tail on all sides, and very distinct from the general colour of the body. A black semicircular line of unequal width (from a quarter of an inch to two inches) separates the white of the rump from the dun of the body. Their summer coat is thin, and the colour a reddish grey.
>
> The head resembles that of the common American deer (*Cervus virginianus*) and of the horse, much more than that of the elk or moose, and is pointed and handsome. The legs are admirably formed for strength and activity, resembling those of the race horse, particularly the hinder. . . . The Wapiti [*sic*] has an oblique slit or opening under the inner angle of each eye, nearly an inch long externally, which appears to be an auxiliary nostril, and secretes a brown granulated substance. He has no voice, like the horse or the ox, and this organ seems to be given him as a compensation; for with it he makes a noise, which he can vary at pleasure, and which is like the loud and piercing whistle that boys give by putting their fingers in their mouth.[1]

The carefulness, clarity, and length of this text is indicative of the era's interest in natural history and hunger to learn more about little-known global species.

1. Cormack, 117.

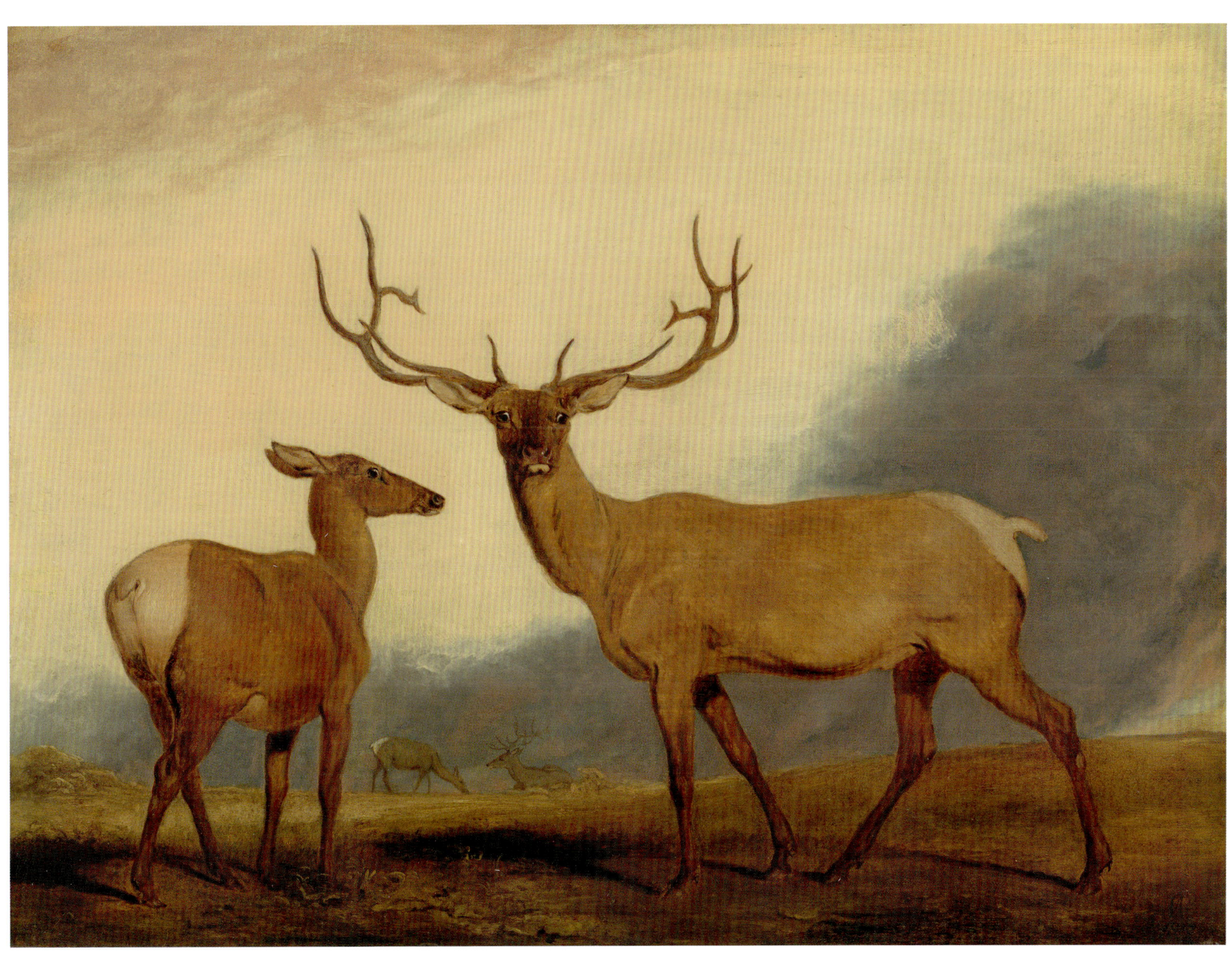

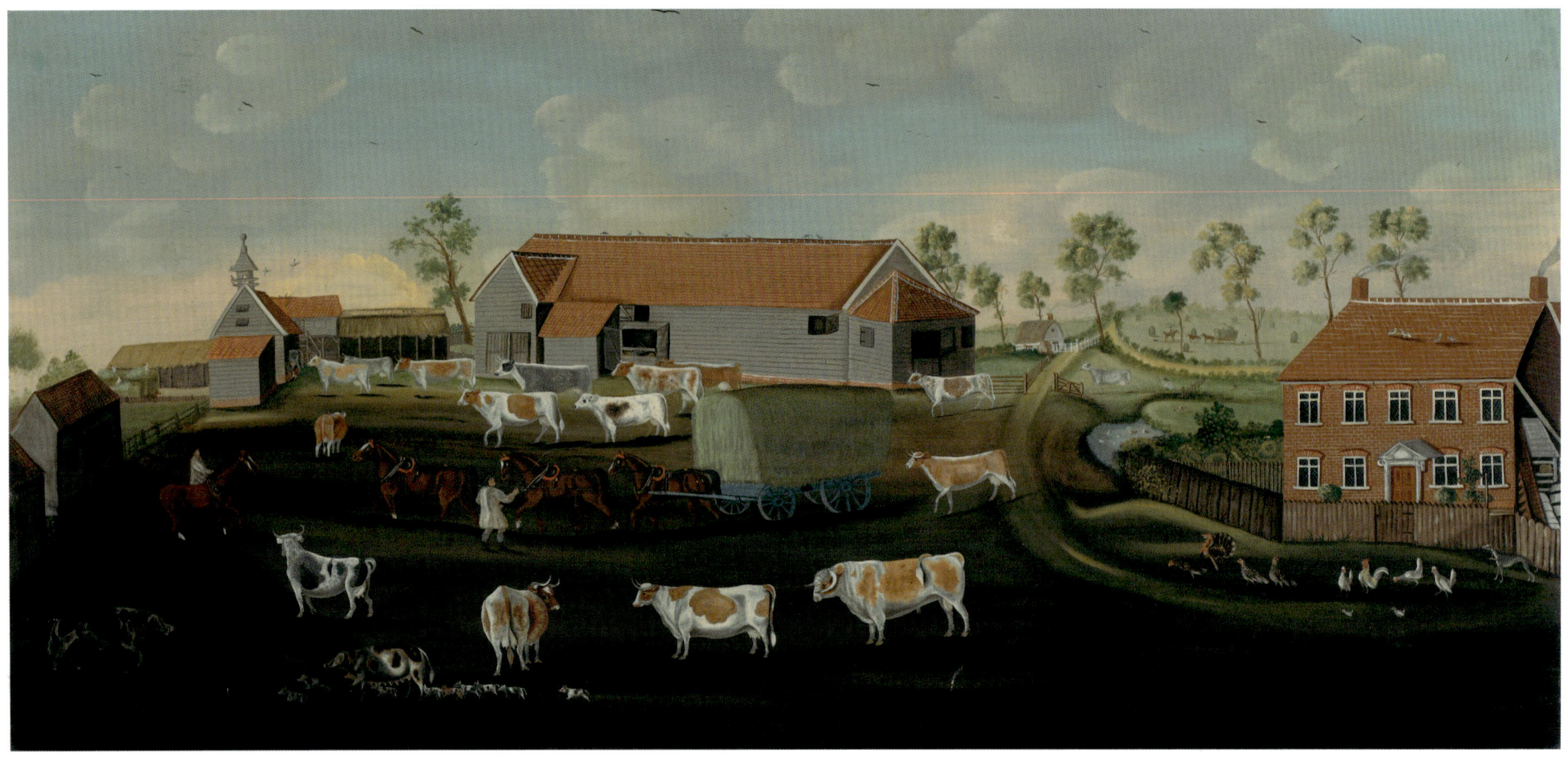

55 William Williams (English, active 1802)

Farm Scene in Summer, 1802

Oil on panel, 28 7/8 x 59 1/8 in., Paul Mellon Collection, 85.479.1

The biography of the artist who signed this ruggedly charming summer landscape and its winter counterpart (cat. no. 56) is unknown. Although he has sometimes been thought to be American, the buildings appear distinctive to East Anglia, particularly Suffolk, in England.

Williams has imagined the daily routines of farm life at opposite times of the year. In both works, the most impressive piece of architecture is a brick house. With its two chimneys, plentiful windows, and classically inspired door, it makes for an imposing edifice among the other wooden structures. Although these buildings may not seem as permanent as the house, the routines of the individuals and animals appear as if preordained by a very British version of nature.

This idyllic summer scene teems with life: the formal garden next to the brick house is in full bloom, and the men and numerous animals—cows, pigs, horses, chickens, ducks, a turkey, and a greyhound—are all living and working together in harmony.

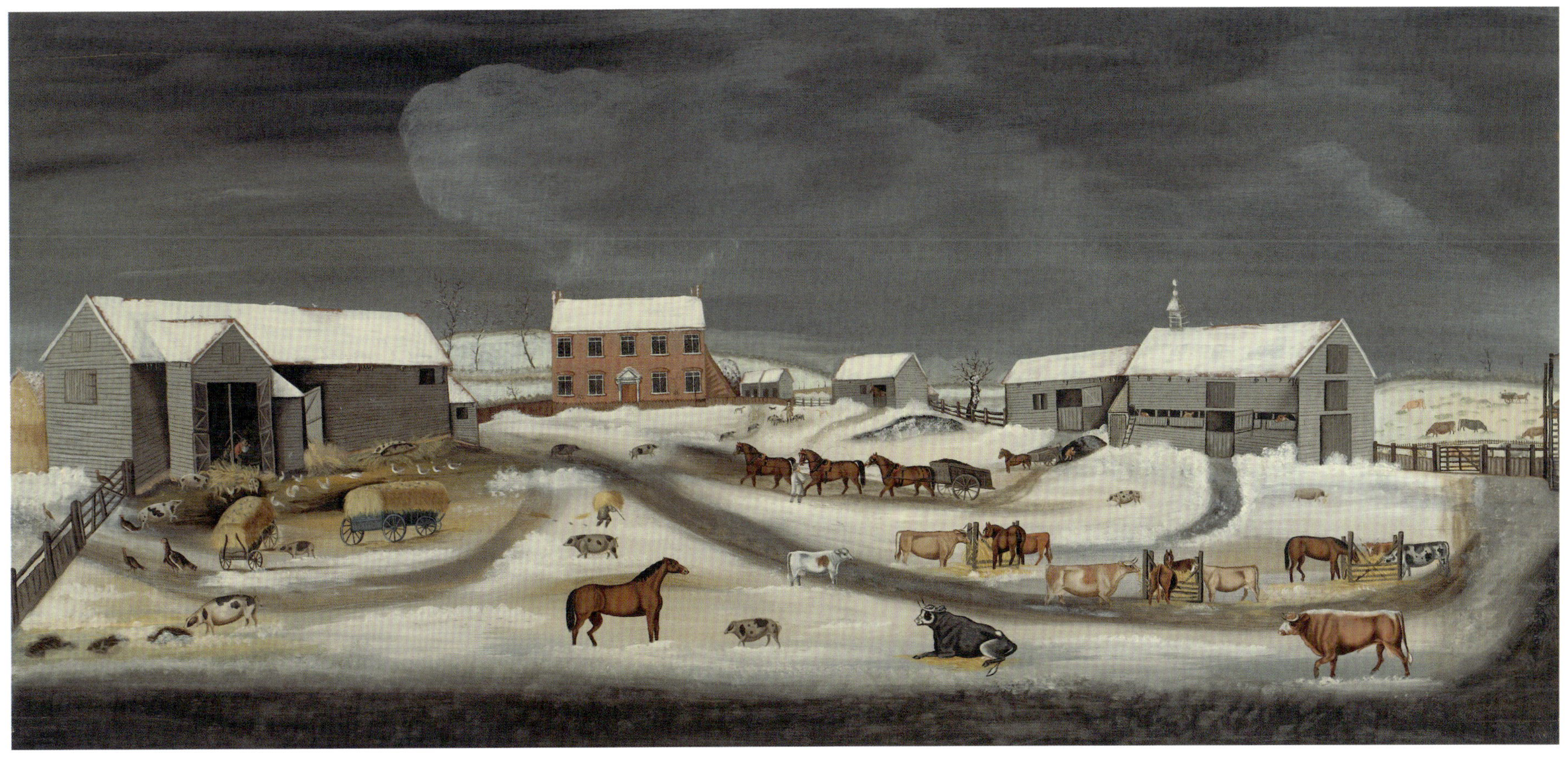

56 William Williams (English, active 1802)

Farm Scene in Winter, 1802

Oil on panel, 28 ¾ x 59 ½ in., Paul Mellon Collection, 85.479.2

In this winter scene, the soft, comfortable summer light has been replaced with a leaden sky. Though a blanket of snow covers the ground and icicles dangle from the sides of buildings, life carries on at the farm. The baby animals have grown older, including the piglets trotting past the brick house toward a farmer passing out feed.

THE WORLD UPSIDE DOWN

THE WORLD UPSIDE DOWN presents several highly comic paintings, taking gravity rather than gravitas as their starting point. However, these images do more than poke fun at those lacking sporting prowess. They encourage sportsmen, sportswomen, and nonparticipants alike to view sport as pure free play, where anything can happen with few consequences—except perhaps on the hunting field. As Mr. Mellon cautioned, "Of course, people get maimed and killed by the way of broken necks while foxhunting, but I have never thought of it as a dangerous pastime, so interesting and healthful and exciting it has always seemed. And I had well-schooled horses, mostly thoroughbreds, so the jumping was always safe and my mounts had lots of stamina to carry me."[1]

This catalogue concludes with Philip Reinagle's *Portrait of an Extraordinary Musical Dog* (1805), a work whose absurdity fits itself well within the idea of the world being turned upside down. Yet, if one moves past its absurdity and considers how a work such as this fits within the larger nature of sporting art, we arrive back at the original challenge Mr. Mellon set for viewers at the opening of the 1963 exhibition *Paintings of England, 1700–1850* at the Virginia Museum of Fine Arts. "Let's take it seriously, let's reevaluate it, let's look at it, let's enjoy it."[2]

---

1. Mellon, 386.
2. Mellon, 290.

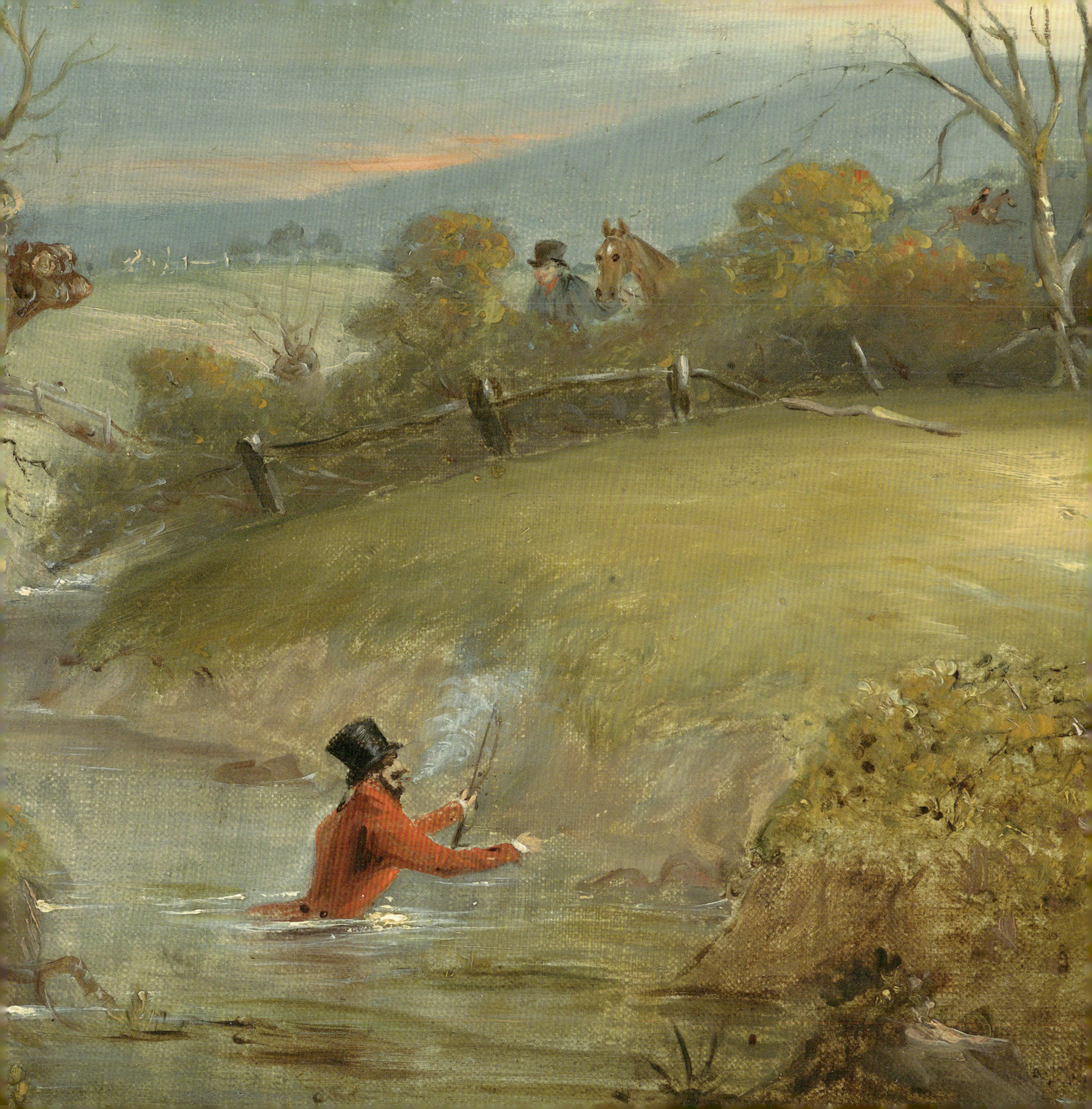

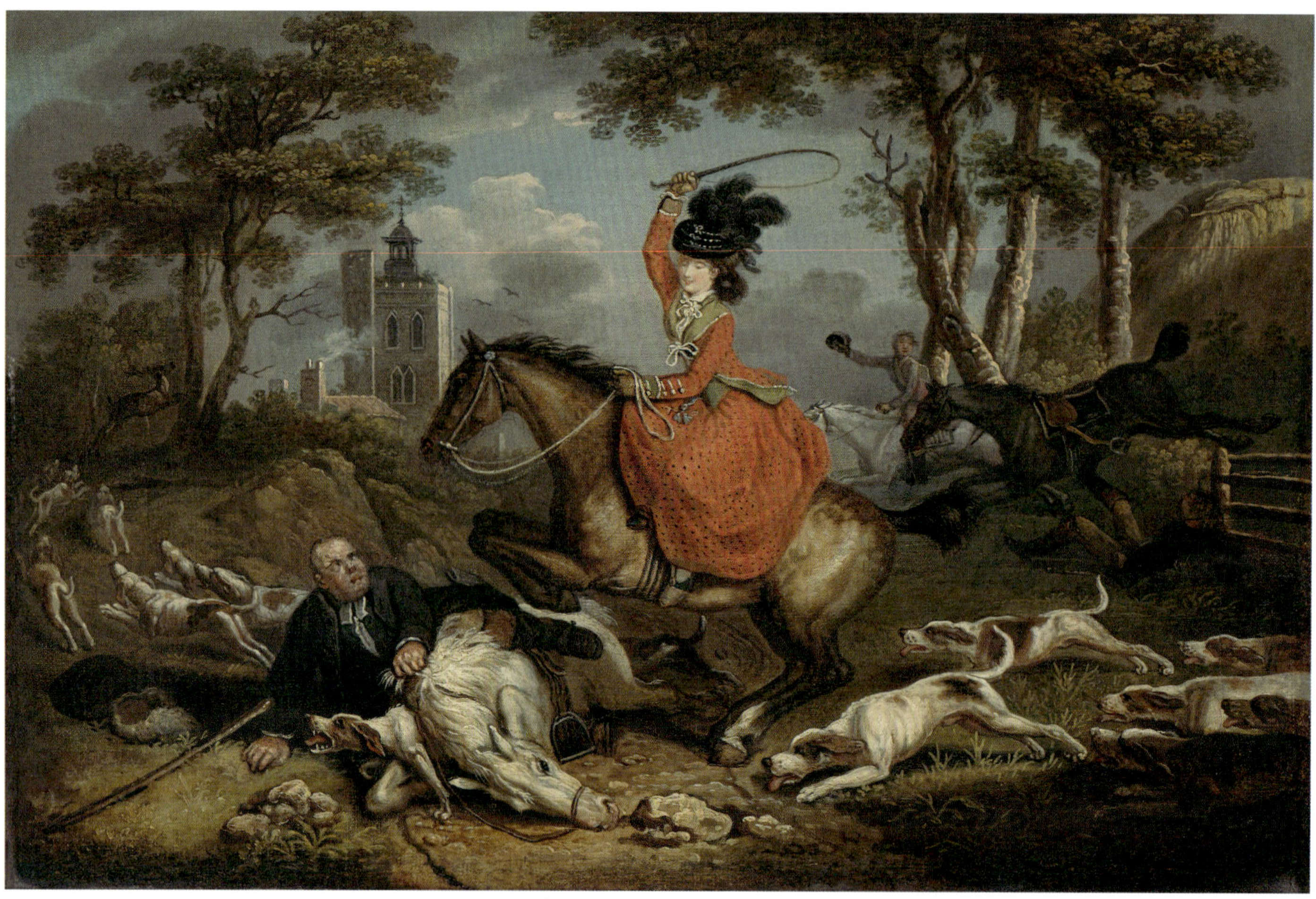

57 John Collet (English, ca. 1725–1780)

"The Joys of the Chase," or "The Rising Woman and the Falling Man," 1780

Oil on canvas, 16 x 23 1/2 in., Paul Mellon Collection, 99.62

John Collet's paintings and engravings portray scenes of the comical and occasionally debauched society in which he lived. Though Collet's works are more satirical than moralizing, he is adept at rendering the characters and costumes of his time.

This unusual scene depicts a woman dominating a stag hunt through the English countryside, suspended in mid-canter above a parson—identified by the bands at his neck—who is pinned under his horse. As he struggles to free himself, his wig and hat have tumbled off his head and lie to his left. At right, there is a second pair of male riders, one of whom has fallen off his horse while attempting to jump over the hurdle. The central female figure ridicules the ability of the horsemen through the authority of her pose and attitude—as she glances downward at the clergyman, she raises her stock whip to urge her horse forward.

Whereas other works in Mr. Mellon's collection privilege men as representing the sporting ideal, this scene celebrates the emergence of a woman who transcends the boundaries of gender by excelling in a traditional male role. Collet blithely illustrates an example of shifting societal views in England during the last quarter of the eighteenth century as upper-class women challenged male-dominated culture and the church began losing power and relevancy. These changing dynamics anticipated the emergence of the Woman's Rights Movement in Britain, North America, and elsewhere in the nineteenth century.

58 John E. Ferneley, Sr. (English, 1781–1860)

a–j. *Count Sandor's Hunting Exploits in Leicestershire, A Set of Ten Sketches,* 1829

A specialist in images of horses, dogs, and hunting who studied briefly under Benjamin Marshall, Ferneley moved in 1814 to Melton Mowbray, Leicestershire, the epicenter of foxhunting. It was an astute decision since he was able to attract commissions from sportsmen who came into the area, Count Sandor included.[1]

Count Moritz Sandor of Hungary came to Melton Mowbray for the 1828–29 season and paid Tilbury, the horse dealer and carriage designer, £1,000 to hire eight horses. The count's daughter, Princess Metternich, described him as "daring to the point of recklessness," a quality admired in Leicestershire. Contemporary sporting writer C. J. Apperley, known as "Nimrod," had this to say about him:

> The Count, however, gave astounding proof of what can be done in a short time in acquiring perfection in bodily arts, when heart and soul are earnestly engaged in them. From a mere tyro, scarcely equal to sit a horse if he shyed, he became in a few months able to go along-side the best men of the day, although at the cost of sundry marvelous escapes from broken bones and watery graves. The prints published by Ackermann, from the pictures Ferneley, of Melton, painted for the Count, descriptive of the various situations, good and bad, in which he exhibited himself in chase, are excellent, and I am not surprised to hear that they have been so eagerly sought after.[2]

Count Sandor himself commissioned this set of small comic paintings from Ferneley, to whom he paid 30 guineas. Unfortunately, repeated falls throughout his life led eventually to his death in 1878 from brain damage.

It was this element of danger led to Andrew W. Mellon's extreme dislike of foxhunting, his son Paul's cherished pastime—and indeed, the younger Mellon had his own share of accidents in the hunting field. Many of his reminiscences mimic scenes in Count Sandor's exploits. The period descriptions that accompanied the prints made from each sketch were provided by "Nimrod" and appear in bold type.

1. Cormack, 451.

2. Nimrod, *Nimrod's Hunting: Comprising Memoirs of Masters of Hounds, Notices of the Crack Riders and Characteristics of the Hunting Countries of England* (London: Lane, 1926), 225.

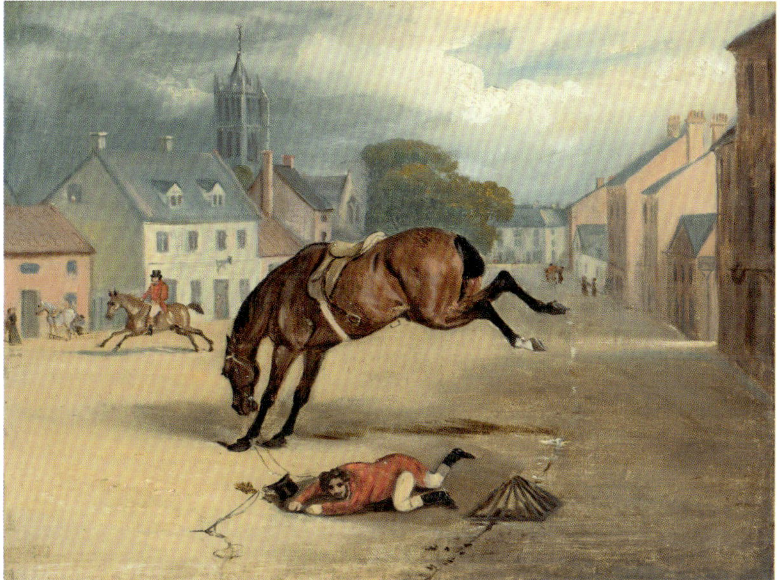

a. *No. 1: The Count Floored in the Street of Melton Mowbray, on the First Day of Going to Cover,* 1829

Oil on canvas, 10 7/8 x 14 1/8 in., Paul Mellon Collection, 99.63

No. 1 represents the Count floored in the streets of Melton Mowbray on the first day of going to covert. He was in the act of putting on his gloves, when his horse, Cruiser, started at a drain, and, sitting loosely at the time, he kissed Mother Earth.

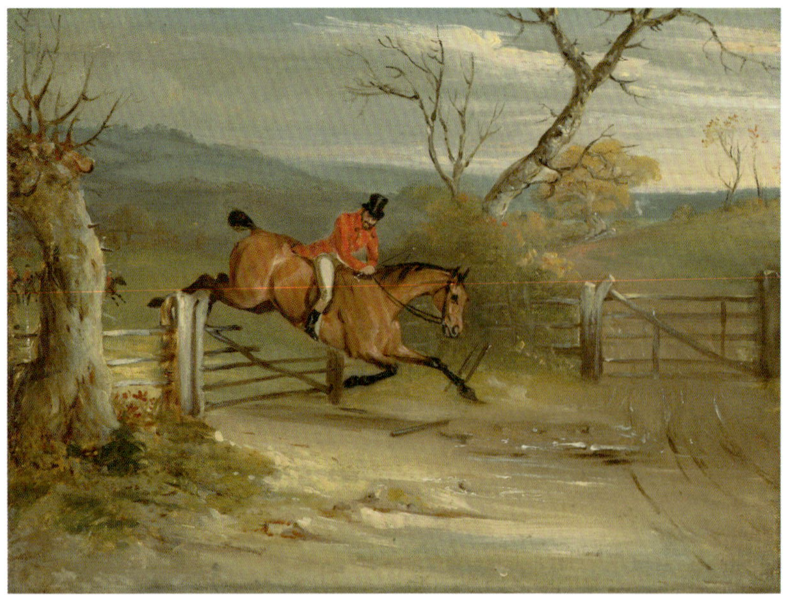

b. *No. 2: The Count Charges a Gate on Comedy,* 1829

Oil on canvas, 10 ½ x 14 in., Paul Mellon Collection, 99.64

No. 2 The Count charges a gate on Comedy, and only avoids a fall by breaking every bar in it.

No. 3 In the rush at starting in a run—a trial of nerve in Leicestershire—the Count on Columbine leaps over Sir James Musgrave, his horse and all. He falls immediately after, and Sir James returns the compliment by riding over him.

No. 4 Columbine . . . having got rid of the Count, goes well up to the hounds, clearing everything in his stroke. The Count, following on foot, comes to a wide brook . . . jumps into the middle of it . . . lands up to his waist in water and mud, and sticks fast. At the end of a quarter of an hour—having lighted a cigar to keep out the cold—he espies a shepherd, and implores his assistance. "Where are you?" said the shepherd, who heard a voice but did not see the little Count. "In the brook! G—d d—n," was the reply.

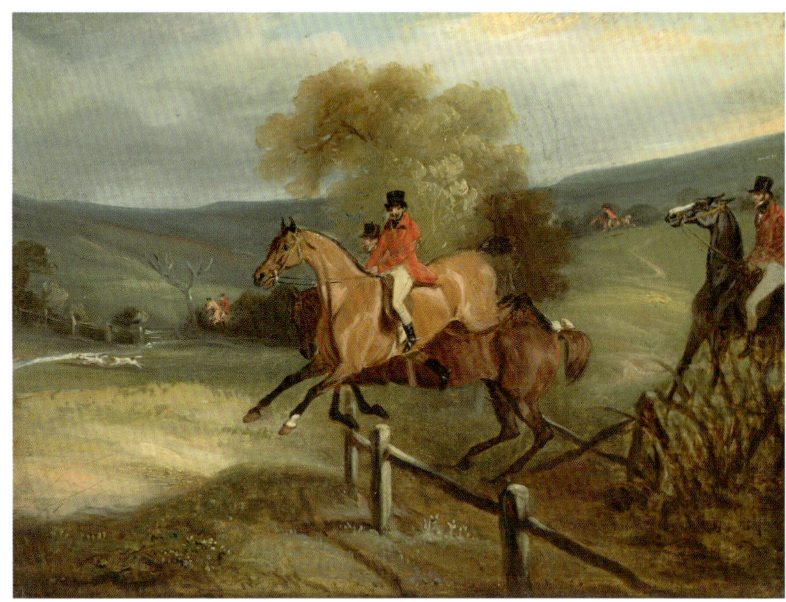

c. *No. 3: The Count Leaps over Sir James Musgrave, His Horse and All,* 1829

Oil on canvas, 10 ⅞ × 14 in., Paul Mellon Collection, 99.65

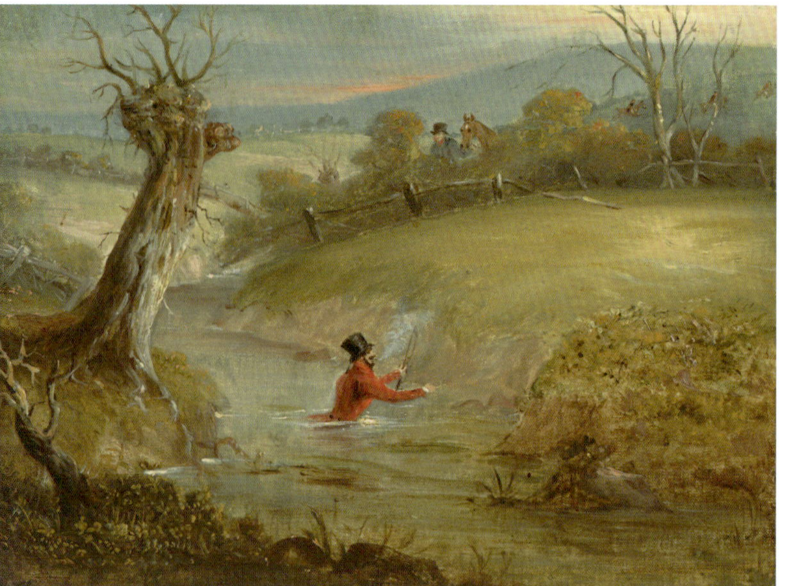

d. *No. 4: The Count in a Brook up to His Waist in Water and Mud,* 1829

Oil on canvas, 10 ½ x 14 in., Paul Mellon Collection, 99.66

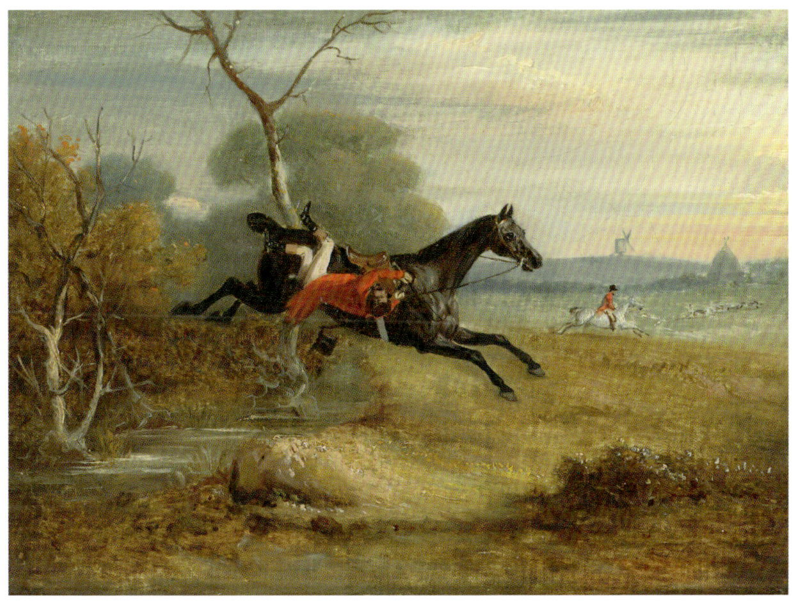

No. 5 The Count on Brigliadora, going a slapping pace, and well up in front, charges a large fence, at nearly full speed. A strong grower catching his knee, he is displaced from his saddle; but, unwilling to part, is carried hanging at his bridle, over another good fence, well into the next field. There a separation takes place.

No. 6 The Count, again on Brigliadora, charges a wide deep drain in the vale of Belvoir. The bank being rotten the horse falls backwards, and, but for the assistance of Tom Wilkins, the whipper-in, would, in all probability, have been drowned . . .

No. 7 The Count is now considered one of the first flight. On Lord Alvanley's very celebrated horse Everitt, he clears a flock of sheep, a stile and a long foot-bridge, landing safe and well in the next field.

e. *No. 5: The Count on Brigliadora Is Displaced from His Saddle, but Is Carried Hanging at His Bridle,* 1829

Oil on canvas, 10 ½ x 14 in., Paul Mellon Collection, 99.67

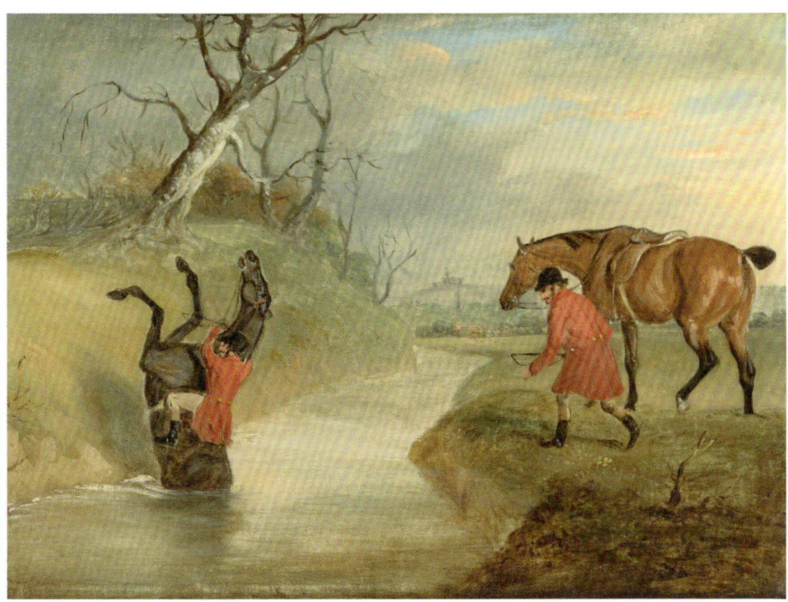

f. *No. 6: The Count on Brigliadora Charges a Wide and Deep Drain in the Vale of Belvoir,* 1829

Oil on canvas, 10 ½ x 14 in., Paul Mellon Collection, 99.68

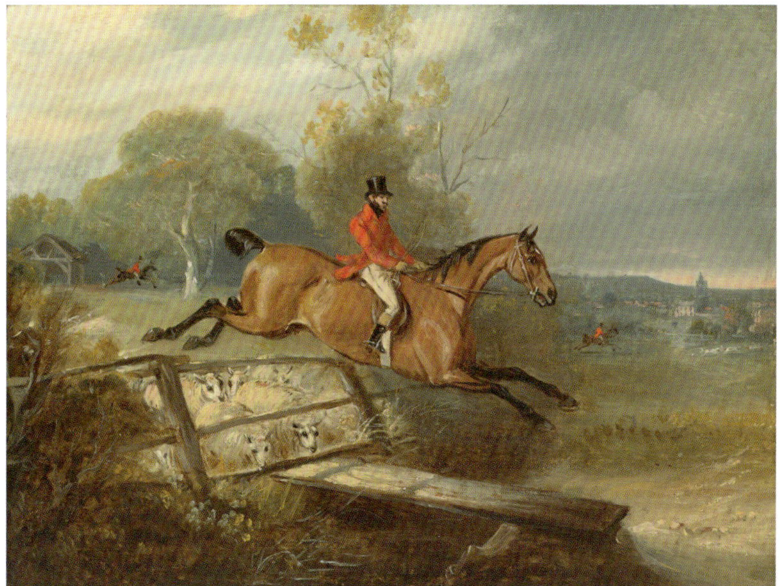

g. *No. 7: The Count on "Everitt" Clears a Flock of Sheep, a Stile and a Long Foot Bridge,* 1829

Oil on canvas, 10 ½ x 14 in., Paul Mellon Collection, 99.69

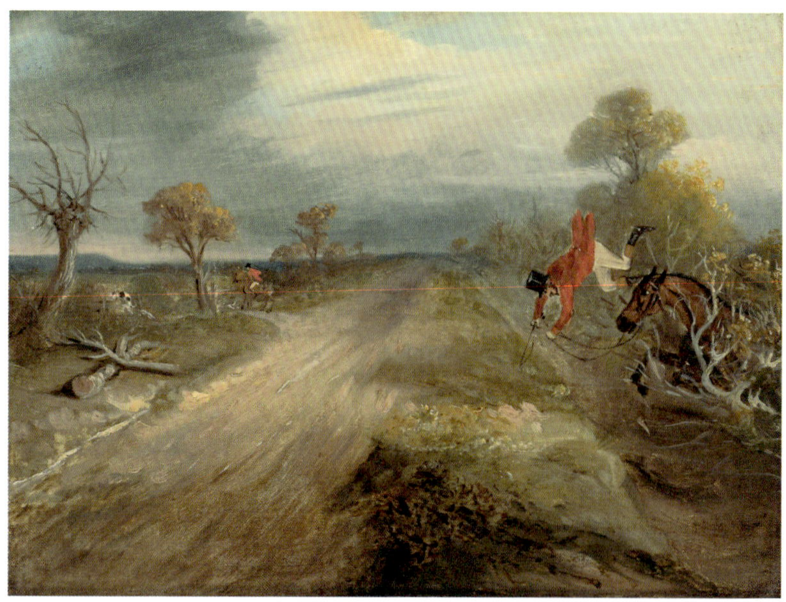

No. 8 Another disaster occurs. The Count, well up with his hounds, had only one alternative—either to lose his place, or charge a most awful bullfinch, on the other side of which was a lane. His horse, Cruiser, goes gallantly at it; but sticking fast in the middle, the Count is exhibited, absolutely flying over his head, into the lane below.

No. 9 The Count here is doing the thing well. On his horse, Nimrod . . . he clears a large ox-fence, at full speed, and comes handsomely into the next field.

No. 10 represents the Count "larking." Returning from hunting, he rides Mother Goose at a gate on the swing, and gets a harmless, but very dirty fall.

h. *No. 8: The Count on "Cruiser" Flying over his Head into the Lane Below,* 1829

Oil on canvas, 10 ½ x 14 in., Paul Mellon Collection, 99.70

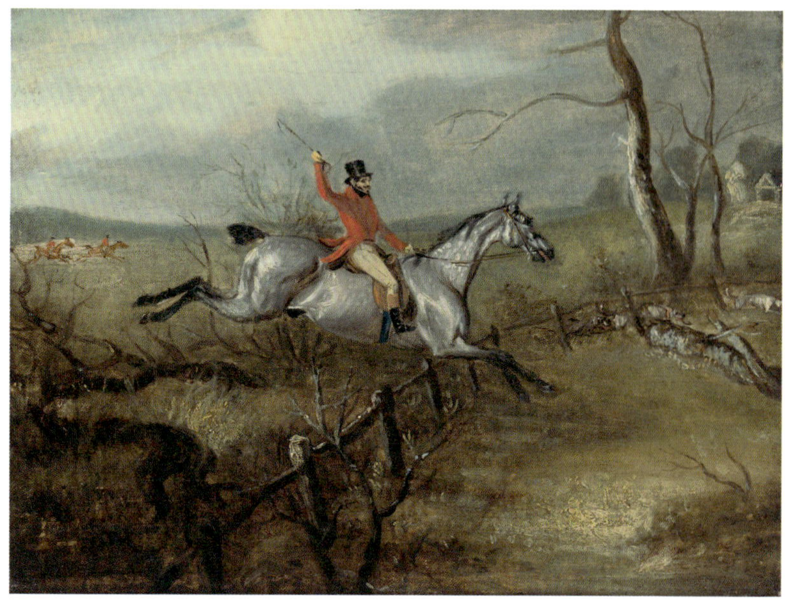

i. *No. 9: The Count on "Nimrod" Clears a Large Ox-Fence,* 1829

Oil on canvas, 10 ½ x 14 in., Paul Mellon Collection, 99.71

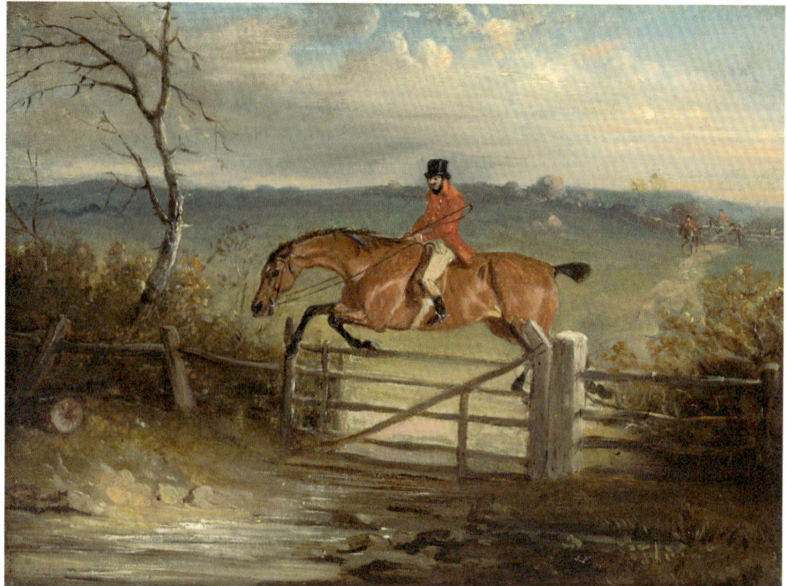

j. *No. 10: The Count on "Mother Goose" Gets a Harmless but Very Dirty Fall,* 1829

Oil on canvas, 10 ½ x 14 in., Paul Mellon Collection, 99.72

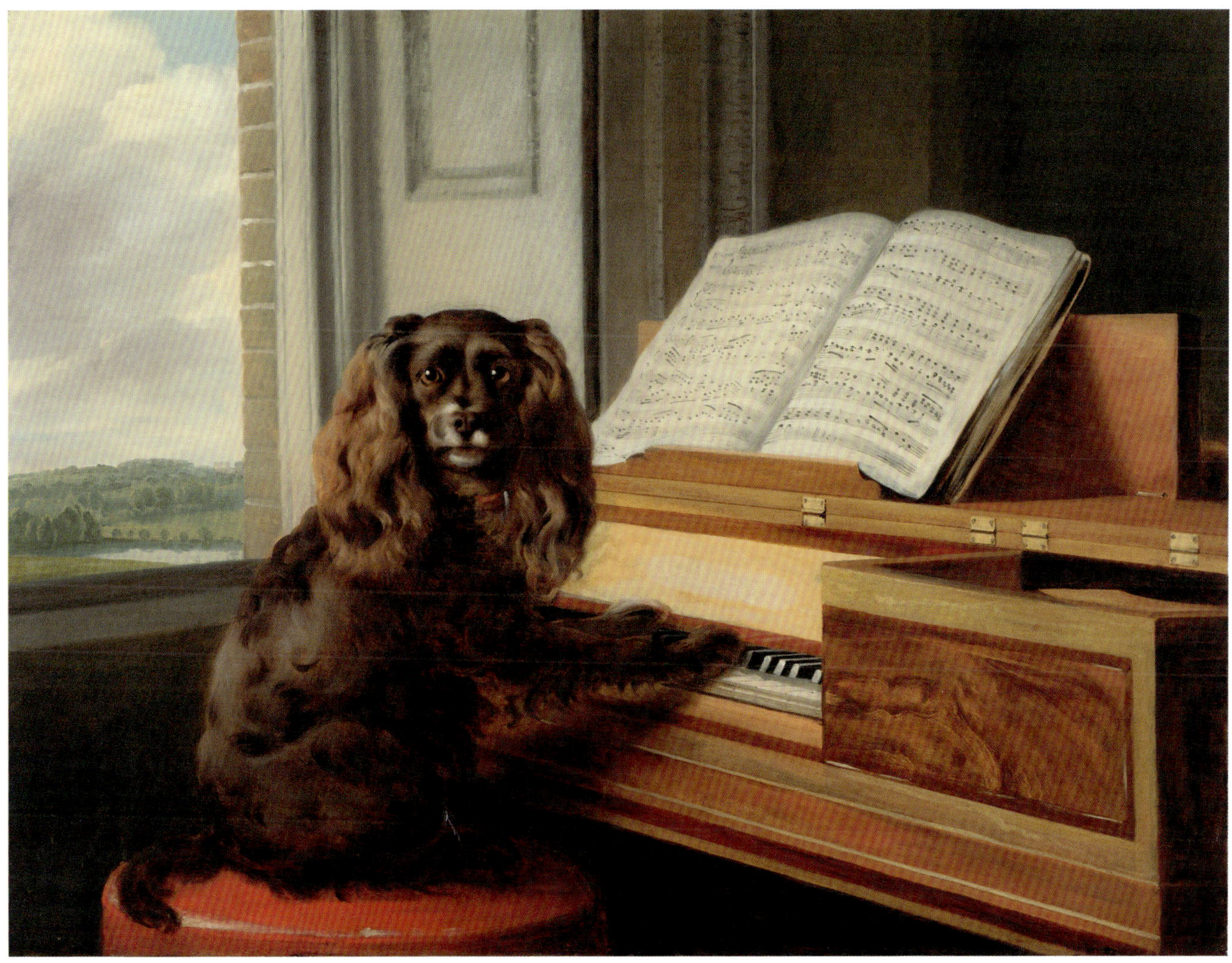

59 Philip Reinagle (English, 1749–1833)

Portrait of an Extraordinary Musical Dog, 1805

Oil on canvas, 28 1/4 x 36 1/2 in., Paul Mellon Collection, 85.465

Philip Reinagle was born in Scotland, the son of a Hungarian musician. He entered the Royal Academy Schools in 1769 and began showing at the Royal Academy in 1773. Reinagle is remembered as a painter of conversation pieces, landscapes, and sporting works.[1]

Here, Reinagle has seemingly appropriated a pose from a portrait of Mozart to depict a spaniel playing a Broadwood square piano.[2] Known for their intelligence, spaniels received praise for their extraordinary capabilities in period texts, such as one that commented, "The various tricks which these Dogs are sometimes taught to perform, seem more like the effect of reasoning powers, than of undiscerning instinct."[3]

Much argument has been made over the meaning of this image. It has been seen as an exemplar of successful spaniel breeding, as a satire on human infant prodigies, or as loyalist propaganda (the music is sometimes identified as "God save the King/Queen"). Without a doubt, however, the artist must have had a strong general appreciation for the remarkable intelligence of dogs if not a somewhat comic attitude toward this "extraordinary" specimen.

1. Cormack, 454.
2. Cormack, 111.
3. Bewick, 362.

Index by Artist